The Emotional Toolkit

Seven Power-Skills to Nail Your Bad Feelings

Darlene Mininni, Ph.D., M.P.H.

St. Martin's Griffin *New York*

www.stmartins.com

Library of Congress Cataloging-in-Publication Data

Mininni, Darlene.
    The emotional toolkit : seven power-skills to nail your bad feelings / Darlene Mininni.
        p. cm.
    ISBN 0-312-31887-1 (hc)
    ISBN 0-312-31888-X (pbk)
    EAN 978-0-312-31888-8
    1. Women—Psychology. 2. Emotions. 3. Self-help techniques. I. Title.

HQ1206.M532 2005
158.1'082—dc22   2004051315

First St. Martin's Griffin Edition: February 2006

The
Emotional
Toolkit

For Bryan
I love you for the person you are and the person
I am when I am with you.

To Sophia
You fill my heart with joy.

To Marilyn
You are the most wonderful mother
any girl could hope for.

To Alfred
You'll always be with me.

Contents

Acknowledgments ix
Introduction xvii

Part One: Opening Your Toolkit

1. It's Time for Your Emotional Education   3

2. A Feeling Is a Full-Body Experience   11

Part Two: Finding Your Tools

3. Understanding Your Feelings   23

4. The Four Gateway Feelings   29

5. What's Underneath Your Emotions   54

6. Your Thinking Mind and Your Moods   61

7. Why You Communicate the Way You Do   79

Part Three: Using Your Emotional Toolkit

8. Finding the Right Emotional Tools for You   97

9. The Voices in Your Head   106
   Tool 1: Thought-Shifting

10. The Power of Quiet   138
    Tool 2: The Meditative Arts

11. Finding Your Voice   165
    Tool 3: Communication

12. Putting It on Paper   178
    Tool 4: Emotional Writing

13. Your Body of Emotions   198
    Tool 5: Physical Movement

14. The Importance of Others   223
    Tool 6: Connection

15. Reaching Out, Reaching In   245
    Tool 7: Psychotherapy

16. The Emotion Tree: A Guiding Formula   261

17. Putting It All Together   269

Appendix A: Common Questions   275
Appendix B: Resource Guide   280
References   287

Acknowledgments

Social support is an emotional tool of great value, and it is the support of many caring others that helped me complete this book. When my ideas were first taking shape, many women eagerly offered to read my early drafts and give feedback. I am grateful to Sue Donnellan, Gail Herndon, Susan Jensen, Janet Miller, Cathy Mininni, Marilyn Mininni, Deb Raupp, Marti Stewart, and Jill Turissini for their help.

It is with great affection that I thank C. C. Holland for her friendship and expert advice. Not only is she an extraordinarily talented editor, but in the beginning of this process, she gave me the emotional support I needed to continue writing.

I am indebted to my remarkable colleagues at UCLA, whose vision, integrity, and professionalism I so greatly value: Susan Jensen, Rena Orenstein, and especially, Pam Viele, whose generosity and wisdom I will always cherish.

Thank you to those experts in the field who took the time to review the manuscript for accuracy and content. They are Sara Lazar, Terry Oleson, James Pennebaker, Steven Petruzzello, Michael Ruff, Catia Sternini, M.D., and Alan Wallace. And thank you to those experts who spent time talking with me about their work: James H. Austin, Leslie Bogart, Karen Koffler, M.D., Larry Payne, and Richard Usatine, M.D. Thanks also to the many investigators worldwide who corresponded with me about their research. And a special thanks to Nischala Joy Devi for her willingness to help me, and for providing me with her creative yoga images.

I am forever grateful to Sharon Simon. Like an angel who was in my life only for a short time, she showed me there were other possibilities. I am also thankful to those individuals who've helped me stay emotionally healthy: Howard Lee, Virginia Mullin, and Shinzen Young.

I am grateful to Lita Singer for being a wonderful role model, mentor, and friend. I am equally grateful to Valerie Pinhas, the first academic woman to influence and shape my ideas about being a professional. Thanks to Aaron Mendelsohn for his sound advice about business and how it all works; to Susan Jensen and Deb Raupp for their constant emotional support; to Jon Entine for his early words of wisdom; and to Robert Doig for being such a great accountant and joke-teller.

Thanks to my agent, Patricia van der Leun, a nurturing soul who enthusiastically believed in this endeavor and helped me realize my dream. Thanks to the outstanding staff at St. Martin's Press, especially my talented editor Diane Reverand for her expertise and commitment to this project, and Regina Scarpa for her kindness and patience. I am also indebted to my publicist Suzanne Wickham-Beaird for her guidance, knowledge, and can-do spirit. Thanks also to Brian Goodman and Gennan Shippen of Public Works Productions for their excellent work.

Finally, thanks to the most important people in my life, my family. It is with gratitude that I thank my extraordinary parents, Marilyn and Alfred, for always believing in me, loving me, and being there when I needed them. And growing up just wouldn't have been much fun without my fantastic brothers, Joe and Gary.

I thank my precious husband, Bryan, for his devoted love, tireless support, and unwavering faith in me. From the first day we met, he's helped me reach my goals in a million different ways with his characteristic sense of caring, generosity, and creativity. I feel truly blessed to know him and cannot imagine my life without him. And thank you to my beautiful and amazing daughter, Sophia, who has taught me as much about life as I'm teaching her.

Last, but certainly not least, a heartfelt thank-you to the kind women who shared their stories with me for *The Emotional Toolkit.* Because of confidentiality, I won't mention their names, but they know who they are. And thank you to my many students and clients who have opened their hearts to me. I hope I have served them well.

The individuals in this book are based on real people. To protect their confidentiality, I have changed identifying information or created composites.

We learn by practice.
Whether it means to learn to dance by
practicing dancing or
to learn to live by
practicing living,
the principles are the same.

—Martha Graham

Introduction

When I was eleven years old, I remember having a disagreement with my mother. At one point in my completely illogical argument, she said, "You think you know everything." And she was right. I did know everything. My eleven-year-old world was very small, and I was the master of it.

As I grew older, things changed. My world got bigger, and suddenly I didn't know so much anymore. My life became complicated, filled with complex feelings, competing expectations, and societal pressures.

As an adult, I had to maneuver my way through the tricky emotions that came with intimate relationships, workplace responsibilities, balancing family and career, and living in a fast-paced culture. Like most people, I had been launched into my adult life without an emotional road map—without the skills I needed to live as successfully on the inside as I was educated to do on the outside.

Joan's Story

Joan, like me, felt unprepared to navigate her emotional world. When Joan and David married, they wanted to start a family right away. For two years, they tried to conceive with no luck. The couple was at odds over whether to give in vitro fertilization a try.

Emotionally, Joan was on a cyclical roller coaster. Each month she was anxious about the prospect of another disappointment, sad when she learned she wasn't pregnant, and angry at the unfairness of her situation.

The stress was wearing on the couple. Joan felt lost and unable to take control of her overwhelming emotions. The only strategies she used to soothe herself were eating junk food and going shopping. What Joan really needed were the emotional skills to understand and reduce her distress. She needed an Emotional Toolkit.

Your Emotional Education

If you're like most people, you've probably taken lots of classes in your life. You went to school and learned all about history and math. You may even have taken piano or swimming lessons. But what about lessons in your emotions? Where were those classes? Which courses taught you the purpose of your feelings or how to calm yourself when you were overwhelmed? Where did you learn how to put the brakes on your runaway thoughts or to express your angry feelings without harming your relationships? Unless you were very lucky, you had no such education.

How could it be that such a critical part of your life—understanding and managing your feelings—could be so glaringly omitted from your formal education? Maybe it's because we are not given awards and accolades for the development of our emotional selves. As author and cultural observer Gail Sheehy writes, "The prizes in our society are reserved for outer, not inner, achievements." As a result, developing emotional mastery seems less significant, and the vital skills we need to create happier lives go unlearned.

In my fifteen years as a behavioral health specialist and educator at UCLA, I saw many young women stumbling in their lives. They were intellectually bright, but they lacked emotional savvy. Most of these women were dealing with the normal challenges of life, but the negative aspects of these situations were magnified by their shortage of coping skills.

Danielle is a good example. When she arrived at college, she found herself living with five other girls in a small room. Each of these girls had wildly different habits and personalities. Every night, one of them would set her alarm for 6 A.M. When it rang the next morning, she would hit the snooze button again and again and again. Danielle, who didn't have class until 11 A.M., would lie awake frustrated, her sleep disturbed and her heart pounding with anger. But she never talked with her roommate about it, because she "didn't want to make a big deal out of nothing."

An alarm clock disagreement is not the end of the world, you may say. And that's true, but let's look at this situation more closely. By not speaking up, Danielle found herself getting increasingly angry with her roommate. She began feeling uncomfortable in her own room and spent more time away from the dorm and apart from her other roommates. She began feeling lonely and sad and started questioning her decision to go away to college. This is the spiraling effect an unaddressed emotion can have.

Although this may sound like college stuff, these types of struggles are not limited to young women. In my work I have seen women of all ages desperately trying to cope with their fears, manage feelings of loss, or stay centered in a demanding world. Adult women, like their younger counterparts, never learned the skills to navigate their emotional lives.

This was the situation for Maya. A financial analyst for a major consulting company, she was highly regarded and highly paid. She had learned her academic and professional lessons well, but her personal life was another story.

Maya's hands shook when she told me about a disagreement she had with her husband. "I get so upset with him sometimes, but I just stuff it all down. I'm afraid to tell him how I really feel."

"How is holding back your feelings affecting you?" I asked.

"Sometimes, when I'm hiding my true feelings, I feel distant from him, like he doesn't know the real me," she said. "But if I tell him how I really feel, it might hurt our relationship. I'm stuck between a rock and a hard place." Danielle could sound like this (or be in the same situation) ten years from now.

It is the rare woman who learns the skills needed to navigate her emotional life successfully, and yet we know from research that having these skills can help reduce distress and increase happiness. So how are you to learn these lessons? Wouldn't it be nice if you could take a class and learn what you need to know—if there were a place where you could obtain an Emotional Toolkit?

A Class About Life

In 1997, my UCLA colleague Pam Viele, and I observed that most students struggled with developmental issues because, in part, they had never learned the critical coping skills they needed to manage their feelings of anxiety, sadness, anger, loneliness, and other difficult emotions. It was my assignment to create a college course that would teach students what their feelings mean and how to reduce their distress. The initial class was designed strictly for women, since our earlier research was based on women and I had a lot of experience working with them.

For two years I worked on developing the course, which we called "LifeSkills." I spent countless hours at the library, combing through dry research studies to make sure the curriculum was based on sound psychological theory. The next step was to create something that the average student could understand, relate to, and enjoy.

When I finally taught my first LifeSkills class in 1999, I was nervous. How would the women respond to the class? Would they find it helpful? Could it in any small way make their lives easier and happier? I would find my answers when the results of our focus groups and anonymous surveys were revealed ten long weeks later.

When the evaluation results finally came in, I was floored by the responses. Many of the women found the course to be life-changing. They talked about feeling less overwhelmed even though their heavy workloads hadn't changed. They spoke of better relationships with romantic partners, parents, and roommates. They wrote about feeling stronger, more confident, and generally happier with their lives. In our initial survey, 100 percent of the students said the class had reduced their distress and had equipped them to manage their lives better. I was elated. Here are some of their comments:

I'm a better person because of this class. I feel like I can handle my life more easily now. I feel stronger and more confident.

I have had decreased anxiety since I started this class. I am a lot less lonely, sad, depressed, and nervous. I have seen a major change in my happiness level. I am much better off physically and emotionally than when I first started. I am happier and able to cope with the problems and stresses that arise in my life.

This course has enabled me to live much differently. I don't think I have even realized the total effects; this will be a lifelong process of continuing to develop and use the tools I have learned here.

This class enhanced my life, my spirit, my personality, and it brought forth my potential and maximized it. I couldn't really be much happier.

The next quarter I taught the class again. By now, word had spread, and there was a waiting list to get in. In eighteen months, the number of applicants to the class would jump from thirty to seven hundred. I was amazed by the sheer magnitude of the course's impact, and I was about to be surprised again.

"I Wish I Could Take Your Class"

Many students told me that they talked with their mothers about what they were learning in class. Some mothers were so interested in the topics that they made regular telephone appointments to talk with their daughters about the latest class lessons. One student even told me that her mother made copies of the course materials and started a discussion group with other women in her hometown. I was beginning to realize I'd struck a nerve.

When I would give talks to community groups of women about issues related to psychology or emotional health, the host would usually mention my work with the LifeSkills course in the introduction. When question-and-answer time arrived, the audience would enthusiastically ask about the class.

"Can I take the class? I really need something like that."

"I'm sorry," I'd say, "it's only for undergraduates."

"Will you ever offer it to the public? And if so, where can I sign up?"

Others chimed in, "Yes, yes." They too, wanted to learn the skills taught in my class so they could better manage their lives. They were having problems with in-laws, with children, with work, with long commutes. Even when my own colleagues, friends, and family learned about my course, they said, "I really need something like that. I wish I could take your class."

What Is an Emotional Toolkit?

It was clear that women of all ages were looking for the emotional education they never had. Listening to this growing chorus of voices, I decided to respond. I distilled the core skills of the LifeSkills course and refashioned them to apply to women of all ages and situations. The result is this book. It is a guide to understanding the purpose of your feelings and changing your unpleasant moods using what I call the Emotional Toolkit.

Part One

Opening Your Toolkit

1

It's Time for Your Emotional Education

Everything has been figured out, except how to live.

—Jean-Paul Sartre, philosopher

Imagine having your own Emotional Toolkit. When you experience a feeling that is confusing or distressing, you reach into your Toolkit and find the tool that helps you cope more effectively. You find a tool that helps you understand your feelings more fully or respond with more clarity. You find a tool that can actually change the chemicals in your body that influence your feelings.

Each tool in the Emotional Toolkit has been scientifically studied at universities and medical centers throughout the country and has been shown to improve emotional well-being. I've done exhaustive research and included only those strategies with a proven track record for success.

The tools are practical, usable skills that help you manage your emotions. They are not academic or theoretical or abstract. They are real skills to use in everyday life.

The Emotional Toolkit is more than a book; it is an opportunity to get what most of us missed: a how-to course in the basic skills of

your emotional life. Even if you are, or have been, in psychotherapy, this book can supplement the process with action-based
strategies that will complement and enhance the therapy experience. This book is for you if you've ever felt:

- confused about what you're feeling
- powerless to reduce the intensity or duration of your
  distressing feelings
- consumed by your thoughts and feelings
- unable to shift your unpleasant moods
- overwhelmed trying to stay centered in a fast-paced world

Why Is This Book Focused on Women?

Let's face it. Haven't we all felt some of the feelings on the preced-
ing list at one time or another? I know I have, and so have most of
my friends, colleagues, clients, and students. And it's not just
women who experience these feelings—men do, too. Men also feel
pressured and confused and overwhelmed, and all the Emotional
Tools in this book work just as well for men. However, I decided to
focus this book on women because I've had many years of experience in teaching, counseling, and writing about women. As such,
I've gathered many people's stories to share—as well as stories
from my own life.

Mind you, confidentiality is of utmost importance to me, and I
would never break that trust. I've removed all identifying information from the stories you'll read in this book, and in many cases,
I've created composites. Still, I think it's critically important that
we share our stories with one another. Although you may sit and
read this book alone, it is my hope that you will feel connected to
some of the women you read about.

The Seven Power-Skills

This book presents seven tools to help you manage your emotional life with mastery:

- **Tool 1, thought-shifting.** Your negative thoughts directly affect the quality and intensity of your feelings. Positive affirmations are not the answer because, for most people, they don't work. Thought-shifting includes four steps that can help you shift your thoughts from judging to supporting.

- **Tool 2, meditative arts.** The meditative arts include belly breathing, mindfulness meditation, and meditation-in-action. These powerful body-mind tools can reduce anxiety, sadness, and anger. They can also increase your happiness and optimism by transforming your thinking patterns and increasing activity in the region of your brain associated with upbeat and happy moods.

- **Tool 3, communication.** The key to becoming an effective communicator is not just learning a few techniques, but also understanding what your communication style is and how it developed. When you use strategies that are consistent with your needs, you will be able to reduce anxiety, sadness, and anger.

- **Tool 4, emotional writing.** It's hard to believe that just writing about your distressing feelings can change them, but it can. People who write about their deepest feelings in a specific way are less depressed, less anxious, and more positive about life than are those who write about trivial things.

- **Tool 5, physical movement.** Emotional exercise, movement that can shift your emotions, can take whatever form you like—walking, dancing, or yoga, just to name a few. When done in a prescribed manner, movement can be as effective as a minor tranquilizer at reducing anxiety-related muscle tension. It can also create an effect in your brain similar to that of antidepressant drugs like Prozac.

- **Tool 6, connection.** Feeling connected to others can decrease your sadness, anxiety, and loneliness and can even increase your self-esteem. Activities like entertaining people at your home or belonging to a bowling team are the happiness equivalent of more than doubling your income.

- **Tool 7, psychotherapy.** Most people who seek therapy report less anxiety and depression as well as better relationships than do those with similar problems who don't go to therapy. Therapy works best when you have a good relationship with your therapist, learn new skills, and are encouraged to take action.

From this array of strategies, you can choose the Emotional Tools that are right for your personality and your situation. Over time they may change. The goal is to know yourself well enough to say, "Yes, when I use this tool, I know I'll feel better." Keep in mind that it is not necessary to incorporate all these techniques into your life at the same time. That would be overwhelming and would defeat the whole purpose of making you feel better. Instead, use the tool or tools that work best for you.

Managing Your Emotional Life

You don't need me to tell you that life has its ups and downs. M. Scott Peck started his classic book *The Road Less Traveled* with the line, "Life is difficult," and it's true. No matter how charmed your life is, you will experience a range of emotions from joy, love, and exhilaration to sadness, anger, and fear. And this is normal.

In addition to your day-to-day reactions to life, there are cyclical emotions you can expect to experience. According to Yale University psychology professor and researcher Daniel Levinson, adults will have predictable crises in their lives separated by times of calm. These crises arrive approximately every five to seven years and have to do with your *evolving identity.*

Your evolving identity is the way you change as a result of time, experiences, and just plain living. For example, the challenges and choices you face in your twenties or thirties—What kind of work will I do? Will I marry? Where will I live?—are different from the ones you face in your forties or fifties when you might ask, Have I made good choices? Is there something I've neglected to do in my life? Each time you reevaluate your life, you may bring up feelings of excitement and anticipation as well as loss and confusion. All of this is to be expected.

Sometimes people strive for great wealth or fame, thinking it will insulate them from distressing feelings and imagining that once they have "arrived" they will be forever happy. They are often surprised to realize that a short while after attaining their goals, they still feel the same way they have always felt, experiencing the ups and downs of life. As author Jon Kabat-Zinn so aptly says, "Wherever you go, there you are."

Your emotions have a purpose: they are signals that can tell you important things about yourself, if you listen. Anxiety can be a sign that you need to be alert to a potential danger. Anger might occur when you feel you've been violated in some way. And sadness can be a validation that you have lost something valuable. It's as if your body is saying, "Look at me; something in your life needs attention!" Our aim is not to remove all unhappy emotions, but rather to reduce the amount of time they exist and to decrease the distress that gets created around them.

Of course, long-term distress may be a sign of a more serious condition, such as clinical depression or anxiety. When emotions debilitate you or remove joy from your life for a significant amount of time, it is helpful to seek professional counseling. This will be discussed in more detail with Emotional Tool 7, psychotherapy.

Becoming Emotionally Fluent

One certainty in life is that things don't always turn out the way you plan. You may be rushing to an important appointment only to find that your car battery has died. Or you may be eagerly anticipating the birth of your first child, only to be overwhelmed by the demands of new motherhood. Or you may have worked hard for a promotion only to be passed over. This is life. You can't always change what happens on the outside. This book focuses on what you *can* change and how you respond on the inside.

By employing the Emotional Toolkit, you will not automatically be happy all the time, although many women taking my course have reported increased happiness. What I can guarantee is that you will be emotionally fluent. In other words, you will be able to use your emotions as a guide to understanding your deeper needs. You will understand more clearly how to identify your feelings. And once you've identified them, you will be able to act on them in a way that will help reduce your distress and ultimately increase your happiness.

Before we discuss the purpose of your emotions and the Emotional Toolkit, let's recap the key points we've discussed so far:

- Your emotions have a purpose.
- If you pay attention to your emotions, you can learn about yourself and your needs.
- The Emotional Toolkit can reduce the amount of time unhappy emotions exist and decrease the distress they create.
- You can't always change the things that happen in your life, but you can affect the way you respond emotionally.

- You can personalize your Emotional Toolkit by using the tools that work best for you.

How to Get the Most Out of This Book

In order for you to get the most out of this book, I offer the following advice:

- **Be patient with yourself as you learn the Emotional Tools.** Many times I've listened to women berate themselves for not using the Emotional Tools more often, with more precision, for a longer period of time, or with a better outcome. These personal floggings defeat the whole intent of the tools. Judging yourself harshly will only increase your distressing feelings, not reduce them. Perfection is not the goal. Congratulate yourself for whatever you do.

- **Understand that change doesn't happen overnight.** You probably didn't learn how to read the alphabet or manage your finances in just one day. Skills take time to master. They also take practice. Some of these skills require a bit of courage along with know-how. Focus on how far you've come, not how far you have to go. As I tell my clients and students, change starts with baby steps.

- **As you read the stories of others, use them as a source of motivation, not comparison.** Seeing that others have struggled with feelings can be comforting, and reading about people using their Emotional Toolkit to help themselves can be inspiring. It becomes defeating, though, if you say, "Gee, she mastered that skill so quickly; why can't I?"

- **Consult Appendix A for answers to questions I'm commonly asked.** Although I'm not there to address each of your concerns personally, this appendix can help you overcome common roadblocks and clear up some of your confusion.

- **Consult the Resource Guide in Appendix B.** Some of the information you'll be learning might stimulate your desire to know more about a specific topic. In the Resource Guide you'll find information on books, videotapes, audiotapes, workshops, and Web sites that can help you with each of the Emotional Tools you'll be learning about.

My Hope for You

As you read this book, I hope that you will see me as your teacher and guide. Although I might be considered an expert in psychology, I can relate to you because I have struggled with many of these issues myself. Almost everyone I know has, regardless of fancy degrees or impressive titles. I have found that having a core foundation of Emotional Tools has helped me navigate my emotional life with more confidence. It doesn't mean I never stumble, but when I do, I'm better equipped to pick myself up—and you will be too.

It is my hope that as you master the Emotional Toolkit, you will experience the same positive changes in your life that many of the women in my LifeSkills class did. I'm remembering the comments of one such student: "I feel much more knowledgeable and confident in myself. I feel like I can communicate if I want to, rather than just holding things in. I am more centered and grounded as a person. I have acquired a new outlook on life because I am more peaceful and more realistic. I have gained a new sense of self, in which I enjoy the moment . . . and feel more relaxed. I have a new sense of internal happiness. I attribute all of this to the Emotional Toolkit."

Now it's time for you to come to class. Welcome and have a seat.

2

A Feeling Is a Full-Body Experience

Every thought we think has a biochemical equivalent.

—Christiane Northrup, physician

Did you know that by simply slowing down your breathing you can stimulate the release of acetylcholine, a chemical responsible for creating a calm and tranquil feeling? Or that talking with a friend about a problem can promote the action of peptides that help create feelings of emotional well-being? In fact, research now shows that some of the old adages, such as "Take time to smell the roses" or "A faithful friend is the medicine of life," are scientifically true.

Using the Emotional Toolkit to Improve Physical Well-Being

A wealth of information confirms that people who use the emotional skills you'll be learning in this book can deliberately improve their physical health. Here are a few of the studies that show the power of some of these tools. I've highlighted the tools in italics.

James Pennebaker, while at Southern Methodist University in Dallas, found that individuals who *wrote about upsetting personal experiences* had higher-functioning immune systems, lower blood pressure, and fewer symptoms of asthma and rheumatoid arthritis than did individuals who wrote about trivial topics. The simple act of putting pen to paper and writing about feelings actually made people healthier.

In another study, David Spiegel, M.D., at Stanford University Medical School, found that women with advanced breast cancer who participated in a *support group* along with their medical treatment lived twice as long as did women who received only the medical treatment. The women in the support group were encouraged to talk about how they felt, both the good and the bad.

Expressive emotional tools—strategies in which you express feelings either verbally or in writing—are not the only ones shown to produce positive physical benefits. Alice Domar of the Mind/Body Center for Women's Health at Harvard Medical School found that women with infertility who practiced *meditation and thought-shifting* were more likely to conceive than were women who did not use these Emotional Tools. And Jon Kabat-Zinn and his colleagues at the University of Massachusetts Medical School found that psoriasis patients who followed a *mindfulness meditation* audiotape while undergoing ultraviolet (UV) light treatments experienced clearing of their skin lesions faster than did patients who did not meditate with their UV treatments.

The Power of the Emotional Toolkit

The power the Emotional Tools can have on the body's natural ability to function and heal is astonishing. What turns out to be equally astonishing is that along the road to getting physically healthier, people who use these tools get happier, more centered, and more optimistic. Even when people were diagnosed as terminally ill, as in Dr. Spiegel's support group, they still felt more connected, understood, and loved. Now science is helping us understand why these Emotional Tools can have such a profound effect on your emotional well-being.

The Biology of Feeling Good

To understand how the strategies from the Emotional Toolkit can biologically enhance your emotional well-being, you need to understand a little about your body. Picture your body as an elaborate communication system in which interaction occurs between every cell in every system. Your nervous system is composed of your brain, spinal cord, and long nerves that project into your body. It has delicate switches that can be flipped on or off, depending on your situation or thoughts. The position in which each switch gets flipped will dictate how your body responds. Let's take a look at what happens when the switch is on.

How Your Body Expresses Emotions

Imagine you're feeling anxious. How do you know you're having that particular feeling? What happens in your body to let you know that things are not quite right? Take a minute to think of a few of the body signals you receive.

Although different people will experience different signals, you may have tense shoulders, a headache, jaw clenching, cold or sweaty hands, rapid breathing, trouble sleeping, racing thoughts, a pounding heartbeat, or difficulty concentrating. These are all signs that the switch for your sympathetic nervous system has been turned on.

The sympathetic nervous system is composed of neuron fibers that are linked to all of your internal organs—heart, kidneys, intestines, stomach, and so forth. Most of the reactions in this system operate without your conscious awareness. Your heart doesn't beat because you get up every morning and tell it to. It beats automatically. It's the same with the functioning of your stomach and intestines. You don't have to tell your digestive system, "Okay, consume that bagel." It knows what to do without instructions from you.

Although highly efficient, this delicate system is primed to respond to situations and thoughts in a primitive way. It was originally designed to allow our prehistoric ancestors to run from a vicious lion or escape natural disasters, but it responds the same way in the modern world to problems like getting stuck in traffic or dealing with an overbearing boss.

What exactly does the sympathetic nervous system do when it's activated? It spits out a chemical called norepinephrine that sends energy to your muscles so you can run or jump if you need to get away from that lion. This fight-or-flight response quickens your heartbeat so oxygen can speed to your muscles and brain to give you energy. It accelerates your breathing so you'll have more oxygen in your lungs for an impending battle. The size of your blood vessels gets smaller to divert blood away from your extremities in case you are wounded in the fight.

The problem is that in our modern lives, the issues and dilemmas we face don't require us to rally our internal troops to such a heightened degree. You don't need a pounding heart or tense muscles to explain to your husband for the hundredth time why you want him to put the toilet seat down. And you can't use your extra energy and muscle strength to pop your boss in the nose for that disapproving sneer he or she's been known to give, although sometimes you might like to.

Tapping into the power of the sympathetic nervous system can be helpful if you're about to run a race or need energy to respond to an emergency. However, people often find themselves becoming anxious or depressed when this system is continually activated by the stresses of daily life. And this, it seems, has become a normal condition in the twenty-first century. Our nervous systems are constantly turned on in anticipation of the next demand or crisis.

A Case of Sympathetic Arousal

When I was in graduate school, I was in a never-ending state of sympathetic arousal. I had left my whole life in New York—family, friends, familiar things—and moved to Los Angeles to attend UCLA. My classes were demanding, with workloads that were challenging and relentless. Although I was doing well in my studies, I was completely unschooled in how to deal with my distressing feelings. I was anxious, wondering how I would make it in a new city with no friends, no car (practically a crime in Los Angeles), and little money. My tense shoulders were practically touching my ears as I sat down to study. My heart would often race with fear as I focused on all the things that could go wrong. If only I had known then what I know now—how to shut off the switch to my sympathetic nervous system.

Calling In the Feel-Good Chemicals

In the late 1960s, groundbreaking Harvard University researcher Herbert Benson, M.D., wondered: if activating the sympathetic nervous system could create feelings of anxiety and tension by revving up the body, what would happen if its counterpart—the parasympathetic nervous system—was purposefully activated?

The parasympathetic nervous system is wired to put the brakes on the sympathetic nervous system. With long, neuron fibers spreading throughout the body, it spurts a chemical called acetylcholine. This chemical is responsible for slowing the heart rate, lowering the blood pressure, promoting blood flow to all the organs, and generally reversing the internal processes the sympathetic nervous system has set in motion.

Dr. Benson worked with volunteers who practiced meditation, a technique we now know directly affects the nervous system among other things. He hooked up the volunteers to various machines and found that when they turned on the switch to their parasympa-

thetic nervous systems—or as he called it, the *relaxation response*—
they not only slowed down their physical reactions, but they positively affected their emotions.

As Dr. Benson describes it, the meditators "felt at ease with the
world, peace of mind, and a sense of well-being akin to that feeling
experienced after a period of exercise but without the fatigue." Indeed, Dr. Benson had shown that the emotions and the body are
linked and, more important, that the physical processes that influence certain emotions can be consciously and purposefully controlled.

The Mind-Body Split

Dr. Benson's work was radical for its time, because traditional
views of biology and psychology had long maintained that the
mind and body are two separate entities. If I were to ask you,
"Where is the mind located?" you might likely say, "In the brain."
Indeed, most people think of the mind as inhabiting the area above
the neck. Seventeenth-century philosopher René Descartes first
declared that the mind and the body are separate, a belief that has
been maintained for more than three hundred years.

We're now learning that this division of the mind and body is
artificial. Research is confirming that brainlike tissue is found
throughout the entire body—in the intestines, the stomach, and all
other organs—suggesting that the mind is not sitting inside the
brain. The body and the mind are continually communicating
with, and directing each other through, the cells. If you know how
to jump into their conversation—by using the Emotional
Toolkit—you can have a profound impact on the chemicals that
contribute to your emotional well-being.

Your Emotions Are Living Things

Pioneering neuroscientist Candace Pert made the remarkable discovery that feelings are created in part from the action of physical substances in the brain and body. Emotions develop from a chain of amino acids called a *peptide*. Peptides carry messages to every cell in your body. According to Pert, if emotions, particularly strong ones, are suppressed, they can clog the biological system, causing both physical and psychological disturbances. When feelings are processed, the peptides move through the system unimpeded, contributing to feelings of happiness.

Have you ever held in a strong emotion like sadness? Maybe you were embarrassed to share it with others, or you didn't want to burden anyone with it, or you felt you should work it out on your own. Then maybe a friend or a family member said, "You look sad; are you okay?" and you just burst out crying. You told your story and talked about your feelings. In a short while, you felt lighter. Even though the situation may not have changed, you felt better. That's an example of unclogging the biological system by processing your emotions. In her book, *Molecules of Emotion,* Pert writes: "When emotions are repressed, denied, not allowed to be whatever they may be, our network pathways get blocked, stopping the flow of the vital feel-good, unifying chemicals that run both our biology and our behavior. . . . When your emotions are moving and your chemicals flowing, you will experience feelings of freedom, hopefulness, joy because you are in a healthy, whole state."

Right In the Gut

Researchers Marcello Costa, M.D., John Furness, and Michael Gershon, M.D., made the stunning rediscovery of a second brain located in the gut, after its original discovery by nineteenth-century

British researchers Bayliss and Starling went nearly unnoticed. Containing more than a hundred million nerve cells, this "belly brain" has its own nervous system, called the *enteric nervous system,* capable of functioning without the help of the bigger brain located in the skull. According to Dr. Gershon, "The enteric nervous system may never compose syllogisms, write poetry, or engage in Socratic dialogue, but it is a brain nevertheless. It runs its organ, the gut; and if push comes to shove . . . it can do it all by itself."

Researchers have shown that in addition to governing the functions of the gastrointestinal tract, the belly brain may also store physical information from past decisions and situations. When new circumstances arise that require judgments, the belly brain sends out "gut feelings" from its past experiences to help guide decision making. Let me illustrate this process.

Lorraine met Thomas, a man who seemed wonderful. They really liked being together and had much in common. As the weeks turned into months, Lorraine noticed that Thomas would put her down. It was subtle at first: "You really like that kind of music? I don't know anyone who likes it." Over time, the putdowns became more obvious. Thomas would roll his eyes when Lorraine talked about something he disagreed with, or he would cut her off in midsentence. Lorraine didn't like being treated this way and decided to end the relationship.

One night several months after the breakup, Lorraine was at a party. A handsome man came over to talk with her. They began chatting about Lorraine's work. "How could you work in a hospital? I'd never want a job like that."

Suddenly, Lorraine got a pang in her stomach. It was a familiar feeling, the same one she used to get when Thomas put her down. "I think I see a friend, would you excuse me?" Lorraine said, moving away.

Lorraine had learned something from her past experience with Thomas, so when she saw it happening again, she knew to stay away. Moreover, Lorraine's belly brain was also giving her signals in the form of gut feelings to let her know that this was not the man for her. So gut feelings are not just in your head, and those butterflies in your stomach have a biological basis.

The purpose of this biology lesson is to help you understand that the Emotional Tools will use the resources of your whole body to affect your emotions in a positive way. The first step is for you to become aware of your emotions and the messages they are sending you.

Part Two

Finding
Your Tools

3

Understanding
Your Feelings

*I believe all emotions are healthy because
emotions are what unite the mind and the body.*

—Candace Pert, neuroscientist

One day I received a frantic phone call from Nancy. Her rapid speech was punctuated with brief moments of crying as she tried to convey all that was happening.

"I don't know what I'm going to do," she said.

"What's going on?" I asked.

"I was laid off from my job on Friday. I don't know what I'm going to do," she repeated.

"Okay, Nancy. Let's take this one step at a time. What are you feeling as you tell me this?" I asked.

"I don't know. It's all just a blur."

As a former client of mine, Nancy was familiar with examining her body and mind to find out what she was feeling.

"Let's begin with your body," I said. "What's happening in your body?"

"My stomach is tight. I keep clenching my teeth, and my heart is pounding."

"Okay. Now let's move to your thinking. What kind of thoughts are you having?" I asked.

"So many thoughts all at once: What if I can't find another job? What if I can't pay my mortgage? What if I can't pay for my son's preschool? I can't sleep because I'm constantly worrying, and I don't have any answers."

"Your body is tense, and your heart is racing. Your thoughts are focused on the future and all that could go wrong. What kind of emotion is that, Nancy?"

Nancy immediately recognized the body and mind connection.

"It's anxiety. I'm afraid. It's fear," she announced. As she spoke these words, her tense body began to relax.

You'd think that realizing she was feeling fear might magnify the emotion, but it doesn't. When you acknowledge the unidentified feeling you're having, your body relaxes, as if to say, "Thank you for noticing me."

Once Nancy identified her feelings, we were able to uncover what was driving her fears. With that knowledge, we then came up with a strategy to reduce her distress by using the Emotional Toolkit.

The next section will help you understand your feelings and what's beneath them. This is the foundation for becoming emotionally fluent. With this insight, you'll be able to choose the Emotional Tools that can help you reduce, and in some cases eliminate, your distressing feelings.

What Are Feelings?

Feelings are expressed in both your body and your mind, and they influence and interact with each other. A feeling is a full-body experience. Feelings are based on a unique combination of your perceptions, thoughts, beliefs, and past experiences, as well as the chemical workings of your body, including your brain, glands, internal organs, and muscles.

In trying to recognize a feeling, it is helpful to be able to identify what's going on in your body and mind. I call this "deconstructing a feeling," which means picking it apart into its basic components so that you can put it back together with a better understanding. That's what Nancy did.

Noticing Your Feelings

Throughout the day you experience many different emotions. Start to become conscious of how you feel. Take a minute to write down all of the feelings you've experienced in the last twenty-four hours. You can use the Feeling Chart on the next page to help you identify them.

The Body of a Feeling

When you have a feeling, your body experiences it. If you become aware of your physical sensations, you can notice how your body "feels" an emotion. One woman may notice she clenches her jaw when she's angry. Another may find that her stomach gets tight when she's worried. This is your body's emotional voice.

As you become more aware of your body, you may begin to notice that you have particular physical and emotional patterns. Tiredness may signal that you're feeling sad. A headache may be a recurrent sign that you're paying more attention to the emotional needs of others than to yourself. When you begin to recognize such patterns, you are becoming acquainted with the language of your body.

Body sensations can quickly change depending on the situation. This was the case for Rachael. She went on an interview for a job she really wanted. She was nervous, and her body expressed that nervousness with a pounding heart, perspiring hands, and a dry mouth.

The Feeling Chart

Accomplished	Foolish	Needed	Tired
Accepted	Forgiving	Optimistic	Trapped
Adventurous	Fortunate	Overwhelmed	Troubled
Afraid	Fragile	Panicky	Trusted
Agitated	Frantic	Passionate	Unappreciated
Angry	Frustrated	Peaceful	Unattractive
Anxious	Fulfilled	Pessimistic	Uncertain
Appreciative	Furious	Preoccupied	Uncomfortable
Apprehensive	Glad	Pressured	Understood
Ashamed	Good	Proud	Uneasy
Awkward	Grateful	Provoked	Unfulfilled
Beautiful	Great	Quiet	Unique
Bored	Guilty	Recognized	Unsuccessful
Brave	Happy	Regretful	Unsure
Calm	Hateful	Rejected	Uptight
Capable	Helpless	Relaxed	Used
Cautious	Hopeful	Relieved	Uplifted
Cheerful	Hopeless	Remorseful	Valuable
Cherished	Hostile	Renewed	Victimized
Comfortable	Humiliated	Resentful	Victorious
Competent	Hurt	Respected	Voracious
Concerned	Ignored	Sad	Vulnerable
Confident	Impatient	Safe	Wavering
Confused	Inadequate	Satisfied	Weak
Connected	Incompetent	Secure	Weary
Curious	Indecisive	Self-conscious	Welcome
Defeated	Inferior	Sexy	Well-balanced
Delighted	Inhibited	Shaken	Whole
Dependent	Insecure	Shocked	Wicked
Depressed	Irritated	Shy	Willing
Desirable	Isolated	Silly	Wishful
Desperate	Jealous	Special	Witty
Devastated	Joyful	Spiritual	Womanly
Devoted	Lonely	Strong	Wonderful
Disappointed	Lovable	Stubborn	Worn-out
Discouraged	Loved	Stupid	Worldly
Disgusted	Loyal	Supported	Worried
Disrespected	Lucky	Sympathetic	Worthwhile
Doubtful	Mellow	Terrified	Yearning
Embarrassed	Miserable	Thankful	Youthful
Energized	Misunderstood	Threatened	Zany
Excited	Needy	Thrilled	

After she left the interview, Rachael sensed that she didn't get the job. She became sad. That sadness felt like a heaviness in her body, a loss of energy, and a desire to cry. These were all physical manifestations of her feelings, the body part of an emotion.

The Mind of a Feeling

The mind part of a feeling is related to any thoughts, beliefs, or perceptions you have about a situation. This aspect of a feeling includes how you interpret things based on your past experiences or temperament and what you tell yourself about those interpretations. After the interview ended, Rachael thought, "I didn't get the job because I'm not smart enough. I said dumb things. I'll never have the career I want. Why even bother trying?"

These thoughts underscore Rachael's interpretation that the interview did not go well because she's not competent. It's easy to see how she would feel sad given her perception of her abilities.

To show how different thoughts can create different feelings, let's look at Ling. She had the same job interview as Rachael, with the same results, but her interpretation of what happened differed: "I really wish this had worked out, but it didn't. I'm not happy, but I know I'm capable. I'm sure there's another job out there that's right for me."

Given Ling's interpretation of the situation, it's obvious her feeling reaction was different from Rachael's—Ling was more disappointed than sad. Psychiatrist Aaron Beck, a chief originator of cognitive therapy, claims that the way we interpret situations can profoundly influence the feelings that result. Being able to identify and shift your thinking patterns is a crucial part of being able to reduce your distressing feelings. You will learn how to do this using Tool 1, thought-shifting.

Becoming Aware of Your Feelings

Becoming aware of your body sensations and thinking patterns is the basis for becoming aware of your feelings. Some people may notice the body signs more easily than their thoughts, or vice versa. This dominance doesn't really matter. Over time, you will be able to put the two together.

What Feelings Give You

Many people label feelings as good or bad. For example, they consider happiness good and anger bad. If you understand the reasons feelings exist, you might not be so quick to judge them.

In some cases, feelings give you needed information. This information might be related to your relationships, emotional needs, or level of safety. A simple example can be seen with Lisa. Usually an outgoing person who easily mingles at parties, she suddenly felt sad when her husband joined a group of his school friends to talk about old times. This sadness gave Lisa some valuable information: she realized that she needed to be included to feel good. Acting on that feeling, she walked over and joined her husband's buddies, who were happy to entertain her with their stories.

Feelings can also provide you with the energy you need to respond to specific circumstances. For example, Donna felt a rush of nervous energy when the high school called to say her son got hurt while playing basketball. Although her son turned out to be fine, Donna's sympathetic nervous system kicked in to help give her the energy she needed to rush to the school and focus on her son.

Given the usefulness of feelings, our aim is not to eliminate all unpleasant emotions. That would be unhealthy. Rather, our goal is to reduce the amount of time difficult emotions exist and to decrease the distress that often accompanies them.

4

The Four Gateway Feelings

Happiness is not being pained in body or troubled in mind.

—Thomas Jefferson, U.S. president

M ost feelings can be categorized into four types: anxiety, sadness, anger, and happiness. I call these *gateway feelings* because they encompass a range of related emotions that share similar characteristics and benefit from the same Emotional Tools. In essence, I believe all emotions can be reduced to the four gateway feelings shown on the list below.

ANXIETY	SADNESS	ANGER	HAPPINESS
nervousness	grief	upset	joy
apprehension	remorse	displeasure	elation
dread	loneliness	outrage	pleasure
panic	guilt	frustration	gratitude
trepidation	shame	resentment	relief
insecurity	inadequacy	judgment	excitement

ANXIETY	SADNESS	ANGER	HAPPINESS
concern	gloom	exasperation	pride
overload	sorrow	annoyance	amusement
jealousy	jealousy	jealousy	contentment
vulnerability	humiliation	irritation	love
fright	hurt	bitterness	delight

You can experience gateway feelings in many different ways. For example, sometimes you might have multiple feelings in the same category. Take the anger category: you could be upset at your sister for being late again to pick you up and resentful that her lack of responsibility will cause you to miss the beginning of your granddaughter's recital.

It's also possible to feel emotions from different categories at the same time. You could feel grief over the loss of a relationship and nervousness about now facing the future alone. Or you could be angry with a friend for not being there to help when you were in crisis, as well as sad that you no longer feel as close to her because of it. Or you could feel lonely now that your youngest child has left for college but happy with your newfound freedom. Let's look more closely at the four gateway feelings of anxiety, sadness, anger, and happiness.

Anxiety

We all experience anxiety. Anxiety is a normal feeling. It gets your attention when there is a threat to your well-being. Certainly it's hard to ignore a pounding heart or shaking knees. Anxiety also activates your body so you'll have the energy you need to take care of yourself if there's a danger.

Anxiety is the racing heart Amanda feels when she's about to give the toast at her sister's wedding; the fearful thoughts that run through Mia's mind when she thinks about life without her mother; and the tense shoulders Loretta feels each time the man she's trying to avoid calls and leaves a message on her answering machine. In order to understand anxiety, let's first deconstruct it into its body and mind components.

The Body of Anxiety

When you feel anxious, there are usually clear signs from your body. For example:

- racing heart
- tense muscles
- sweating
- dry mouth

- feeling on edge
- shaking
- shallow breathing
- difficulty sleeping

Different people will experience different signals, but in general everything just seems to go faster (heartbeat, breathing) or feel tighter (tense muscles, clenched jaw). This is because the switch to your sympathetic nervous system has been turned on, and your body is producing norepinephrine so you can run from that vicious lion we mentioned earlier. Even though there is probably no lion in your immediate vicinity, there is a feeling of danger. This danger is often a psychological one.

The Mind of Anxiety

For many people, a familiar component of anxiety is what happens to their thoughts. It can feel like a tornado is spinning through your head. Your thoughts race fast and furious, and it seems as if there's no way to stop them. For this reason, when you're feeling anxious, you may have difficulty concentrating or sleeping.

A common characteristic of anxious thoughts is *what-if* thinking: What if I can't do this? What if it doesn't work out the way I want? What if they don't like me? Nancy had these kinds of thoughts after she was laid off from her job.

Note that these anxious thoughts are focused on the future. That's a hallmark of anxiety: *worrying thoughts are focused on the future and all that could go wrong there.* They are also coupled with the belief that if things go wrong, you might not be able to handle it.

It's All About Your Fear

The many forms of anxiety include feeling overwhelmed, panicked, or scared, and they all have one thing in common. If you were to break anxiety down, you'd find fear at the bottom of it. Amanda is afraid she'll forget her wedding speech, and people will judge her harshly. Mia is afraid she won't be able to stand on her

At the Bottom of Your Anxiety Is Fear

Anxiety	I'm Afraid That . . .
Amanda is about to give the toast at her sister's wedding.	"People will criticize me if it isn't good. I'll look like a fool, and I'll disappoint my sister."
Mia thinks about life without her mother.	"I won't make good decisions without my mother's guidance, and negative things will happen as a result."
Loretta doesn't answer the phone when the man she's trying to avoid calls and leaves a message.	"If I tell him I'm not interested, I'll hurt his feelings, and he'll think less of me because of it."

own when her mother dies. Loretta is afraid of hurting her suitor's feelings with a rejection.

Two Kinds of Fear

Fear can be divided into two types: *danger fear* and *loss fear*. Danger fear creates anxiety if you feel the threat will cause harm to your physical well-being. Such a threat might be finding out you have a life-threatening illness, living in a dangerous area, or walking alone in a dark parking lot.

DANGER FEAR

Diana knows about danger fear. While she and her husband were making love, he found a lump in her left breast. Diana knew she needed to make an appointment with her doctor first thing in the morning. While she lay in bed waiting for the sun to rise, a million thoughts raced through her mind: What if it's cancer? What if they say I need to have chemotherapy? What if the treatment doesn't work? Diana felt the fear wash over her tense body.

As soon as the clock struck 9 A.M., Diana made an appointment to see the doctor. Tests revealed a small benign cyst. It wasn't cancer. Diana's relief softened her tense body, and her thoughts shifted from panic to gratitude.

LOSS FEAR

Loss fear occurs when you are anxious about a real or imagined future loss—for instance, the loss of a job, relationship, status, or regard from others. Benita experienced this type of fear when she was deciding whether or not to tell her family she is gay.

Benita grew up in a close-knit, loving family. The clan would gather once a month for her mom's classic Sunday dinner. Benita treasured this time, but always felt that something was missing. That something was a part of her, the part she was afraid to share with those she loved the most.

Benita had the same recurring thoughts. She would reveal to everyone that she was gay, and suddenly everything would change. They would never disown her, but somehow an air of disappointment would forever linger. Benita wanted to tell her family, but was afraid of their disapproval.

Finally, one day while they were sitting alone in her family kitchen, Benita decided to tell her mother. At first, her mother was in shock. Although Benita had many years of knowing about her sexual identity, her mother didn't. She was clumsy and embarrassed by her daughter's sudden revelation. Benita could see her worries becoming a reality. Finally, with tears in her eyes, her mother said, "I loved you from the day I first held you in my arms, and there's nothing that will ever change that. I'll always be proud of you." In that instant, Benita's anxiety vanished.

Of course, it's possible that both these stories could have ended differently. Diana could have been diagnosed with breast cancer, and Benita's family could have rejected her. At that point, their anxieties may have intensified, shifted to sadness or anger, or included any combination of the three. We'll talk more about these feelings later.

It's Not Just Fear

It isn't just fear alone that characterizes anxiety. In most cases, it's fear coupled with a feeling that you can't handle the situation causing the fear. Diana might believe that she can't cope with the realities of a life-threatening illness. Benita may believe that she won't be able to manage the loss she would feel if her family disapproved of her. In this respect, if anxiety were a mathematical formula, it would look like this:

Anxiety = A Threatening Scenario +
A Belief You Can't Cope

Sylvia's Anxiety

Sylvia was juggling many balls, like a lot of women today. She was married, working full-time, and was the mother of two teenage sons. At the end of a long workday, she began her second job—the job of cook, shopper, teacher, and maid. It never dawned on Sylvia that she simply had too much to do. Her concern was that she wasn't excelling at everything she was doing. Sometimes she would forget to defrost the chicken for dinner or lose track of her husband's work schedule. With so much on her plate, Sylvia had, in her words, "become mediocre at everything."

When Sylvia came to see me, she was worried. She was having tension headaches and difficulty sleeping. "I'm going and going from morning until night, but I just can't seem to stay on top of it all. I don't know what to do." As I listened to Sylvia, I heard the voice of anxiety.

"What are you afraid will happen if you're not on top of everything, Sylvia?" I asked.

"It will all fall down like a row of dominoes. I have to be on top of everything. If I'm not, who will be?" she replied.

Sylvia grew up in a chaotic home with little parental responsibility. Her father, an alcoholic, was often gone—even when he was sitting next to her in the living room. Her mother, unable to deal with the stress, retreated to evenings out at church, her mother's house, or wherever her husband was not. The children were often left to fend for themselves.

Because Sylvia was the oldest, she assumed the role of family caretaker for herself and her two sisters. She felt the need to take care of everything. If she didn't, who would? Without a stable adult figure, Sylvia feared her world would fall apart, and there would be no one there to pick up the pieces. The anxiety she felt as a child was decreased by her taking charge, but this same take-charge behavior as an adult was actually increasing her anxiety.

Anxiety and Clinical Anxiety:
What's the Difference?

All of us worry about things from time to time. All of us feel the racing thoughts or pounding heart associated with anxiety. So what's the difference between this and clinical anxiety?

The first difference is the duration. Clinical anxiety usually lasts at least six months, and you'll probably feel a sense of anxiety on most of those days. It may also be more intense. The constant worry and body symptoms of tension, difficulty concentrating, or feeling on edge often affect your relationships or your ability to work and play. The nature of the worry is often different too. In clinical anxiety, your level of worry greatly exceeds any real threats to your well-being. In some cases, you may worry excessively about specific things, like getting sick, your weight, or your safety. In most cases, your anxiety doesn't diminish with your efforts to relax or rest.

If you're experiencing clinical anxiety, it's a good idea to seek out the help of a trained clinician. We'll talk more about that when we discuss Tool 7, psychotherapy.

Understanding Your Anxiety

When you feel anxious, or experience any of the emotions related to anxiety—nervousness, insecurity, panic, or being overwhelmed—ask yourself this question: what am I afraid of?

Sadness

Sadness is also an emotion we all experience, a normal reaction to the ups and downs of life. It's the tears Tanya sheds upon realizing her family's heirloom ring was stolen; the "down in the dumps" feeling Jeanne gets when she discovers none of her colleagues voted for her to become president of their organization; and the lethargic heaviness Anita feels when she learns she won't have enough money to buy the home she's dreamed of all her life.

The Body of Sadness

There are a variety of body signs you may experience when you feel sad. As with any feeling, not everyone will experience all of these sensations:

- tiredness
- heaviness
- crying

- decreased or increased appetite
- oversleeping or insomnia
- tearfulness

Unlike anxiety, which is expressed in the body as a speeding-up, sadness is usually expressed physically as a slowing-down.

The Mind of Sadness

When you feel sad, you're likely to find your thoughts focused on the negative aspects of a situation or yourself. These thoughts often revolve around the same theme: *loss*. This loss could be related to an object you value, or something less tangible like a dream, the esteem of those you care about, a relationship, or time.

Catherine's Sadness

During Catherine's high-school years, she was popular and active in school events. She was class president and yearbook editor, and everyone enjoyed her quick wit and dedication to her class. After graduation, she went away to college and lost touch with many of her hometown friends.

Catherine moved to a large city, got married, and became a cardiac nurse. One day she opened her mailbox and found an invitation to her twenty-fifth reunion. Catherine was overjoyed. She couldn't wait to see her old friends and catch up on their lives. She bought plane tickets and filled her husband in on the names and stories of all her old friends.

Catherine walked into the crowded hotel ballroom looking for familiar faces. Her friend Francine screamed when she saw her. "Caaaaathrine, how are you?" she cried. Catherine mingled, laughed, chatted, and shared stories with all her old friends. But as the night wore on, she found herself becoming increasingly sad.

"Why are you sad?" her husband asked. "Your friends seem so nice, just as you described them. Aren't you glad to be here?"

"I'm glad," said Catherine, "but everything has changed so much. Not that I expected my friends to be the same, but it's all so different."

The images Catherine had had in her mind for twenty-five years were of fun-loving sixteen-year-old girls going to the beach and dating boys. They were replaced by the faces of forty-three-year-olds working and raising families. For Catherine, the sadness came from the loss of her memories. She would never be able to think of her gang in the same way again.

What Does Loss Mean?

The loss connected to sadness comes in two forms: *specific loss* and *collective loss*. Specific loss is one particular loss that triggers feelings of sadness. This was the kind of loss Catherine experienced.

Collective loss is a series of losses—or an ongoing loss—that can lead to sadness. For example, Denise has experienced the breakup of a number of relationships. Her son joined the navy, her daughter got married, and her longtime boss moved to another company. Patricia is experiencing an ongoing loss in the gradual weakening of a cherished friendship. Since her friend Helen moved to another part of the country, they don't talk on the phone as often. And when they do talk, they seem to have less and less to chat about. Slowly, bit by bit, Patricia is losing Helen's friendship.

At the Bottom of Your Sadness Is Loss

Sadness	I've Lost . . .
Tanya's family heirloom ring was stolen.	"The history associated with this ring and the opportunity to pass it along to my child."
Jeanne learns none of her friends voted for her to become president of their organization.	"The positive impression I thought my friends had of my ability to lead."
Anita realizes she won't be able to buy the home she's wanted all her life.	"My lifelong dream to live on the lake."

Emotions Related to Sadness

Other emotions that share the theme of loss are related to sadness. Any of the following emotions can result in the same body and mind signs as sadness.

EMOTION	THE LOSS OF . . .
Grief	Someone or something loved
Regret	An opportunity
Loneliness	A connection to another person

Guilt	Self-esteem when you don't live up to someone else's standards
Shame	Self-esteem when you don't live up to your own standards

Jealousy can also be related to sadness if you perceive that another person's gain is your loss. For example, Judy is jealous of Mark's musical accomplishments, because she feels it highlights her inability as a musician. "I'll never be able to play the piano like that," she says. Watching Mark play highlights the loss that she will probably never realize her dream of becoming an accomplished pianist.

Sadness and Depression: How Do They Differ?

Although the emotional and physical signs of sadness can feel similar to those associated with depression, there are significant differences. In depression, the feelings are more intense, last longer, and often disrupt your relationships and the ability to work and play.

Typical symptoms of depression include feelings of negativity, hopelessness, worthlessness, and guilt. When you are depressed, you get less pleasure from things you used to enjoy, and you may withdraw from others. You may find yourself sleeping less or more than usual, and you feel a constant state of tiredness regardless of how much sleep you get. When depressed, you may have difficulty concentrating or you may find yourself uncharacteristically indecisive. In some cases, you may find yourself thinking about your own death.

Unlike sadness, depression usually colors every aspect of your life with a dark cloud that you can't seem to get out from under. The things you might usually do to help lift you from a bad mood don't seem to work. Depression, in some cases, can be paralyzing, and in extreme cases it can be life-threatening. For this reason, seeking out the care of a trained clinician is critical. This is something we'll talk about with Tool # 7, psychotherapy.

The Purpose of Your Sadness

Sadness has several purposes: it clarifies your values, signals a period of growth, and motivates you to change.

Sometimes, sadness validates the importance of what you've lost, and in doing so, it helps you clarify your priorities and values. Many Americans, saddened by the horrible events of September 11, 2001, reevaluated their lives and made changes that reflected their true priorities. Some changed their jobs, ended relationships, or started families. For many people, the sadness of this terrible time ultimately became a catalyst for positive change.

Sadness can also be a sign of growth. Often when you are in the process of growing and stretching yourself in new ways, you feel sad. In order to develop a new part of your identity, you may lose another part of yourself—usually a part that no longer fits. That's why women will sometimes feel sad when they get married, have a child, get a promotion, or make a decision to alter their lives for the better. Even though the changes are positive and frequently planned, there is still a letting-go and grieving that occur simultaneously.

Growth sadness can be magnified if a woman feels the need to change her old ways, but is unsure of what the change should be. This was the case for Miriam. For ten years Miriam worked as an accountant in a large organization. She enjoyed her job, but as time went on she found herself frustrated by the bureaucracy, stymied by the politics, and generally bored by her work. She knew it was time to move on. But to what? Miriam no longer wanted to be an accountant, but she wasn't sure what she wanted to do with her life. The sadness she felt was underscored by her confusion. Her old identity as an accountant no longer fit her, but her new identity had not yet emerged.

Miriam decided to create a plan to figure out what her new passions were. She talked with people in other fields to find out about their work, met with a career counselor, and looked to her childhood to remember the things that gave her joy. During this time, she still felt sad going to a job that no longer fit her identity, but she was consoled by the fact that she was on her way to discovering what her new identity was.

Finally, feeling sad can also be a motivator for change. The discomfort of being sad can compel you to find ways to get rid of that feeling, just as the pain of a thorn in your finger compels you to pull it out. This was the case for Elaine. She felt sad that she and her husband no longer shared the same connection they once did now that they had three children. The sheer effort of raising a family, taking care of a home, and working left little time for the two to be together. The sadness Elaine felt motivated her to talk with her husband about her feelings. The two of them came up with a plan to swap babysitting with a neighbor twice a month, and to put the kids to bed earlier so they'd have more time alone. By simply sharing her feelings with a responsive partner, Elaine felt more connected. It was this connection she felt she had lost. She could feel her sadness beginning to dissipate.

Understanding Your Sadness

When you are feeling sad, or experience any of the emotions related to sadness—grief, regret, loneliness, guilt, shame, or envy—ask yourself this question: what have I lost?

Anger

Anger can be a tricky emotion. Some women feel guilty for experiencing it. Others are scared of it. Some are quick to express it, but don't get the results they hope for when they do.

Anger can be mild, as when you're annoyed or peeved, or it can be strong, as when you're irate or outraged. Keisha is incensed that her husband expects her to cook dinner every night even though both of them work full-time. Sandra is bothered that her married sister is having an affair. Nicole is upset that her friend won the scholarship for which both of them applied.

For many women, anger can be a confusing and complex emotion. Let's begin to understand anger by deconstructing it into its body and mind components.

The Body of Anger

The body signs connected to anger are often similar to the body sensations of anxiety. In most cases these signs are speeding-up and tightening sensations.

- rapid heartbeat
- tense muscles
- shaking
- voice becomes louder
- crying

- increased energy
- clenching jaw
- fast breathing
- red face
- becoming hot or cold

These strong reactions occur because the switch to your sympathetic nervous system has been turned on. Your body is now producing norepinephrine to provide you with energy to defend yourself. Unlike in primitive times, the defense required is usually more psychological than physical. Today you are more likely to have to defend your integrity, your values, your self-worth. In that sense, the body sensations of anger are a potent message that something is not right in your personal world.

The Mind of Anger

Physically, anger is similar to anxiety in that your body gets rigid and charged up, but the accompanying mindset is different. Instead of fearful thoughts about the future producing anxiety, negative thoughts about the person or situation you feel has wronged you create anger: Who does she think she is? How could they do that to me? I should give him a piece of my mind!

Anger alerts you to the fact that your sense of self has been violated in some important way. Your focus is on the unacceptable or unfair nature of the situation or the other person's behavior. This violation involves your beliefs, values, or sense of right and wrong. That's why you can get mad at someone you don't even know, like a politician whose ideas you disagree with or a stranger who treats a child badly. As social psychologist Carol Tavris writes, "Anger is . . . an emphatic message: Pay attention to me. I don't like what you are doing. Restore my pride. You're in my way. Danger. Give me justice."

Sandra's Anger

One day Sandra's sister JoAnn invited her to lunch. "I've got a secret to tell you," JoAnn said.

"Oh, I hope it's a good one," Sandra said excitedly. "I'll meet you at noon."

That afternoon the two met at a local restaurant. Right after the waiter brought the bread to their table, JoAnn announced, "I'm having an affair."

"What do you mean you're having an affair?" Sandra asked in disbelief.

"It just happened. I didn't plan it. You're the only one who knows. I know you won't tell anyone else."

Sandra was in shock, but her shock turned quickly to anger. By the time she returned home from their lunch date, she was fuming. She tried to tell herself that she had no right to be angry. After all, it was JoAnn's marriage, not hers. So why was she so angry?

Sandra was angry because she felt violated. Although it wasn't a physical violation, her sense of right and wrong had been attacked. In Sandra's worldview, married people shouldn't have affairs. JoAnn's behavior was symbolically attacking that deeply held belief. And JoAnn's request that Sandra keep it a secret made Sandra an unwilling partner in something she disapproved of.

When Your Anger Is Really About Fear or Loss

Sometimes, anger can cover feelings of anxiety (fear) or sadness (loss), or both. This can occur when a violation or threat not only gets you mad but also leaves you feeling vulnerable or hurt. Often,

At the Bottom of Your Anger Is a Feeling of Being Violated

Anger	What's Been Violated?
Keisha is incensed that her husband expects her to cook dinner every night even though both of them work full-time.	Her value as a person. Her rules of a relationship.
Sandra is bothered that her married sister is having a secret love affair.	Her personal values and beliefs of what's right and wrong.
Nicole is upset that her friend won the scholarship that both of them applied for.	Her belief in fairness, since Nicole believes she has better credentials than her friend does.

identifying and managing these underlying feelings of fear or loss can defuse your anger. To determine if fear or loss is at the bottom of your anger, closely examine your angry emotion. Ask yourself what's underneath your anger by using the Layer Technique, as shown in the box below.

The Layer Technique

What's Underneath My Anger?

What am I angry (upset, peeved, annoyed, etc.) about?

Am I sad (hurt, disappointed, etc.) about this situation? If so, how?

Am I anxious (afraid, worried, frightened, etc.) about this situation? If so, how?

What's Underneath Keisha's Anger?

Keisha and Ray have been married many years and describe themselves as happy. But things have changed since Keisha took a new job that requires her to work long hours. She's upset because her husband Ray expects her to cook dinner every night even though both of them work long days. Each night after work, Ray flops down onto the couch and turns on the television. Meanwhile, Keisha runs into the kitchen and starts chopping vegetables and making salad.

Every time she glances into the living room, she sees Ray sprawled out, enjoying his program. With each look she feels her teeth clenching, her heart pounding, and her mind filling with thoughts about how inconsiderate and lazy he is. Finally she says something.

"It must be nice to come home and relax, Ray. I wish I could do that."

"Do you need something, honey?"

"Oh, no, that's okay; you just keep enjoying yourself. Don't worry about me."

"Thanks, dear, because I really had a rough day."

Inevitably, Keisha would become even angrier as her negative thoughts about Ray intensified. She didn't feel she should have to tell him to join her in the kitchen. He should just know that sitting on the couch while she is busy making dinner is rude and uncaring. Each night the scenario is the same as the tensions between the couple grow.

What was really going on here? Keisha felt that she was being attacked. Ray's behavior symbolized a threat to her sense of self and the "rules" of their relationship. Her inability to articulate these feelings to Ray only magnified her anger. Although it was clear that Keisha was upset, I decided to see if there were any other feelings beneath her anger. The box on the following page shows what we found.

As you can see, underneath Keisha's anger was the fear of re-creating her parents' marriage. This was unlikely given that Keisha and Ray had been married for twenty-eight years and had a completely different type of relationship from that of her mother and father. Still, that anxiety made her particularly sensitive to any situation that made her feel like "I'm doing it all, and you're doing nothing."

Before Keisha started her new job, she had come home from work much earlier than Ray. In that scenario, she was happy to make the dinner. It seemed fair to her. Now that her day was just as long as Ray's, however, she wanted the two of them to make din-

The Layer Technique

Underneath Keisha's Anger

What am I angry (upset, peeved, annoyed, etc.) about?

I'm upset because I feel like the responsibility for dinner falls on my shoulders, even though I've been working all day.

Am I sad (hurt, disappointed, lonely, etc.) about this situation? If so, how?

I'm hurt you don't recognize that I work just as hard as you do, and I'm tired too.

Am I anxious (afraid, worried, frightened, etc.) about this situation? If so, how?

I'm afraid that we're re-creating the kind of marriage my parents had, where my mother did everything and my father did nothing.

ner together, or at least take turns, but neither of them talked about how Keisha's new hours would change their dinner routine. Keisha just assumed Ray would do things differently without having to discuss it. Ray didn't really think much about it since Keisha had always been in charge of cooking and seemed to enjoy it.

Understanding Your Anger

When you feel angry or experience any of the emotions related to anger—upset, annoyance, frustration, resentment, or judgmental—ask yourself this question: Is my anger masking my feelings of fear or loss? If not, what part of me or my belief system is being violated?

Happiness

Happiness exists on many levels. Since people often think of it as a euphoric state, it can be easy to miss its more subtle moments, such as the happiness you feel when you look at a flower garden or hold a child's hand.

Happiness can be the dizzying excitement Joan feels upon learning she is pregnant after two years of trying to conceive. Or it can be the quiet contentment Colleen feels as she and her husband of three decades sit in their backyard sipping lemonade.

The Body of Happiness

The body sensations of happiness may vary depending upon your level of excitement. If you are elated, you're likely to experience an arousal in your body sensations. Sometimes people describe this feeling as "being so happy I could burst." In those moments, you may even cry like a newly crowned Miss America. If your happiness feels more like a quiet sense of serenity, you probably feel a calmness in your body sensations. Here are the body sensations associated with happiness.

EXCITED HAPPINESS	QUIET HAPPINESS
• racing heart	• feeling of lightness
• fast breathing	• relaxed muscles
• increased energy	• slow breathing
• smiling	• calmness

The Mind of Happiness

Just as sadness is related to loss, happiness is related to *gain*. When you feel happy, it's usually because you believe you've gained something. This gain can be material—a new coat or car—but just as often it is a gain to your self-esteem, values, or interests.

For something to be considered a gain, it must be consistent with your values. For example, a job promotion might be a cause for happiness. But if you are promoted to a job you don't want, you won't be happy. You may feel sad because to you the new job feels like a loss—a loss of your satisfying position, your work friends, or a less demanding worklife.

When you perceive something as a gain, you're likely to find your thoughts focused on the positive aspects of the situation or yourself. Your confidence is boosted, your sense of opportunity expands, your values are reconfirmed. Often, these positive thoughts lead you to anticipate future happiness as well. With the happiness of a new relationship comes the anticipation of loving times together. With the excitement of a new job comes the expectation of learning opportunities that will lead to greater skills.

At the Bottom of Your Happiness Is Gain

Happiness	What's Been Gained?
Joan learns she is pregnant after two years of trying to conceive.	The role of mother. The anticipation of family life.
Linda walks in the newly fallen snow.	A feeling of peace. A moment of quiet away from her busy world.
Nina learns how to play tennis.	A sense of competence. The anticipation of good times playing tennis with her best friends.

Colleen's Happiness

Colleen feels a sense of quiet contentment as she and her husband Frank sit in their backyard drinking lemonade. Her thoughts are focused on the present and the past. She reflects on how far the two of them have come and how much they have grown from those skinny kids who were married in the old town church so many years ago.

Their life has not been easy. They've experienced Frank's heart attack, the deaths of Colleen's parents, and economic struggles. Although each of these experiences was difficult, Colleen looks back on them now with the distance of someone who has learned what those losses have brought her: a closer connection to her husband, a greater appreciation of life, and an understanding that change needs to be surfed like a wave on the ocean.

As she sips her lemonade, Colleen enjoys the sound of the ice cubes clinking in her glass and the taste of the tart lemons made sweet with sugar. She is calmed by the feeling of the soft breeze on her face and the warmth of the sun on her shoulders. Colleen can truly say she is happy.

Understanding Your Happiness

When you feel happy or experience any of the emotions related to happiness—contentment, excitement, joy, or gratitude—ask yourself this question: what have I gained?

The Body and Mind of Emotions

By deconstructing your feelings, you can see that various combinations of body and mind reactions often produce specific emotions. In the case of Nancy, who called to tell me she had just been laid off from her job, a combination of body tension and speed (quick heart rate, fast talking) combined with constant fearful thoughts about the future and what-if thinking suggests anxiety. Use the Body-Mind Feeling Guide to review the body and mind combinations of the gateway feelings.

The Body-Mind Feeling Guide

Feeling	Body	Mind
Anxiety	Racing heart	Constant worry, what-if thinking
	Tight muscles	Fear about the future
	Sweating	Fear you can't cope with the challenges before you
Sadness	Tired	Focus on what's been lost
	Feeling of heaviness	Focus on what's wrong
	Crying	Focus on the past
Anger	Increased energy	Negative thoughts of the person/situation that has wronged you
	Rapid heartbeat	A desire to confront or distance yourself from the "attacker"
	Tight muscles	
Happiness	Racing heart	Positive thoughts
	Relaxed muscles	Focus on what has been gained
	Smiling	Anticipation of future pleasure

If Your Body and Mind Signs Don't Match

If you are confused because you experience the body sensations of one emotion but the thoughts of another, follow your thoughts. Although the body-and-mind link shown in the Body-Mind Feeling Guide works for many people, not all bodies will experience emotions in the same way.

Some women may find that worrying thoughts and fears about the future create body sensations of tiredness and crying rather than tension and a racing heart. Although this could indicate that they are experiencing anxiety and sadness at the same time, it could also be that their worrying mind has worn the body out. If this is the case for you, follow the feeling connected to your thoughts to discover what's underneath it all.

5

What's Underneath
Your Emotions

*The degree of one's emotion varies inversely with one's knowledge
of the facts—the less you know the hotter you get.*

—Bertrand Russell, philosopher

Once you've identified your gateway emotion, the next step is to explore what's underneath that feeling. Since most people can easily recognize when they're feeling happy and since happiness is not usually associated with distress, we're going to focus on the first three gateway feelings: anxiety, sadness, and anger.

As we've discussed, beneath feelings of anxiety, sadness, and anger are the core issues of fear, loss, and violation. These core issues drive your thoughts and body sensations, and thus your emotions. What is causing the fear, loss, or violation? Sometimes that's easy to see; other times it's not. If you can figure out what's underneath your feelings, you can develop a strategy to reduce your distress.

This is what Sarah tried to do. All her life she dreamed of moving away from her small country town to the big city eight hundred miles away. She worked two jobs to save the money she needed. Finally, on a warm July day, Sarah and her fiancé packed up all their possessions and headed to their new jobs in Boston.

At first Sarah was delirious with the giddiness that comes from the realization of a dream. As time went on, however, Sarah's happiness started to diminish. She often found herself weepy and tired. Her thoughts turned increasingly negative. "I don't understand," Sarah thought. "I have everything I've always wanted, but I'm not happy. I don't know what's wrong with me. Is it my demanding job, my relationship, being in a new city? I just can't figure it out."

Looking at her body and mind signs, it's easy to see that Sarah was sad. Now we know she's experiencing a loss. The question is, what has she lost? Sarah didn't know. To answer that question, Sarah tried internal questioning.

Internal Questioning

To get to your underlying issue, you may need to do some digging. Internal questioning is one way to do that. This process involves first becoming relaxed, and then silently asking yourself a series of questions. The response that has the most meaning for you will be reflected in your body's reactions.

To begin internal questioning, find a comfortable position to sit or lie down in. Make sure you won't be interrupted by ringing phones or other people. Carve out about ten minutes of quiet time just for you.

STEP I: RELAX YOUR BODY

Start by relaxing your body. You can do this in any way that feels right for you. Here's what I say to my clients:

Close your eyes. Take a deep breath in through your nose, and as slowly as you can, let it out. Take another breath in, and this time as you let it out, feel your shoulders melting and getting heavy. Take a slow breath in, and on the out breath, feel your whole body getting heavy and loose. Feel yourself sinking into the chair. Continue to slowly breathe in and out. As you do, feel all the tension leave your body. Think of your spine as a clothes hanger, strong and erect, with your body just hanging off the hanger like a shirt or a dress. Your whole body is heavy and limp. Continue to breathe slowly, at your own pace, until the distractions of the world seem a little farther away.

STEP 2: THE QUESTIONS

Once your body is relaxed, you can begin the next step: silently asking yourself questions. If you've already identified your gateway feeling through your body and mind signs, you can start there. Say to yourself, "I'm feeling anxious," or "I'm feeling sad," and so on. Then wait for a response. If this feeling is accurate for you, you may feel a slight sense of body relaxation or a gentle realignment in your body.

If simply acknowledging your feeling doesn't evoke any reaction or it just doesn't feel right for you, continue further. Ask yourself, "What else am I feeling?" Then wait. Give yourself time for an answer to emerge. If it doesn't, try running some possible feelings through your mind: afraid, lonely, frustrated. You can also use the list of feelings in Chapter 4 for help. When you find the feeling that accurately describes your emotion, your body will react in one of two ways. Your body will deeply relax or you may cry. Sometimes both will happen.

Once you've identified the feeling, continue probing further. Ask about the nature of this feeling: "What's the worst of this feeling?" Or you can ask about the core issues: "What is it I'm afraid of (if it's anxiety), or what am I losing (if it's sadness)?" When you find the underlying issue, your body will deeply relax or you may cry.

You'll know the process is complete when you feel a sense of closure. This closure may signal that you've figured out what you need to know. Or maybe you've just figured out all you can handle right now or all you can absorb for today. Whatever you find, it's enough.

Pioneering psychologist Eugene Gendlin showed that people could use the sensations from their bodies to uncover and shift their emotions. According to Gendlin, "The body is a biological computer, generating . . . enormous collections of data and delivering them to you instantaneously when you call them up."

In the next section, we'll see how Sarah used the internal questioning process to identify the issues underlying her feelings of sadness.

Sarah's Internal Questioning

One day when she was home alone, Sarah sat on her living room couch. She let her body completely relax by taking slow, deep breaths and allowing her body to feel heavy and limp.

When she felt ready, she began by silently saying to herself, "I'm feeling sad." She waited for a response from her body. Although she noticed a slight sense of relaxation with this statement, she intuitively sensed that sadness was not the whole story. She continued.

"What else am I feeling?" Sarah ran a variety of feelings through her mind that might apply to her situation. "Afraid, frustrated, overwhelmed, lonely?" Her body didn't react much to her words, until she said "lonely." At that moment, she began to cry. "I'm lonely," she said to herself with the sense of relief that comes with acknowledgment. She allowed herself to feel her loneliness.

Loneliness is one of the feelings related to sadness. So Sarah was on the right track by becoming aware of her sadness. She just needed to fine-tune what form of sadness she was feeling. Some people will need to do this; others won't.

Upon recognizing her loneliness, Sarah could have easily moved into her thinking mind: "What do I have to be lonely about? I've met lots of nice people in my new job, and I still keep in touch with my family and friends from home. Isn't this just a normal adjustment feeling?" But she refrained from doing this and stayed with her body sensations.

"What am I lonely about?" she asked. She waited patiently for a response to her question. She pictured her relationships. Family. Friends from home. New friends from work. Her fiancé. When she got to her fiancé, she again began to cry.

She pictured her fiancé and allowed herself to continue crying. She waited. Suddenly a thought popped into her head: "Even when we are together, I feel alone." At this, her body fully relaxed, and she sobbed with a deep feeling of recognition. This was her underlying issue.

Since their move to Boston, the couple had been out of sync. Their vision of a life together was crumbling. Sarah saw herself as an adventurer climbing the administrative ladder at her new job, while her fiancé was ready to start a family and live a more domestic life. They'd been bickering over little things, and their relationship had become increasingly strained.

Since sadness and its correlate loneliness are related to loss, what was Sarah losing? Her sense of connection with her fiancé. This loss was magnified because her family and lifelong friends were far away and unable to provide her with the support she needed. Once Sarah identified her feelings and underlying issues, she could select the Emotional Tools that would best address her situation.

Teresa's Internal Questioning

Teresa made a bold decision. At the age of forty-one, she was going to college. Her family was proud of her for taking on this new challenge, but no one was more proud than Teresa herself. She had married young and quickly had three children. She was dedicated to her family but felt it was now time to nurture her own dreams.

As the first semester approached, Teresa began acting in an uncharacteristic way, snapping at her children and her husband. They didn't clean up the kitchen the right way, they talked too loudly on the phone, they were late for dinner. Everyone asked, "What's wrong?" but Teresa could only answer, "I don't know. I guess I'm just having a bad day."

Teresa couldn't understand why she was upset about things that never bothered her before. She racked her mind to try to figure it out, but no answers came. She decided to try internal questioning.

She started by finding ten minutes of quiet time and space. Sitting in a comfortable chair, she closed her eyes and began taking deep breaths. She allowed her body to become heavier and heavier with each breath until she felt like she was sinking into the chair.

Teresa felt ready to begin. She decided to ask herself about the core issues related to anger, because she was losing her patience with everyone. "How am I feeling violated or attacked?" Teresa felt no response. Her body didn't shift or relax in any way. "Maybe my impatience is related to loss or fear," she thought, so Teresa asked about that. "What am I losing?" she silently asked herself. Again, no reaction. She continued. "What am I afraid of?" Teresa's eyes began welling up with tears. She knew she had unlocked something.

"What am I afraid of?" she silently asked again. Teresa was patient. She didn't use logic to figure this out. She could feel the knot of fear in her stomach. A thought came to her: "What if I can't do this? What if I let everyone down?" Her stomach relaxed with the recognition of her fear, and she began to cry.

When Teresa made the decision to go to college, everyone in her family was excited. "You'll be such a wonderful role model for your children," her brother said. "You'll make our family proud," her husband said. "We can study together," her children said. Suddenly, Teresa was beginning to feel the pressure of everyone's expectations, and she was scared of letting them down. After all, it had been twenty-three years since she'd been in a classroom. Instead of dwelling on her fears, Teresa used the information she had learned from internal questioning to choose the Emotional Tools that would help her cope with her fears.

Internal Questioning Process

Quick Guide

- Find a quiet place, and sit or lie in a comfortable position.

- Relax so that your body feels heavy.

- Silently say how you're feeling (for example, "I'm feeling anxious"), and wait for a physical response.

- If you don't get a physical response, silently list other emotions until you find one that feels right.

- When you find a feeling that is accurate for you, you will deeply relax, cry, or do both.

- Silently ask about the nature of this feeling with questions such as, "What is the worst of this?" "What am I afraid of?" "What have I lost?" Patiently wait for a response.

- You will experience a feeling of deep relaxation or crying when you find the answer that's right for you.

- Continue asking questions until you feel ready to stop.

A Word About Internal Questioning

Some people find internal questioning difficult to do. Like any new skill, it takes practice to notice the subtle sensations of your body. Recognizing the sense of deep relaxation I've talked about is easier to do once you've actually experienced it. In time, you'll begin to find it easier to relax your body, gain access to your body's emotional voice, and ask the right questions to elicit the information you need.

6

Your Thinking Mind and Your Moods

We don't see things as they are, we see them as we are.

—Anaïs Nin, writer

I've been away from the adult world so long, I don't think I could go on a job interview without asking the employer if he needs to go potty," Carol, a former corporate attorney, said half jokingly. "Maybe I don't have what it takes anymore. What if no law office wants to hire me? Sometimes I think I should just forget about the whole thing. I don't have much to offer."

"Don't worry, Carol," her friend said. "Just think positive thoughts. You'll be fine."

If only it were that easy. Negative thoughts are sticky little things. And once they appear, it can be hard to shake them. No matter how hard Carol tried, she had trouble shifting her thinking. Before you learn how to reduce your distressing thoughts, it is helpful to understand how they get created.

Your Thoughts and Emotions

Sigmund Freud believed that the unconscious is the source of troubling feelings and negative thinking. Once you become aware of the suppressed memories and conflicted wishes that reside deep inside your unconscious mind, your emotions will change.

As a practicing psychoanalyst, Aaron Beck believed this too. That is why he was surprised to find that his clients' moment-to-moment thoughts influenced their emotions as well. He discovered that when he helped his clients become aware of their thinking patterns and how to modify them, their distressing emotions diminished. From this experience, he created a cognitive psychology to help individuals develop new ways of thinking and feeling in a direct and accessible way.

Some research in cognitive psychology goes so far as to quantify the ratio of positive to negative thoughts a person needs to be happy. In general, studies show that people with a ratio of 1.7 positive thoughts to 1 negative thought are happy, while those with a ratio of 1:1 are distressed.

Your thinking patterns influence bodily reactions as well. Your body doesn't know the difference between a perception and a fact. It believes that what you think is fact, so it responds accordingly to whatever you tell yourself. With anxious thoughts, you're likely to have a rapid heartbeat or a clenched jaw. With sad thoughts, you'll probably feel a sense of heaviness or a desire to cry. And with angry thoughts, you will feel increased energy and muscle tension. Because of this body and mind connection, actors often experience physical changes when playing a role that requires them to act anxious, sad, or angry because they are focused on thoughts that elicit those emotions.

What Is Self-Talk?

You don't often pay attention to your self-talk. You may not even be aware of it, but like the Muzak that you don't notice in an elevator, self-talk becomes the background music to your life. Your self-talk interprets events, monitors your behavior, and makes assessments about you.

Sometimes your self-talk is encouraging and supportive: for example, "I know I can do this. I'll just take it slowly." When it is critical, unrealistic, excessive, or rigid—like "What's wrong with me?"—it can contribute to distressing feelings. The most damaging type of self-talk is the kind that harshly judges you.

Positive Affirmations?

It would seem at this point that the best advice I can give to reduce your anxiety, sadness, or anger is this: just say more positive things to yourself. This should make you feel better, right? Well, the answer is yes and no.

Let's take a look at two women about to take their real-estate licensing exam. Jane and Mary are feeling nervous before their tests. Both studied just as hard and know the material just as well, but Jane passed and Mary failed. Assuming both women are similar, what happened?

If we step back and look at each person's self-talk, we see a difference. Jane said, "I'm nervous because I want to pass this exam. It's okay to be nervous. My nervousness is just a way for my body to give me extra energy. It's a good thing. I'm sure I know this material as well as anyone else here. I'll just do the best I can, and take it one question at a time."

By contrast, Mary said, "The fact that I'm so nervous just goes to show how unprepared I am. I really want to get my real-estate license. If I don't do well on this test, I'm in big trouble. Without it, I'll have to stay in my crummy job. All my dreams will be ruined just because of this test."

It's likely that Mary's negative self-talk helped create her test anxiety. Some people believe that if Mary had said some encouraging words to herself before the exam, like "C'mon, Mary, I know you can do it," she could have passed too. It's possible, but in my opinion this approach is too simplistic.

Look at the Stuart Smalley character from *Saturday Night Live*. Struggling with low self-esteem, Stuart looks into his mirror every day and says out loud to himself, "I'm good enough, I'm smart enough, and doggone it, people like me." But it's clear that his positive affirmations haven't changed the way he feels about himself. Why? In part, because he doesn't believe them. And Mary probably wouldn't believe positive affirmations about her superior test-taking abilities either.

Before you can change your negative self-talk, you need to understand its source. Such self-talk is often a function of habit, unsupportive schemas, or your temperament type. Understanding the origin of your self-talk can be a valuable first step in changing it.

Negative Self-Talk as a Habit

For some people, negative self-talk is a habit formed when a negative experience or comment from another is internalized and reinforced over time by a cue to respond. Let me show you how this happened with Jackie.

JACKIE'S NEGATIVE SELF-TALK HABIT

Jackie comes from a large Midwestern family. Every year they gather for a lavish Christmas celebration. Included in the festivities is a gift exchange. As the family has grown, so has the gift exchange. Jackie now starts shopping in August to buy presents for all the nieces, nephews, cousins, and in-laws. What started out as an enjoyable experience has now become a stressor, not only on her time but on her pocketbook as well. She used to look forward to the holiday celebration, but now she dreads it. She decided it was time to say something.

When Jackie saw her oldest brother during the summer, she said, "I've given it a lot of thought, and I think we should end our gift-giving ritual. Our family has grown so large that buying gifts has become more of a burden than a pleasure. It is the pleasure of everyone's company that is the greatest gift."

"Boy, Jackie, you really are cheap, aren't you? How can you deny the kids a real Christmas? Maybe I should call you Ms. Scrooge," her brother said.

Stunned by his words, Jackie retreated. His words hurt. Maybe he was right. Maybe she was being petty and cheap. By August, she was Christmas shopping once again.

Jackie never took the time to examine whether her brother's words were fact. Was there any evidence to back up his claim that she was cheap? Instead, she accepted his assessment for fear that, even if she didn't see herself as miserly, others might. The negative thought had been planted.

Now each time Jackie was in a situation to spend money, she recalled her brother's words. Out shopping for a birthday gift, she looked at a sweater that was on sale and a more expensive sweater. "I don't want to appear cheap, so I'll get the expensive sweater," she thought. Any situation that tested her perceived frugality was her cue to respond. Each time she felt the need to prove she wasn't cheap, she was reinforcing the negative self-talk that said

Is Your Negative Self-Talk a Habit?

Ask yourself, do I say negative things to myself because they are facts or because they are just what I always say to myself?

she was. Numerous opportunities arose to cue her negative self-evaluation: tip-seeking waiters, company fund-raisers, cookie-selling Girl Scouts. The negative self-talk ("I'm cheap") had now become a habit.

Negative Self-Talk and Unsupportive Schemas

From infancy, you began to make assumptions about the world based on your experiences. If your caretakers were loving, changed your diapers when needed, fed you when you were hungry, and were generally available to you, you got the sense that the world was basically a good place. As you grew older, in addition to your family, you interacted with other people and had more experiences. You went to school, developed relationships, and had new opportunities and responsibilities.

The quality of these experiences and interactions created your *schema*. Your schema is the way you view yourself, your relationships, and life in general. It's an invisible filter that influences your perceptions and feelings. Early experiences that are ongoing or particularly significant have the most impact on your schema, as do cultural values. Messages that teach, directly or indirectly, how a woman should behave contribute to your schema.

You're probably not consciously aware of your schemas, but they color how you interpret your life. Since your schemas influence the way you understand and explain your world, they shape your self-talk. When painful early experiences get translated into unsupportive schemas, they can contribute to negative self-talk. That's what happened to Shoshanna and Karen.

SHOSHANNA'S SCHEMA

Shoshanna grew up with two parents who loved her. They were both there for her on parent-teacher nights, to watch her at ballet recitals, and to hear her sing in the temple chorus. Then when

Shoshanna was eleven, one evening her parents sat her down and told her they were getting divorced.

Within a matter of months, Shoshanna and her mother moved into a small apartment, and her father moved to another city. In the beginning, he called his daughter often and sent cards, but over time his calls were less frequent and his cards were often late. Within a year, her father remarried, and during the next three years he had two new daughters. When Shoshanna stayed with her father and his new family during the summer, she felt like an outsider. By the time she was sixteen, she stopped going.

Shoshanna could have made a number of interpretations about this situation. The one many children make is that their parents divorced because of them. Although her father told her otherwise, Shoshanna believed that if only she'd been smarter, nicer, or less noisy, her parents would have stayed together. This belief solidified into a schema that affected Shoshanna's adult love life.

When she met a man she liked, she would often feel that once he got to know the real Shoshanna, he would leave. She spent much of her time in relationships trying to please her partner and be whoever he wanted her to be so he would stay. Over time, men would become frustrated by Shoshanna's passivity and end the relationship. This would only serve to reconfirm Shoshanna's beliefs that men leave relationships, creating a perpetuating cycle.

Shoshanna's schema might have looked something like this:

Myself: *"I'm flawed and unlovable."*

Relationships: *"Relationships never last."*

Life: *"Life is unpredictable and unsafe."*

SHOSHANNA'S SELF-TALK

Knowing Shoshanna's schema, you can probably predict the kind of self-talk she might have. Upon meeting a new man, she often says to herself, "I hope he likes me. . . . He probably thinks I'm too opinionated. . . . I've got to put my best foot forward." Notice she hasn't said anything about the man and what she wants from him. This is because her schema is guiding her to focus critically on herself.

When Shoshanna does get into a relationship with a nice man, her self-talk is often negative. "This probably isn't going to last," she tells herself. If her partner is late calling, her self-talk is filled with more negative thoughts, even when there's no basis for them. "He's probably avoiding me" or "Maybe he doesn't want to see me," she thinks, instead of "Maybe he's stuck in traffic" or "Maybe he's tied up at work." Such negative self-talk only fuels her distressing feelings of anxiety, sadness, and anger.

KAREN'S SCHEMA

As the youngest child, Karen was often compared to her siblings. "Why don't you play sports like Susan does? Why don't you have better grades in math like David does?" Karen's mother would never look for the good in what Karen had done, but would search to find what was wrong with it. "Your dance moves are good, but your arms need to be straighter" or "That hair style is nice, but it makes your face look fat." These were the ongoing comments Karen heard from her mother. Her father was conspicuously silent.

As an adult, Karen no longer needed her mother's presence to hear her critical words. She had already internalized her mother's comments and was saying them to herself: "Karen, you can't do anything right. . . . Karen, I can't believe you don't know that." When her colleagues asked her to join them in sailing lessons, she declined. She told them she was too busy, but in reality she was afraid of looking stupid in front of them. Her life was joyless because everything she did became a referendum on her competence and worth. She took the smallest suggestions from her loving husband and supportive boss as criticisms of her abilities.

Karen's experiences growing up created the belief that she had to be perfect in order to be loved. She tried so hard to do everything right, hoping that one day her mother would say, "Yes, Karen, I love you just the way you are." But her mother never did.

Karen's schema might look like this:

Myself: *"I'm inadequate."*

Relationships: *"I need to be perfect to be loved."*

Life: *"Life is hard work."*

KAREN'S SELF-TALK

It's easy to see what drives Karen's self-talk. She has a running dialogue in her head that monitors, grades, and critiques everything she does; she's always on the lookout for errors. "What's wrong with you, Karen?" she often asks herself. Her self-talk prods her to keep seeking perfection and scolds her when she doesn't achieve it. This pattern of self-talk creates an alternating sequence of anxiety and sadness. The anxiety comes as she strives to be perfect. The sadness results when she doesn't achieve perfection, or worse, when she does achieve it and her mother still can't reward her with the approval and love she craves.

UNDERSTANDING UNSUPPORTIVE SCHEMAS

Schemas serve a purpose. They can help you organize and make sense of a difficult or confusing world. Because they are mostly developed in your early years, the world you sought to understand may no longer exist. Take Shoshanna. Her parents divorced when she was a child. She made some assumptions about that experience in order to make sense of what was happening. But now that she's an adult, her belief that relationships never last and men will always leave isn't accurate. This once useful organizing system has outlived its usefulness and is causing Shoshanna a lot of pain.

LOOKING FOR PATTERNS

The key to knowing whether your self-talk is related to your schemas is to look for patterns. As a psychology professor of mine used to say, if it happens once, it's an incident; twice, it's a coincidence; and three times, it's a pattern. If you continually have the same distressing reactions to situations or people regardless of the circumstances, it may be related to your schemas. Karen, whose schema dictated that she must be perfect, believed that most people—her husband, her boss, her colleagues—were critically judging her even when they weren't. That feeling of being judged emanated from her schema ("I need to be perfect to be loved"), not from reality. Regardless of the facts, her reaction was often the same: "I'm not good enough."

Here are some common schemas I see among women:

SUPPORTIVE SCHEMAS	UNSUPPORTIVE SCHEMAS
• I am a valuable person.	• It's important that everybody likes me.
• In the end, most things work out the way they should.	• I am responsible for other people's feelings.
• I deserve to be in a loving and happy relationship.	• I should never disappoint others.
• I can handle most things that come my way.	• I need to be beautiful to be loved.
• Even if I make mistakes, I'm still okay.	• I must never make a mistake.
• I deserve to have good things in my life.	• Everything must be perfect before I can be happy.

Uncovering Your Schemas

If you'd like to gain some insight into your schemas, complete the Uncovering Your Schemas exercise (page 72). Answer each statement with a complete sentence or any random words or thoughts that come to mind.

The secret to doing this type of exercise is to do it quickly, without much deliberation. Don't ponder your answers. Pondering engages your intellectual mind. That's not where your schemas live. They live in a place beyond your intellect and reason. So write down what pops into your head first, even if you don't like or agree with what you write.

Once you've finished the schema exercise, review your responses. Ask yourself these questions:

- Are these beliefs supportive or unsupportive?
- Do the original circumstances that created these beliefs still exist?
- Are any of these beliefs negatively influencing my self-talk?
- How might these beliefs be guiding my behavior?
- How might these beliefs be affecting my emotions?

For those schemas that are unsupportive or creating distress in your life, the Emotional Tools of thought-shifting (1), connection (6), and psychotherapy (7) can be extremely helpful. New experiences, caring relationships, and your evolving identity may also shift some of your schemas over time.

Is Your Negative Self-Talk Related to Unsupportive Schemas?

Ask yourself these questions: Do I say these negative things to myself because they are fact or because they are connected to my early life experiences? Do I have a pattern of reacting this way regardless of the situation?

Uncovering Your Schemas

Being female . . .

Being male . . .

My body . . .

I'm happy when . . .

I'm scared when . . .

Most men are . . .

Most women are . . .

Love relationships . . .

Friends . . .

My mother . . .

My father . . .

I am . . .

As a kid . . .

What I want most . . .

My future . . .

My most vivid childhood memory . . .

When I make mistakes . . .

When others don't agree with me . . .

When others expect things of me . . .

Negative Self-Talk and Your Temperament

When I was teaching the LifeSkills course, I asked my students to use one tool from the Emotional Toolkit and to write about the experience. They repeated this exercise with several different tools throughout the quarter. Since we had developed a strong bond of trust, the women often wrote in intimate detail about their innermost thoughts and experiences.

During my years of teaching, I carefully read more than fifteen hundred student journals. In these journals, I began to notice a pattern emerging. Some women would consistently view their world in a threatening or negative way, apparently unrelated to their circumstances or schemas. This view, in turn, influenced the content of their self-talk. As one woman, Renee, wrote, "I worry a lot about what other people think of me. I'm very sensitive to even the slightest comment or criticism. I think about it for days and can't let it go. I don't know why I do this. I don't think it's my schema. My parents have never been overly critical of me. I know they love me. When I was younger, I didn't have any terrible experiences. I have many great friends and am in a wonderful relationship. My life is good. I can't figure out why I worry about these things, but I do, and I always have."

Her words, "and I always have," stuck in my mind. From my conversations with Renee, I knew she wasn't clinically depressed or experiencing an anxiety disorder. She was well-adjusted and successful in her endeavors. I began to wonder if there was a connection between temperament type and self-talk. Was this young woman just temperamentally more sensitive than others?

WHAT IS TEMPERAMENT?

Temperament is the behavioral and emotional style with which you're born. Your genes significantly influence it. You may have inherited Aunt Tilly's sensitive nature or Uncle Fred's love of adventure. Your style affects the way you interpret and respond to the world, and it shows up soon after birth.

Pioneering researchers and psychiatrists Stella Chess and Alexander Thomas conducted a landmark study of temperament in the late 1950s. They observed babies in the first months of life and found that they had distinct differences in the way they responded to the world. Some babies were generally happy and easy to soothe, while others were fussy and cranky even with caring and attentive mothers. Some babies delighted in new faces and experiences, while others cried and turned away. Chess and Thomas noted nine distinct differences in the way babies respond to their world. Although a baby's temperament can be modified by experiences in life, these traits often endure over time.

Developmental psychologist Jerome Kagan of Harvard University conducted studies showing that certain temperament types are hardwired into the structure and function of your central nervous system. These differences in emotional circuitry can, for example, make some people more excitable or more sensitive.

Not only are certain dispositions inherited, but they often affect a person's self-talk and mood. According to research psychologist David Watson of the University of Iowa, the one temperament style that is most associated with distress is called a *negative emotionality trait*. People with this inherited trait are often critical of themselves, overly sensitive to perceived criticism from others, and tend to focus on the negative aspects of a situation. This focus on the negative leads to negative self-talk, which leads to distressing feelings, which leads back to a focus on the negative. Thus a pattern is created. It's possible that my student Renee's worrying style was inherited as part of her temperament.

ASSESSING YOUR TEMPERAMENT TYPE

Knowing the specific characteristics of your disposition may shed some light on the origins of your self-talk and moods. I've created a questionnaire that assesses the nine categories of temperament identified by Chess and Thomas. Although not a clinical tool, it can give you some insight into your temperament. It's important to note that all nine categories used in this questionnaire are considered normal. Taken in combination, they create a profile of your unique characteristics.

To determine your temperament type, complete the following assessment. Circle the number on each of the nine dispositions that most closely relates to how you usually feel.

Energy level: Do you get antsy if you sit too long? Do you like to be on the move? Or do you enjoy doing things at a slow and leisurely pace?

1	2	3	4	5	6	7
QUIET						ENERGETIC

Rhythmicity: Are you predictable in when and how much you need to sleep and the times you need to eat? Are you unhappy if you don't meet those needs on schedule? Or are your basic body needs variable?

1	2	3	4	5	6	7
UNPREDICTABLE					PREDICTABLE	

Initial reactions: How do you react to new ideas, situations, or places? Do you enjoy the novel and unexpected? Or do you like things that are familiar and comfortable?

1	2	3	4	5	6	7
SHY AWAY FROM NEWNESS				DRAWN TO NEWNESS		

Adaptability: How quickly do you adjust to change? Do you have a hard time accepting new situations that might not be what you're used to? Or do you roll with the punches?

1	2	3	4	5	6	7
HARD TIME WITH CHANGE					FLEXIBLE	

Sensitivity: How conscious are you of the sounds, colors, or smells in your surroundings? Are you affected by temperature changes? Are you affected by other people's emotions?

1	2	3	4	5	6	7
NOT SENSITIVE					HIGHLY SENSITIVE	

Emotional intensity: How strongly do you react to things? Are you dramatic in both your pleasure and displeasure? Or are you generally quiet with your feelings?

1	2	3	4	5	6	7
QUIET EMOTIONS				STRONG EMOTIONS		

Overall mood: How would you generally describe your overall disposition? Are you most often happy or optimistic? Or are you serious or melancholy?

1	2	3	4	5	6	7
HAPPY					MELANCHOLY	

Distractibility: How easily is your attention diverted from what you are doing? Do noises or other people's conversations grab your attention when you're doing other things? Does your attention wander? Or can you easily stay focused on the task at hand?

1	2	3	4	5	6	7
EASILY DISTRACTED					FOCUSED	

Persistence: If you can't figure something out quickly, do you lose interest or give up? Do you give yourself frequent breaks when involved in a demanding project? Or do you stick with a demanding task for hours? If you are interrupted while doing a task, can you easily shift gears, or do you get upset?

1	2	3	4	5	6	7
LAID-BACK					DETERMINED	

WHAT YOUR TEMPERAMENT TYPE TELLS YOU

The point in knowing your particular disposition is not to change it, but rather to work with it. The temperamental qualities you uncovered in this questionnaire will give you the knowledge you need to create what Chess and Thomas call a "goodness of fit." For example, from this assessment Renee learned that she is highly sensitive, has a hard time with change, and tends toward a melancholy nature. Although these characteristics may contribute to her worrying nature, they also make her highly attuned to other people's feelings and appreciative of the world around her.

Knowing her particular temperament, Renee should allow herself more time to feel comfortable with new experiences and realize that she's the type of person who feels things deeply. She should also avoid comparing herself unfavorably to people with temperaments that differ from her own. Renee can interrupt her worrying self-talk with statements such as, "This is what I do: I worry. What else can I do besides worry about this situation?"

IS BIOLOGY DESTINY?

Although your temperament may reflect your automatic way of responding, it is not the only way you can respond. Your temperament provides you with a range of possible reactions. And these reactions can be altered with new experiences and practice. According to University of Iowa psychology professor David Watson, "We ultimately are not constrained by our genetic endowment: we

Is Your Negative Self-Talk Related to Your Temperament?

Ask yourself, do I say these negative things to myself because they are fact or because it's always been in my nature to see things this way?

are still free to move around within our 'range' and to increase our overall level of well-being."

SOMETIMES A CIGAR IS JUST A CIGAR

One last caveat on the origins of negative thinking: not all negative self-talk is related to habit, schema, or temperament. Sometimes it's just a natural reaction to the things that happen in your life. A client who had been in a three-year relationship came into my office one day and said, "Paul ended our relationship last night. I'm so upset. I guess it's because of my schema."

No, it was not because of her schema. Or her temperament. Paul was an important part of her life, and it's natural for her to have sad thoughts about the breakup. There is no deep psychological mystery. Keep in mind that patterns of behavior suggest a relation to your schema or temperament, not isolated incidents. If several months had gone by and my client was still unable to shift her thoughts, then it might have been necessary to look deeper, but it's natural to have thoughts that lead to sadness, anxiety, or anger. Even Freud would agree that sometimes a cigar is just a cigar.

MAKING THE SHIFT

Whether it's due to habit, schema, temperament, or just a natural reaction, how do you reduce your negative thinking? The best way is to replace negative thoughts with a positive thought.

"But didn't you say just thinking more positive thoughts doesn't work?" you're probably thinking. You're right, it doesn't work unless it is done in the specific way you'll learn with Tool 1, thought-shifting. But first let's talk a little more about what's underneath your feelings and how it affects your moods.

7

Why You Communicate the Way You Do

The hardest times for me
were not when people challenged
what I said,
but when I felt my voice was not heard."

—Carol Gilligan, psychologist and scholar

When it comes to communicating feelings of anger, anxiety, or sadness, most of us have problems. We either say too much, too little, or things that just make the situation worse.

Each of you has your own way of communicating. Your dominant communication style is determined by your goal. That means you express yourself in a way that reinforces what you value most in your relationships. However, you're often not consciously aware of your communication goals.

There are four basic styles and goals:

STYLE	YOUR GOAL
Passive	To be liked
Attacking	To be right

STYLE	YOUR GOAL
Passive-aggressive	To express your anger while still being seen as a nice person
Effective	To create mutual respect

Although people tend to have a dominant way of expressing themselves, not everyone uses purely one style or another. A person can have a combination of styles that varies depending on the situation. For example, Vanessa is an effective communicator when telling a salesperson she wants a refund on a damaged sweater, but a passive communicator when telling her mother she doesn't want her advice on how she should raise her children.

A description of the four communication styles follows. Your particular communication style can pretty much predict the areas you'll struggle with most as a communicator. For example, if you're a passive communicator, you'll likely have a hard time bringing up a distressing subject if you fear it could hurt someone's feelings. If you're an attacking communicator, you'll probably have difficulty expressing yourself clearly without leaving the other person feeling defensive.

THE FOUR COMMUNICATION STYLES

Passive
- Your goal is to be liked.
- You want everyone to be happy, even if it's at your own expense.
- You seek to preserve your relationships at all costs.
- Your desire not to stir up distressing feelings in others often keeps you silent about your own needs.

Attacking
- Your goal is to be right.
- You are afraid of being taken advantage of.

	• You can be quick to blame.
	• You often speak impulsively without thinking of what's best for the situation.
Passive-aggressive	• Your goal is to express your anger and still be liked.
	• You question your right to be angry.
	• You fear your angry feelings will damage your relationships.
Effective	• Your goal is to mutual respect.
	• You feel you have a right to all of your feelings.
	• You care about others, but you don't let that caring prevent you from expressing yourself in an appropriate way.

It's important to look now at how your communication style developed. This will help you use the emotional tools with greater success. The next section presents three explanations for how your particular communication style came to be. I believe all of them contribute in some way to creating your unique way of expressing your needs and thoughts.

How Your Communication Style Developed

Your Female Identity Formed in the Context of Connection

By the time baby Elizabeth is eighteen months old, she will have a solid understanding that she is a girl. In order to know what it means to be female, she identifies with her mother. Given that they are the same sex, there is a familiarity and knowing in the way they relate to each other. Psychologically, they are joined.

Since her female identity is built around connecting with her mother, Elizabeth develops a core identity that is based on relating to and *connecting* with others. Her identity becomes fused with attachment. The ability to feel others' feelings becomes built into her character.

This experience is different from Elizabeth's brother, Luke. Luke's mother loves him just as much as she loves Elizabeth, but in order to know himself as male, Luke must separate from his mother and identify with his father or some other male figure. Luke develops a core identity that is based on *separation*. As a result, his ability and inclination to empathize will not be woven into his fabric to the degree it is with his sister.

Luke's and Elizabeth's differing ways of being in the world will be played out and reinforced by our culture all through their lives. Given her propensity for connection, Elizabeth will likely have a best friend to whom she tells all her secrets. She'll enjoy playing such noncompetitive games as dolls or jump rope, the goal of which is to spend time with and talk to others. She'll be rewarded for being kind and caring.

Luke, on the other hand, will more likely play competitive games with groups of boys. In these games, following the rules and winning are more important than the feelings of Luke's playmates. He'll be rewarded for being strong and brave.

According to the pioneering research of scholars at the Stone Center of Wellesley College, because of their early gender experiences, women look for ways to sustain and strengthen relationships throughout their lives. This is not to suggest that men don't care about relationships. They do, but it is not tied to their identity in the same way it is for women. For this reason, women, unlike men, often develop rich networks of intimate relationships. Their connection orientation is also the reason women fear being disliked or misunderstood more than men do.

Women's orientation toward relationships—a desire to be joined with others, caring about other peoples' feelings, and feeling threatened by rejection—significantly influences the way most women communicate. When you communicate with others, you are more likely than a man to care what people think about you or how people feel in response to what you've said. You're also more likely to want to talk about something that affects the quality of your relationships.

I'm not a huge fan of theories that state "all women do this, and all men do that." There are always individual variations, but in general, this is the way the pattern tends to go. It's worth reminding yourself that having a connection orientation is neither better nor worse than a separation orientation. It's just different. And it affects the way you communicate.

THE PASSIVE COMMUNICATOR

For women, connection is important to their well-being and a rich source of support. But for some women, the preservation of a relationship becomes more important than their own needs. This dynamic often contributes to a passive communication style. That was the case for Malena.

Malena's Story

Malena is a bright and loving woman. Her family and friends form a core foundation of strength for her. As a result, her fear of losing their approval has kept her silent about her own needs. In our counseling session she had the following insight about her passive communication style: "Somewhere along the road, I lost myself. I look back and try to find all the little ways it happened. I remember all the times I could've spoken up, but didn't because I didn't want to rock the boat or risk rejection from the people I love. And a piece of me got chipped away. I pushed myself to exhaustion helping everyone else, even though I was the one feeling overwhelmed and depleted. I know I should've expressed my feelings, but I always found ways to discount them: I need to be a good daughter, a good mother, or a good friend. I'm at the point now where I don't even know what I'm feeling anymore."

Malena confused submission with caring. This was understandable since the people she loved rewarded her for her "self-less" behavior. When conflicting needs arose, she could not imagine advocating for herself. Instead she spoke up for the other person's needs, because she feared that speaking up for her own needs would harm the connection.

Lily's Story

In some cases, an extreme focus on the emotional needs of others at your own expense can create tormenting feelings of sadness. That was the case for Lily. In her journal she wrote: "I am always trying to figure out how to make this or that person happy: what I can do to help my sister with her boyfriend problems, how I can be the least bothersome roommate, how to spend as little of my parents' money as possible. Basically, I am trying to figure out, to the extent that I am able, how I can cease to exist."

To Lily, it's an either-or proposition: either I give unceasingly of myself, or I will be rejected. According to psychologist and scholar Carol Gilligan, "For many women, the threat of disruption of an affiliation is perceived not just as a loss of a relationship, but as something closer to a total loss of self." Lily's passive communication style is driven by the fact that her value as a person is defined by whether she's made the people in her life happy. This definition is, in a sense, killing her.

THE PASSIVE-AGGRESSIVE COMMUNICATOR

For many women, it is critical that they be viewed by others as caring and nice. Any hint that they might be seen as selfish or insensitive could be devastating. So what happens when you get angry with someone? If your connection to that person is your top priority, and you believe anger is a destructive emotion, how can you express your anger to that individual without harming your identity as a kind person? You're in a bind.

The unconscious strategy developed by some women in this dilemma is to use a passive-aggressive communication style. In this style, women use covert ways to express their anger while appearing to be calm and nice. That's what Naomi did.

Naomi's Story

Steve's ex-wife would often call to tell him about her latest problems, and he would spend considerable time talking with her. This bothered his wife Naomi. She felt uncomfortable with the closeness the two shared, but felt selfish asking Steve to curtail the relationship. As his wife, Naomi wanted to be "above that." She trusted Steve and wanted him to feel free in this relationship, something he didn't feel in his first marriage. "Still," Naomi thought, "if Steve really cared about me, he would know how difficult this is for me without my having to tell him."

One morning, Steve readied himself to leave for work a little earlier than usual so he could mail an important letter. Since Naomi passed by the post office on her way to work, she offered to mail it for him.

That night over dinner, Steve asked, "Did you mail that letter, honey?"

"Oh, Steve," she said, "I completely forgot. I had it in my purse, but I was so rushed running out the door this morning that it completely slipped my mind. I'm sorry."

"I understand. Do you think you can do it tomorrow? It's really important that the letter get there by Friday."

"Absolutely, I won't forget."

When Steve asked about the letter the next evening, Naomi again apologized for forgetting to mail it. Steve was annoyed.

"Never mind," he said. "I'll take care of it myself."

"Are you sure? I'm happy to help."

Naomi may or may not be consciously aware that she's in a psychological bind, but on some level she manages to express her anger while still remaining nice. Interestingly, Steve is now the one who is angry. He is expressing Naomi's anger for her, while she remains helpful and caring.

THE ATTACKING COMMUNICATOR

Just as an orientation toward connection can silence you, it can also promote what I call *ineffective venting*—that is, an attacking style of communication that doesn't help the relationship or the situation. This can range from merely sarcastic remarks to tirades that are downright hostile.

It seems unlikely that this communication style can coexist with a person's desire to maintain a connection, but it often does. This was the case for Sheila. It was her desire to maintain a relationship with Gail that contributed to her simmer-and-explode pattern.

Sheila's Story

Sheila and Gail are coworkers. They live about five miles from each other, so they decided it would be great to drive together to the restaurant where they work. Since Gail likes to drive, she offered to be the twosome's chauffeur.

The first day of their carpooling, Gail arrived ten minutes late. Sheila, typically a punctual person, didn't want to make a big deal out of it. Maybe Gail had trouble finding her house. She said nothing.

The next day Gail was fifteen minutes late. Sheila was annoyed, but again said nothing. "It's not easy for Gail to get her two kids ready for school and get herself ready for work," Sheila thought. "I don't want to say anything that would make her feel more pressured than she already is." Gail's pattern of lateness continued, and each time Sheila made excuses for her.

The next week, Gail arrived late again. Sheila ran out to the car. As she settled into the front seat, she realized she forgot something.

"Oh, no, I forgot my purse. I'll be right back," Sheila said.

"You know, if you had everything ready to go before you left the house, we wouldn't be late," Gail said.

"What?" she exploded. "You're the one who's always late. I kept my mouth shut only because I felt sorry for you. You've got some nerve."

"Well, I'm the one doing you a favor by driving, Sheila," Gail retorted.

After that fight, their relationship was never the same. It's ironic: Sheila didn't voice her concerns to Gail because she wanted to preserve their connection. She didn't want to be perceived as uncaring or selfish. It is precisely because she didn't speak up that the relationship suffered. Who knows? Maybe Sheila and Gail were not destined to be friends anyway. But if Sheila had communicated—either through the right choice of words or appropriate actions—instead of first being silent and then exploding, she could have at least had a good working relationship with Gail. As it is now, the two try to avoid working the same shift, and when they do, they don't speak much. This has made work uncomfortable for Sheila, and she's thinking of finding a new job.

Tamika's Story

Sometimes an attacking style of communication occurs within a romantic relationship, because you feel something is threatening your connection. This is so frightening that you desperately try to change your partner or the situation to be what you want in order to make things "right" again.

Tamika had a vision of the perfect relationship. The man she would marry would be funny, romantic, and ambitious, just like her. When she met Gerald, he seemed to be everything she dreamed of.

Their courtship was like a fairy tale to Tamika. Gerald showered her with flowers every month to celebrate the anniversary of the day they met. As a successful manager at a growing company, Gerald's future looked promising. On the day they married, Tamika glowed.

As time went on, Tamika began to realize they weren't exactly two peas in a pod. They had their differences. One difference in particular caused them to fight.

Gerald was often offered the opportunity to work overtime, but he routinely turned it down to spend time with Tamika. This infuriated her. "How will you ever get ahead if you don't show you're a team player?" Tamika yelled. He said that getting ahead didn't really matter to him. He was happy just where he was. He didn't want the added responsibility and pressure of a high-level position, to which Tamika replied, "Are you crazy or just lazy?"

The more Gerald resisted climbing the corporate ladder, the angrier Tamika became. The angrier Tamika became, the more Gerald refused to work harder. They were stuck in an emotional tug-of-war, and it was threatening their marriage.

These endless conflicts arose in part from Tamika's need to create a relationship that fit the vision she had imagined. "If only he would change," she thought, "we'd have the perfect relationship." It was in the name of connection that Tamika argued. And it was in the name of separation that Gerald withdrew.

IS NAGGING A COMMUNICATION STYLE?

The label "nag" is uniquely female. Why is that? Based on the research of Deborah Tannen, professor of linguistics at Georgetown University, it is due to the dynamics of connection and separation. Since men develop a sense of masculinity created in part on the notion of separation, they are particularly sensitive to the threat of being controlled by others. When Virginia asks Kevin to "please take out the trash," he may be happy to do it—when he's ready. When he resists doing it in what Virginia considers a timely way, she asks him again. Given her connection orientation, she thinks, "If he asked me to do something that made him happy, I'd do it for him when he asked." If Kevin resists again, Virginia may ask again. Kevin now sees Virginia's request as nagging. The couple is unaware of how their differing orientations are influencing their communication styles.

Your Schemas Influence Your Communication Style

Earlier I described a schema as an invisible filter that affects the way you see yourself, your relationships, and life in general. You're probably not consciously aware of your schemas, but they can influence not only your self-talk and your emotions, but also your communication style.

Your way of communicating may vary in different situations, depending on your schemas for those areas. For example, Darcy's schema—"I deserve to be in a loving and happy relationship"— makes it likely she'll be an effective communicator if her date treats her rudely. However, her schema "I must take care of everything myself" will probably make her a passive communicator when it comes to asking her friends for help.

Schemas that contribute to a passive communication style may include "I am responsible for others' feelings" and "It's important that everyone like me." Those schemas contributing to an attacking style might include "I must always win" and "Other people will try to take advantage of me." A person with an effective style may hold schemas such as "My opinions are valuable" and "People in love can disagree."

ROBIN'S SCHEMA AND COMMUNICATION STYLE

"People see me as strong," Robin said during our counseling session. "If I express any doubts, they respond with, 'Oh you can handle it. You always do.' "

"From the look on your face, I can see that this kind of reaction doesn't feel too good," I said.

"No, it doesn't. I feel lonely when they say these things," she said. "Maybe they need me to stay strong because they rely on me so much, but I don't want to be the stoic one anymore."

"Can you think of any time in your life when you got the message that you had to be the strong one?" I asked, looking to see if a schema might be contributing to her feelings.

"I'm the oldest of four kids. My mom died when I was young, so I tried to act like I was in charge so all the other kids would feel safe and my Dad would have less to worry about."

"Do you still hear that voice in your head saying, 'I have to be strong'?" I asked.

"Yes, I think I do," she said.

"What do you think would happen to the people in your life if you weren't so strong all the time?"

There was a long pause. "I don't know," she said.

As she continued, Robin said that her difficulty expressing her feelings was taking a toll on her relationship with her husband and her children. She was able to articulate her needs clearly and assert herself in many situations, but she was not able to communicate her vulnerabilities to the people she loved most. She understood that this old schema was no longer working for her. She had reached a point at which she finally felt strong enough to show her weakness.

LYNN'S SCHEMA

Lynn grew up in a rigid household. Her parents directed everything she did: what she wore, whom she could date, what she should choose as a career. When Lynn was old enough to move away, she did so quickly.

As she became involved in romantic relationships, her schema followed along with her: "The people who love you will try to control you." This schema contributed to Lynn's attacking style of communication.

When her boyfriend asked what she was doing the next weekend, she would interpret his question as an attempt to control her. "I don't have to report to you like a servant!" she snapped. These outbursts created problems in her love life. When Lynn recognized that her schema was controlling her more than any man, she was able slowly to unravel its hold on her and the way she communicated in relationships.

The Biology of Your Communication

Women are always the ones to bring up relationship problems. Men don't like to talk about feelings. Are these just stereotypes? Not necessarily. According to some researchers, the way women and men communicate has to do with biology as well as psychology.

Anthropologists propose that during prehistoric times, labor was divided along physical lines. Given their smaller upper-body size and their ability to nurse their babies, women became the caretakers, while men, with their greater upper-body strength, became warriors and hunters.

Through evolution, men's and women's bodies adapted to meet their survival needs. According to John Gottman, professor of psychology at the University of Washington, women developed nervous systems that were able to calm them quickly after stress so that their milk supply would not be threatened and their babies could thrive. Men, on the other hand, developed nervous systems that were easily aroused so they would be physically ready to chase and kill their prey.

What does this have to do with communication styles? A lot, according to Gottman's research. Given that men's sympathetic nervous systems are easily engaged—causing pounding heart, sweating, and high blood pressure—they are more likely than women to avoid confrontation. Women, who are less physiologically reactive than men, are often the ones to bring up the touchy topics. In fact, Gottman's studies show that wives bring up sticky marital issues more than 80 percent of the time.

In an attempt to elude conflict that might cause them to feel physically overwhelmed, men use a variety of communication strategies, all with the goal of silencing the conversation. Men become mute, defensive, or even mean. Often these reactions serve only to make the woman more persistent, even combative. That's what happened with Neil and Peggy.

"You're always inviting people over without consulting me," said Peggy. "It's as if I don't even live here."

"It's not like that, and you know it," said Neil.

"Yes, it is," Peggy snapped. "What's wrong with you? Don't I matter to you? Don't my feelings count for anything?"

"What do you want me to say?" said Neil.

"Do I have to tell you what to *say* too?" asked Peggy, shaking her head.

Neil looked away, saying nothing.

"Do I?" said Peggy.

Neil sighed and stared into space.

"Well, do I?" said Peggy.

Peggy's harsh comments triggered the switch to Neil's sympathetic nervous system. As she continued to badger him, he withdrew as a way to protect himself from being overwhelmed.

It's obvious that Peggy's style of communication doesn't work. But with more effective communication tools, Peggy could express her concerns in a manner that will increase the likelihood that Neil will respond positively to her.

Getting Clear

The first step in becoming an effective communicator is to be clear about what drives your communication style. Here are some of the points discussed in this chapter:

- You will most often communicate in a style that reinforces what you value most in your relationships: being liked, needing to win, or having mutual respect.

- As a woman, the desire to connect with others is part of your core identity, and it significantly affects the way you communicate.

- Societal and familial messages that socialize you to be nice can considerably influence how and when you express yourself.

- Schemas, particularly if they are unsupportive, can affect your communication style.

- Biology can influence how women and men communicate when they are angry.

Part Three

Using Your Emotional Toolkit

8

Finding the Right
Emotional Tools for You

That which we persist in doing becomes easier for us to do.

—Ralph Waldo Emerson, philosopher

Now it's time to find the Emotional Tools that are right for you. The seven tools are:

Tool 1, thought-shifting

Tool 2, the meditative arts

Tool 3, communication

Tool 4, emotional writing

Tool 5, physical movement

Tool 6, connection

Tool 7, psychotherapy

The Emotional Tools you choose should fit your personality and personal needs. For example, walking will not work for you if you have a physical condition that prevents it. Likewise, emotional writing may not be helpful if you hate to write. Although research shows that each of the Emotional Tools can be effective, the goal is to find the tools that are effective for you.

Either because of their enthusiasm or their desperation, some people try to use as many Emotional Tools as they can all at once. This usually leaves them feeling overwhelmed, creating more distress. Behavior change works best when it's done slowly and is consistent with your lifestyle. Start with one Emotional Tool at a time, and slowly integrate others as you feel the need to do so.

The Emotional Tools for each gateway feeling include strategies to manage the distress in your body and your mind. As such, the solutions are consistent with the way I've divided the problems into body and mind components. In the next section you'll find a description of the emotional tools that work best for the gateway feelings of anxiety, sadness, and anger.

Emotional Tools for Your Anxiety

The Emotional Tools used to decrease anxiety should do two things: (1) calm your body from its speed and tension and (2) decrease your mind's fearful and racing what-if thinking. The tools should also include an effective way to deal with your fear.

If you recall, anxiety is created when you feel threatened, coupled with a belief that you can't cope with that threat. The easiest way to diminish anxiety is to get rid of the fear-inducing situation. Of course, this is not always possible, but when it is, it works like a charm.

Do you have an erratic boss who constantly threatens to fire employees who don't meet his unrealistic expectations? Quit. The threat that's causing the anxiety will be gone, and you'll feel better, assuming you can get another job you like.

Are you taking a course with a tyrannical professor and panicking that you won't pass the class? Drop the course, and take it next semester with a sane instructor. Anxiety gone.

When looking to reduce anxiety, removing the threat is the quickest way to peace. Of course, life doesn't always present you with such easy solutions. It's not always possible to quit your job, drop a tough class, avoid a difficult conversation, or take a leap into the unknown. When that's the case, the best thing to do is to strengthen your ability to cope with the threat. This approach may not completely eliminate your anxiety, but it will make it more manageable so you can more easily handle the situation and the feelings that come with it.

BODY TOOLS FOR ANXIETY

When you are anxious, your body generally seems to go faster (heartbeat, breathing) or feel tighter (tense muscles, clenched jaw). The body tools for anxiety are designed to reverse that trend.

- To calm the speed and tension of anxiety, mindfulness meditation and belly breathing are helpful (Tool 2, meditative arts). Not only do they turn on the switch to your calming, relaxing parasympathetic nervous system, but they also reduce the presence of blood lactate, a chemical associated with anxiety.

- For those who like to move their bodies, meditative movement or yoga (Tool 5) can provide similar results. Many people find that physical exercise like walking or swimming helps release the excess energy created by anxiety's fight-or-flight response while providing a time-out from stressful situations.

MIND TOOLS FOR ANXIETY

Addressing the mind of anxiety is critical because it is the swirl of worrying thoughts that fuels your fears. Finding ways to reduce and shift your worrying self-talk is essential. But this won't happen by simply telling yourself to stop thinking fearful thoughts. Anyone who has ever had a friend say, "It'll be fine; just stop worrying," knows this. In fact, trying to will yourself to stop thinking fearful thoughts may actually make you more anxious. You need some specific strategies to do this.

- Thought-shifting (Tool 1) can help you understand, examine, and reduce your worrying self-talk in a way that will change your anxious feelings.

- Mindfulness meditation or meditation-in-action (Tool 2) can help reduce your worry by shifting your thinking away from future-oriented what-if thoughts to present-moment experiences.

- Anxieties sometimes arise when you need to talk with a spouse or close friend about a touchy subject, and you're afraid of how they'll react. Knowing how to communicate effectively without harming the relationship (Tool 3) can help strengthen your ability to cope and thereby reduce your anxiety.

- Emotional writing (Tool 4) can help you uncover thinking patterns that may contribute to your anxiety and help you make sense of your feelings.

Emotional Tools for Your Anxiety	
Body Tools	**Mind Tools**
• Tool 2, meditative arts	• Tool 1, thought-shifting
• Tool 5, physical movement	• Tool 2, meditative arts
	• Tool 3, communication
	• Tool 4, emotional writing
	• Tool 6, connection
	• Tool 7, psychotherapy

- Connecting with others can be helpful (Tool 6). Talking with a caring friend or relative can give you support, help you get another perspective on possible ways to deal with a threatening situation, and promote the flow of hormones that produce feelings of calm and relaxation.

- If you find your anxiety is compromising your happiness, you may want to talk with a therapist (Tool 7). Psychotherapy can provide you with a safe and confidential haven for the expression of your anxious feelings. The right therapist, acting as an ally and knowledgeable guide, can help you understand and shift your anxieties.

Emotional Tools for Your Sadness

The Emotional Tools used to decrease your sadness should do two things: (1) get your body moving and (2) reduce your mind's negative thinking. The tools should also include an effective way to deal with your feelings of loss.

BODY TOOLS FOR SADNESS

Sadness is usually expressed physically as a slowing down. You may feel tired or heavy. The body tools for sadness are designed to increase your energy. They can also include slow, focused movements that help redirect your negative thinking patterns.

- Moving your body can be a helpful antidote to the heaviness and lethargy of sadness. Physical movement such as walking, running, swimming, or bicycling (Tool 5) can help energize you. Physical movement can also stimulate the release of brain chemicals that can help elevate your mood: namely, serotonin (related to happiness) and norepinephrine (related to increased energy). The availability of these two neurotransmitters can help lift your sadness.

- The meditative arts (Tool 2: belly breathing, mindfulness meditation, and meditation-in-action) can help reduce sadness by increasing activity in the part of your brain associated with upbeat and happy moods.

MIND TOOLS FOR SADNESS

When it comes to the mind of sadness, the goal is to diminish your negative thinking pattern and shift it to a nonjudging one. This is not easy to do without a strategy. The following tools can help.

- The Emotional Tools found in thought-shifting (Tool 1) can help you examine and shift your negative thought patterns in a way that feels authentic and useful. Emotional writing (Tool 4) can also provide you with insight and a new perspective that can help shift your feelings.

- It can sometimes be difficult to talk with a significant other about your sadness, especially if he or she is the cause of it. In some cases, it is wise to talk about it. In other cases, it might be wise to refrain. Knowing good communication skills (Tool 3) can help you cope with these difficult situations more easily.

- Managing the feelings of loss associated with sadness is important. A valuable way to do this is through connection with others (Tool 6). Studies show that individuals who have close relationships with people they can confide in cope better with various stressors. This includes the stress of loss, whether it be the loss of a job or the loss of a dream.

- When sadness interferes with your day-to-day happiness or ability to function, you might want to see a therapist (Tool 7). In a caring and accepting environment, a good therapist can help you understand your feelings of loss and develop effective coping strategies to elevate your mood.

Emotional Tools for Your Sadness

Body Tools	Mind Tools
• Tool 2, meditative arts	• Tool 1, thought-shifting
• Tool 5, physical movement	• Tool 3, communication
	• Tool 4, emotional writing
	• Tool 6, connection
	• Tool 7, psychotherapy

Emotional Tools for Your Anger

The Emotional Tools used to decrease your anger should do two things: (1) calm your body from its speed and tension and (2) reduce the negative thoughts that trigger your anger. The strategy should also include an effective way to deal with your feelings of violation or your underlying feelings of loss or fear, or both.

BODY TOOLS FOR ANGER

For many people, anger is one of the most difficult feelings to alter, but studies have consistently shown that using a body and mind approach can effectively shift this emotion. The Emotional Tools should calm your angry body from its revved-up state.

- Belly breathing, mindfulness meditation, and meditation-in-action are effective tools to reverse the speeding up and tightening sensations of anger (Tool 2). Being able to calm your body from its angry state is particularly important if you decide to talk to the person you're angry with.

- Slow and focused activities such as meditative movement or yoga (Tool 5) can help decrease the physical tension of anger. Some people even find vigorous exercise, like running or swimming, can help. This may seem like a contradiction since these kinds of exercises would appear to charge your body up, not relax it. But for some, a good workout can make you tired and, in effect, relax your body.

MIND TOOLS FOR ANGER

- For the mind, you want to stop obsessing on the thoughts that are triggering your anger—for instance, thoughts about how unfair a situation is, or how rude the other person is, or how you've been wronged. But just willing yourself to stop these thoughts won't work. You need to replace them with new ways of thinking. To learn how to do this, you can use the Emotional Tool of thought-shifting (Tool 1).

- Emotional writing (Tool 4) can help you make sense of your anger, especially when it's masking feelings of fear and loss.

- If you decide to talk with the person you're upset with, you'll want to do it in a way that won't inflame the situation or, if it matters to you, harm the relationship. To do this, you'll need to know about communication strategies (Tool 3). This approach includes not only what to say to the other person, but also a look at how your patterns of interacting with each other may be contributing to your anger.

Emotional Tools for Your Anger

Body Tools	Mind Tools
• Tool 2, meditative arts	• Tool 1, thought-shifting
• Tool 5, meditative movement	• Tool 3, communication
	• Tool 4, emotional writing
	• Tool 7, psychotherapy

Finding Your Emotional Tools

A Quick Guide

- Emotional Tools for Anxiety: These tools should calm your body from its speed and tension and lessen your mind's fearful and racing what-if thinking. The tools should also include an effective way to deal with your fear.

- Emotional Tools for Sadness: These tools should get your body moving to help increase your energy and shift your body chemistry while reducing your mind's negative thinking. The tools should also include an effective way to deal with your feelings of loss.

- Emotional Tools for Anger: These tools should calm your body from its speed and tension and reduce the negative thoughts that trigger your anger. The tools should also include an effective way to deal with your feelings of violation or underlying feelings of loss or fear, or both.

9

The Voices in Your Head

Tool 1: Thought-Shifting

Happiness is not a state to arrive at, but a manner of traveling.

—Margaret Lee Runbeck, author

Have you ever noticed that it's easy to think positive thoughts when you're happy? If you try to think positive thoughts when you're anxious, sad, or angry, they slip off your brain like a fried egg from a greased pan. Why can it be so difficult to think positively when you're distressed?

It's because thoughts exist in an associative network. Your thoughts are linked by a common emotion. Carol, the mother who felt insecure about job hunting, was having difficulty thinking positively about her impending job search. As soon as she had one negative thought ("What if nobody wants to hire me?") another would quickly follow ("I don't have much to offer.") These links, like bridges, made it easy for her negative thoughts to hop from one to another.

In this way, an anxiety-provoking thought will likely lead to another anxiety-provoking thought via their jointly associated emotion. When you're feeling distressed, those thoughts are just more available.

The intent of shifting your thoughts is first to stop the negative thoughts before they have a chance to jump further into the network of distressing thoughts and strengthen their links. The sooner you can stop the cycle of negative thinking, the sooner your unhappiness will be reduced. However, you should not try to will yourself to stop thinking negative thoughts. It doesn't work.

Not only that, it can increase your distress. If I were to tell you not to think of an orange, you'd probably have trouble doing that. The harder you tried, the more tension you'd feel as you tried to suppress your orange-thoughts.

The Goal of Thought-Shifting

Thought-shifting can help you increase your positive thinking and decrease your negative thinking in a way that works. It will not strengthen the network of distressing thoughts available to you or create the tension associated with thought suppression. It will allow your thoughts to leap into a new thinking pattern.

Keep in mind that the goal of thought-shifting is not to think happy thoughts all the time. As I've said before, constant happy thoughts might block important messages you need to hear. However, if your distressing feelings are stubbornly hanging on long after your need for them has ended, it may be time to shift your thinking patterns. Let's begin by looking at *rumination,* a common form of negative self-talk.

RUMINATION

Rumination occurs when you think over and over about your problems and how terrible you feel without taking action to shift those feelings. Women are more likely to engage in rumination than men, because women are more likely to focus inward when unhappy, and men are more likely to focus outward. When I talked to a male friend about the concerns many women have and the things that cause them distress, he said, "Do women really think about these things?"

"We do," I said. "What do you think about when you're upset?"

"I don't think. I play basketball."

That's a perfect example of how men use their outward focus as a way to distract themselves from their problems. Women are more likely to turn inward and ruminate. Women say they ruminate in order to better understand themselves or their problems. But here's the rub: research shows that ruminating may actually interfere with your ability to solve your problems. It also prolongs your distressed mood. Keep in mind that there's nothing wrong with introspection. It can be a positive thing. But introspection turns to rumination when you stay focused on your problems and ignore solutions.

How do you know if you're ruminating? Ask yourself these five questions:

1. Do you feel your distressing emotion more intensely the more you think about it, but continue to think about it anyway?

2. Do you replay upsetting events over and over in your mind?

3. Do you worry that others might reject you because of how you feel?

4. Do you focus on your bad feelings rather than on what you can do to feel better?

5. Do you focus on the body symptoms (tiredness or headache) of your distressing emotion without taking action to relieve them?

The Thought-Shifting Process

A key to reducing negative thinking, including rumination, is to create self-generated positive statements based on fact, not fluff. If you just say to yourself what you think you should say or what someone else has told you to say—like, "C'mon, Mary, I know you can do it"—it's not likely to work, because *you won't believe it.*

In order for thought-shifting to work long-term, you must take the following four steps:

1. Become aware of your negative self-talk.

2. Directly examine and challenge your negative assumptions.

3. Generate new and realistic messages that you create.

4. Develop an action plan.

Let's look at how to do that.

Step 1: Become Aware of Your Negative Self-Talk

The first step in shifting your negative thoughts is to become aware of their existence. Sounds simple enough, but the presence of negative self-talk can be so subtle it's like noticing yourself breathing—you have to focus on it. Many people are surprised at the general negativity of their self-talk.

Distress gets created when negative thoughts are repeated on an ongoing basis. How often do you say things to yourself that make you feel bad about yourself, intensify your fears, or keep you in a bad mood?

One way to become aware of your thought patterns is to notice the thoughts you have as you lay in bed at night. It's also particularly helpful to observe what thoughts you have just before you experience a strong emotion.

Think about an intense or distressing feeling you've had recently. Try to pinpoint the self-talk you had just before that feeling started. You may have said many different things to yourself, but focus on the one that seems to be most connected to your mood.

DEE'S JUST-BEFORE SELF-TALK

Dee was asked to give a speech for her company retreat. She'd never spoken in front of so many people before. She was nervous. As she lay in bed at night, she thought about her speech: *I'm terrible at giving speeches. What if I mess up or bore people to death? I'm going to make a fool of myself. Then my boss will realize I'm not as competent as he thought I was.*

As you can see, Dee's self-talk influenced her emotions and increased her anxiety. For her, this type of thinking was a habit. When she was in the seventh grade, she gave a speech in her history class. She stumbled over her words, and a few students laughed. Ever since then, she's internalized the notion that she is a terrible speaker. Any time she is asked to speak publicly, the negative self-talk about her speech-giving abilities is restimulated.

GLORIA'S JUST-BEFORE SELF-TALK

It was a beautiful day, and Gloria was on her way to work. She needed to stop at the store to pick up a few supplies for the office before the morning meeting. As she came out of the store and walked to her car in the parking lot, she saw her rear tire was completely flat. Here's what she thought: *I can't believe this. What's wrong with tire manufacturers these days that they can't make a decent tire? Companies only care about the bottom line and not about people. And these store parking lots are a mess. You'd think these stores would have a little pride and keep this area free from the junk that causes flat tires. No one cares about anything anymore.*

Gloria's self-talk was typical for her temperament. Her temperament assessment showed she had a strong emotional intensity, a hard time coping with change, and difficulty being distracted from her goals. This explained why she was often quick to anger. It is not likely Gloria will be able to change her initial reactions to situations, but she can become aware of how her thinking style affects her emotions and address that directly, so she can calm herself down more easily.

Become Aware of Your Negative Self-Talk

Ask yourself, what thoughts do I have when I lay in bed at night, or what thoughts did I have just before my distressing feelings started?

Once you recognize your thought patterns and their connection to your emotions, you're in a position to have power over your reactions. That takes us to step 2: directly examining and challenging your negative assumptions.

Step Two: Directly Examine and Challenge Your Negative Assumptions

A major problem with negative thinking is that we rarely question whether our thoughts are accurate. Instead, we reflexively believe our negative thoughts are facts. And the more negative thoughts we have, the more we believe them. After all, if there's so many of them, they must be true, right?

The first step to taking the bite out of a negative thought is to question it. Just because you think something, doesn't make it a fact. Question your negative thoughts as a trial lawyer would. How do you know it's true? What evidence do you have to support your negative assumptions? Examine your thoughts. Put them under the microscope. Break those associative links.

Remember, your habits, schemas, or temperament may be clouding the facts. Only you can uncover the truth. In the following pages, we'll take each of the distressing gateway emotions—anxiety, sadness, and anger—and turn it inside out. You should do this any time you are experiencing one or more of these emotions.

Anxiety and Self-Talk

One of the hallmarks of anxiety is worry. Mark Twain said, "I have spent most of my life worrying about things that have never happened." If that's the case, then why do we worry? People worry for two reasons. One is psychological, and one is physical.

THE PSYCHOLOGICAL REASONS YOU WORRY

As noted in Chapter 4, if anxiety were a mathematical formula, it would be:

$$\text{Anxiety} = \text{A Threatening Scenario} + \text{A Belief You Can't Cope}$$

One of the difficult things about a threat is the feeling that you have no control over it. People often worry as a way to gain control.

I've heard many women say that worrying helps them feel prepared, as if they are doing something in the face of an unforeseen problem. It makes them feel responsible.

But here's the interesting thing: worry is self-reinforcing, because most of what you worry about never happens. Each time you worry about a potential problem, and your worst-case scenario doesn't materialize, you may unconsciously conclude that somehow your worrying played a role in averting the crisis. Your worrying has been positively reinforced, and so you worry more the next time a threat arrives.

Worry is difficult to stop, because your associative links are strengthened by repetition so that worrying thoughts are now more available to you. In other words, the more you worry, the more you worry. With all your worrying, nothing about your problem or your ability to cope has been improved. You're still going around and around in your thoughts. You're still in the same boat dealing with the same threat.

THE PHYSICAL REASONS YOU WORRY

For most people, worry is about thoughts not images. You talk to yourself about your problems: what they mean, why they are happening, or how upsetting they are. Studies show that there may be a reason why people tend to worry with the words of self-talk rather than with visual images.

When people visually imagine their worst fears coming true, the switch to their sympathetic nervous system gets turned on. When this happens, they experience the pounding heart, rapid breathing, or sweaty hands of anxiety. But when people think about their fears with negative self-talk, there is little or no nervous-system activation. Worry can actually suppress the activation of the sympathetic nervous system, leading to fewer body symptoms of anxiety. In this sense, worry becomes a calming coping tool.

Although worry may calm your body, it doesn't do much for your mind. Instead, it leads to distress. A better strategy is to use an Emotional Tool that will calm your body, such as Tool 2, belly breathing or meditation. These body tools also have the added benefit of reducing the worry in your mind.

Tool 1: Thought-Shifting for Anxiety

I. BECOME AWARE OF YOUR NEGATIVE SELF-TALK.

First, become aware of your anxiety self-talk either through your just-before thinking or simple observation. As noted earlier, this type of self-talk usually starts with the phrase "what if." It's usually focused on the future and all that could go wrong there. It will often be about the threat you fear, your perceived inability to cope with that threat, or both.

2. DIRECTLY EXAMINE AND CHALLENGE YOUR NEGATIVE ASSUMPTIONS.

Once you've become aware that you're worrying, it's time to challenge your worries. Like a trial lawyer, your job is to examine the evidence. Break those associative links. Is the threat really as bad as you think? Are your coping skills really as poor as you believe?

One of the most common errors people make about a threat is to magnify it. People imagine the worst possible outcome of the threat and act as if it's already true. The fear of a missed employment opportunity leads to "My life will be ruined if I don't get this job," or the fear of a phone call not returned turns to "I'll die if they don't call me back." Will your life really be ruined? Will you really die?

Challenge Questions

Following is a list of questions you can ask yourself to challenge your anxiety-producing self-talk. You may have some of your own:

- What is the worst thing that could happen in this situation?

- How do I know that will happen?

- If it did happen, could I survive it?

- Have I ever had a situation in the past where I experienced this kind of threat? Did I survive it?

- Is there anything at all good about this situation?

- Can I view this situation as a challenge or opportunity rather than a threat? How?

- Is my worrying helping me deal with the threat?

These questions are helpful because they allow you to pick apart your worries instead of just slapping positive messages on top of them like Band-Aids. As you pick your worries apart, they become less powerful. Figuring things out for yourself leads to a greater emotional change than would occur if someone else figures things out for you.

Step 3: Generate New and Realistic Messages That You Create.

When negative self-talk arises, respond to it with a statement you have created. Think of a comforting or soothing statement to say to yourself. It needs to be right for you, not one that someone else told you to say. It needs to be something you can believe. Say this statement to yourself to create new and positive associative links.

Keep in mind that it took many years to create the thinking patterns you have now. Whether your anxiety-producing self-talk is a result of habit, unsupportive schemas, or temperament, changing thinking patterns takes time.

Following are some examples of things you can say to yourself when a worry arises. Use them only if they resonate with you.

- Just because I think it, that doesn't make it true.
- Look at this situation in another way.
- Stay in this moment, not the future.
- I'm going to change the channel.
- There goes my worrying mind again.
- One step at a time.

Step 4: Develop an Action Plan.

Once you've realistically assessed the threat, it's time to strengthen your coping skills. You can do this with an *action plan*. An action plan is your opportunity to mobilize your resources to address your fear. This plan may include emotional coping strategies such as gathering the support of your family and friends, meditation, physical exercise, asking for help, emotional writing, and/or psychotherapy. It may also include such problem-solving strategies as making a phone call, confronting a friend, researching a topic, writing a letter, finally making a decision, or redesigning your schedule.

Remember, the pounding heart and muscle tightness of your anxiety is your body's way of giving you the energy you need to address this problem. It does not mean that you are unable to handle it. In certain situations, expect to feel fear. Don't try to fight it. The goal is to create an action plan so that your fears will become manageable.

Action Plan Questions

Here are some questions to help you figure out your action plan:

- What else can I do besides worry?
- What do I want to happen?
- How can I make this happen?
- What is the worst that can happen if I pursue my plan?
- What is the worst that can happen if I don't pursue my plan?
- What resources (family, friends, skills, time, etc.) can I use to make this happen?

Let's look at how Neda used the four steps of thought-shifting to help with her anxious feelings.

Neda's Thought-Shifting for Anxiety

As a little girl, Neda dreamed of becoming a painter. Colors and shapes and textures dazzled her. She relished the sensation of the paint gliding across the canvas. Although no one in her family had indulged in such "impractical" dreams, Neda became an art major in college.

In her junior year, Neda fell madly in love with a man fifteen years her senior. She made the difficult decision to drop out of school so she could move across the country to marry him. Her intention, however, was to continue to pursue her art.

Shortly after getting married, Neda unexpectedly became pregnant. Two other children quickly followed. To help make ends meet, Neda took a job in a bank. Although she found this job uninspiring and at odds with her artistic temperament, Neda worked at the bank for more than twenty years.

With her children now grown, her husband about to retire, and their nest egg sufficiently incubated, Neda began to think about her dream of painting. Her husband encouraged her to call the local art studio, but when she contemplated picking up the receiver, she was filled with dread.

Here's how Neda used the four steps of thought-shifting to help reduce her anxiety.

1. BECOME AWARE OF YOUR NEGATIVE SELF-TALK.

Neda asked herself, "What thoughts am I having just before I think about calling the art studio? What thoughts do I have when I lay in bed at night?" Here's what she found:

- What if I fail at painting? What if I'm no longer any good?

- What if this dream I've harbored all these years is just a pipe dream?

- Maybe I'm too old to start a new profession. It will take years to refine my skills.

- No one in my family has ever done anything in the creative arts. What if my family judges me as indulging myself or as being impractical?

These are Neda's worries. These are the thoughts that contribute to her anxiety. With a clear understanding of her thinking pattern, Neda can now move to step 2.

2. DIRECTLY EXAMINE AND CHALLENGE YOUR NEGATIVE ASSUMPTIONS.

To challenge her distressing thoughts, Neda used some of the challenge questions. Here's what she found:

- **What is the worst thing that could happen if I enroll in art school?** The other students will laugh at me. Or the instructor will look down on my work. Maybe I won't be very good.

- **How do I know that will happen?** I don't know for sure.

- **If it did happen, could I survive it?** I would be uncomfortable. I would be sad. But I could survive it.

- **Have I ever had a situation in the past where I experienced this kind of threat?** I was completely out of my element when I went to work at the bank. I had no idea what I was doing.

- **Did I survive it?** Yes, I did. I figured things out and picked it up. And these were skills I'd never used before. Painting is something I know. I may be rusty, but I know painting.

- **Is there anything at all good about this situation?** I'm learning how to go after what I want even though I'm scared. The timing is right. In four years I'll be fifty whether I go back to painting or not. So why not paint?

- **Can I view this situation as a challenge or opportunity rather than a threat? How?** Yes, this is a chance to pursue something that will make me happy. This is an exciting opportunity. Even if I'm not a great painter, I'll still have the chance to do something I love. And that's the whole reason to do it in the first place, isn't it?

- **Is my worrying helping me deal with the threat?** No, it's just my way of stalling.

3. GENERATE NEW AND REALISTIC MESSAGES THAT YOU CREATE.

Neda recalled the words of an inspiring art teacher she had as a girl. When fearful self-talk filled her head, she repeated his words: "My art is my own. I am not ahead or behind anyone else. The journey is only with myself."

4. DEVELOP AN ACTION PLAN.

By challenging her negative self-talk, Neda has taken some of the power out of the threat of going to art school. Now it's time to strengthen her coping skills by taking action. Neda reviews the action plan questions.

- **What else can I do besides worry?** I can talk with my husband about my concerns. He's good at helping me see the bigger picture.
- **What do I want to happen?** I want to go to art school.
- **How can I make this happen?** I can call the art studio and sign up for a class even if I'm afraid. I need to keep in mind that my pounding heart is just a way for my body to give me energy. It doesn't mean I'm not up to this challenge. I'll just take this one step at a time.
- **What is the worst that can happen if I go to art school?** I may not be very good in the beginning.
- **What is the worst that can happen if I don't go to art school?** I will forever regret that I never tried.
- **What resources can I use to make this happen?** I have the support of my husband and children. I need to hear their words of encouragement. And I need to stop worrying about what my extended family thinks about my dreams.

Neda made the decision to call the art studio. After she hung up the phone, she still felt some anxiety, but it was now manageable. Most important, it did not stop her from pursuing her dreams. Neda can probably expect to feel some anxiety in the future. She may feel nervous going to class the first day, using a new technique, or showing her work to other students. At those moments she will remind herself that her art is her own. She is not ahead or behind anyone else. The journey is only with herself.

Sadness and Self-Talk

"Sadness is but a wall between two gardens," said poet and philosopher Kahlil Gibran. True, but sometimes it's very difficult to see that garden when you're stuck on the other side of the wall.

With sadness, your mind is often filled with negative thoughts and rumination. Well-meaning family and friends tell you to look on the bright side, but such advice rarely helps.

As mentioned, one of the most common errors people make is to imagine the worst possible outcome of a threat and act as if it's already true. Sadness gets sustained by its own common errors— that is, by *selective abstraction* and *negative projection*. Although these thinking styles can also contribute to anxiety, they are often a feature of sadness.

SELECTIVE ABSTRACTION

With selective abstraction, your radar is primed to notice only the negative things about a situation. Although your circumstances may truly be difficult—for example, a tense relationship or a dull job—you only notice the elements of the situation that reinforce your sadness.

I once heard a speaker describe an exercise that perfectly illustrated how selective abstraction works. He asked people to look around the room and notice everything that was brown. He gave them a minute or two to do this. Then he asked them to close their eyes. "Now," he said, "try to recall everything in the room that is green." Not surprisingly, people had a hard time doing this. They were so focused on noticing the brown, they didn't even see the green.

That's how selective abstraction can prolong sadness. You get so immersed in focusing on your loss and all its implications that you can't see anything else. Positive thoughts are nowhere to be found—at least not positive thoughts that you believe. And you already know that you have to believe your positive thoughts for them to have any power.

NEGATIVE PROJECTION

Another common error is negative projection. With this thinking style, you interpret all situations, life events, or other people's reactions in a negative way. Do you remember Shoshanna in Chapter 6? She used negative projection when her boyfriend was late calling her. Although she had no reason to believe he had lost interest in her, she still said to herself, "He's probably avoiding me."

You up the ante on negative projection when you blanket your negative assessment with the words *everything* or *always,* as in "Everything in my life is terrible" or "I'll always feel this way."

An interesting study conducted at Dartmouth University highlights the way negative projection can contribute to sadness. Researchers created facial scars on college women using theatrical makeup. The women were told that they would be interacting with female strangers to assess how people reacted to their disfigurement.

What the women did not know was that the scars were removed before their meeting with the strangers. They also didn't know that the strangers were in on the experiment and were told to act in a neutral way during their conversations with the study participants.

When asked how the strangers reacted to their looks, the study participants were more likely, compared to a control group that wasn't given scars, to say the stranger avoided eye contact, stared at them, and acted nervous and uncomfortable. This study illustrates how projecting your negative self-talk onto experiences can create a mindset that prolongs sadness.

Tool 1: Thought-Shifting for Sadness

I. BECOME AWARE OF YOUR NEGATIVE SELF-TALK.

Begin by becoming aware of your sadness-producing self-talk, either with your just-before thinking or as you lay in bed at night. As described earlier, this type of self-talk usually focuses on the negative elements of a situation and on your loss or your perceived loss. Sometimes you may hear yourself using the words *everything* or *always*.

2. DIRECTLY EXAMINE AND CHALLENGE YOUR NEGATIVE ASSUMPTIONS.

Once you've become aware of your negative thinking, challenge those thoughts directly. Your job is to investigate the evidence. This will help break the associative links. Is your thinking style increasing your sadness? Is there anything you can do to get past your sadness?

Challenge Questions

You can ask yourself the following questions to challenge your sadness-producing self-talk:

- Am I spending a lot of time wishing things were different? If so, how does that make me feel?
- Am I blaming myself for this situation? If so, is that making me feel sadder?
- Am I using *everything* or *always* in my self-talk?

- If yes, are these statements true?
- Is my self-talk filled with "why" questions, such as "why do these things happen to me?"
- Am I comparing myself to others? If so, how does that make me feel?
- Is focusing on my loss helping me to feel better?
- Are my sad feelings intensified because I'm ruminating?
- Is there anything I can learn from this situation?
- Is there anything at all that is good about this situation?

As you review these questions, you'll note several things. First, wishful thinking is almost guaranteed to lead to sadness. Certainly there are times when we all wish things were different, but staying with wishful thoughts like "I wish this hadn't happened" or "I wish my life was different" will prolong sadness.

Blaming yourself in a given situation is another way to increase sadness. "It's all my fault" or "If only I'd done more" are judgments that serve no useful purpose except to make you feel bad. It's better to shift to a question like "What else can I do to make things better?"

Last, notice whenever you start a question with *why*—for example, "Why do these things happen to me?" or "Why am I the only one without a happy life?" Since humans are always trying to make sense of the world, your brain will find an answer to your questions. Given the negative nature of the question, the answers you find will likely be equally negative, leading to more sadness. Try shifting to "how" questions, like "How can I get over this?" or "How can I make this situation work for me?"

3. GENERATE NEW AND REALISTIC MESSAGES THAT YOU CREATE.

Once you've challenged your negative thoughts, respond with a different type of thought. Again, it should be a positive response that you have created, something you can believe. Say this statement to yourself whenever you have a sadness-producing thought.

Keep in mind that you may need to use this new self-talk again and again. Stopping the speeding train of your negative self-talk isn't always easy.

Following are some examples of things you can say to yourself when negative thoughts of selective abstraction, negative projection, or self-blame arise. Use these only if they resonate with you.

- There goes my negative mind again.
- Just because I think it, that doesn't make it true.
- I'm going to change the channel on these negative thoughts.
- I don't have to listen to this right now.
- I'm going to focus on what's possible rather than on what's wrong.

4. DEVELOP AN ACTION PLAN.

Now it's time to create your action plan. Sometimes this plan will require specific steps to change the situation that is contributing to your sadness. These may include looking for a new job, getting back into the dating scene after a divorce, or setting firmer boundaries with your family so they don't impose on your limited time.

Other times it will mean selecting Emotional Tools that will support you during a difficult time. This may include the support of family or friends, spending time alone meditating, physical exercise, or emotional writing.

As mentioned before, sadness can provide you with important information about what you value or when you need to grow further. However, when it is prolonged, the following action plan questions can help you take specific steps to move beyond those feelings.

Action Plan Questions

Following are some questions to help you figure out your action plan:

- Am I ready to start feeling better?

- Am I judging myself harshly? If so, how can I let go of that?

- What do I need to feel better—support? time alone? a plan?

- Whom do I know who can support me in feeling better? When will I talk with them?

- Are there any actions I can take to make this situation better? For example, can I get help managing my finances, eat healthier, meet new people?

- If I can't change this situation, how can I accept it?

- What resources do I need to feel better? Family, friends, skills, time, etc.?

Let's look at how Louise used the four steps of thought-shifting to help with her sad feelings.

Louise's Thought-Shifting for Sadness

All her life, Louise focused on one thing: becoming a successful doctor. When her friends were out having fun, Louise could usually be found in the library. This was not a sacrifice to her. It was a step she gladly took to get closer to her goal of becoming Dr. O'Neal.

As a young physician, Louise impressed her superiors with her keen intellect and ambitious enthusiasm. Her hard work landed her a spot on a prestigious research team that was developing cutting-edge surgery techniques.

One night, for the first time, Louise felt a pang she didn't expect to feel. Her friend Ellen called to tell her she was getting married, and she asked if Louise would be her maid of honor. "Of course," Louise exclaimed. But after she hung up the phone, she started to cry.

Many of her friends were getting married and having children. For the first time, Louise thought about what she was giving up to pursue her all-consuming career. She spent much of her time at the hospital, often sleeping and eating in the doctors' lounge. Little time was left for a meaningful personal life. Sadness washed over her.

Here's how Louise used the four steps of thought-shifting to help reduce her sadness.

I. BECOME AWARE OF YOUR NEGATIVE SELF-TALK.

Louise asked herself, "What thoughts was I having just before I started crying?" Here's what she found:

- I'll always be alone.
- I always saw myself ahead of all my friends in life. Now I feel terribly behind.
- I was stupid to think that a career would be the only thing I needed to be happy.
- I wish I could be Ellen. She seems so happy.

These are the negative thoughts that contribute to Louise's sadness. Having acknowledged her thinking pattern, Louise can now move to step 2.

2. DIRECTLY EXAMINE AND CHALLENGE YOUR NEGATIVE ASSUMPTIONS.

To pick apart her sad thoughts, Louise turned to some of the challenge questions. Here's what she found:

- **Am I spending a lot of time wishing things were different? If so, how does that make me feel?** Yes, I keep wishing I had Ellen's life. I think about her spending time with her husband while I'm all alone. Wishing things were different only makes me feel much worse.

- **Am I blaming myself for this situation? If so, is that making me feel sadder?** Yes, I blame myself for not having the foresight to see that I was creating a one-sided life. These thoughts just make me feel bad about myself. The truth is, how could I have known how I would feel at thirty-four when I was just eighteen?

- **Am I using *everything* or *always* in my self-talk?** Yes, I feel I'll always be alone.

- **Is it true that I will always be alone?** It certainly feels that way right now, but just because it feels that way doesn't make it a fact. A feeling is not a fact. Besides, always is a long time.

- **Is my self-talk filled with "why" questions, such as "why do these things happen to me?"** Yes, I keep asking myself why can't I have everything? Instead I need to ask, "How can I have what I want?" I need to be realistic. I can have everything, maybe just not all at the same time.

- **Am I comparing myself to others? If so, how does that make me feel?** Yes, I've always done that. Now I'm comparing my personal life to that of friends who don't have such consuming careers. It makes me feel terrible when I do this.

- **Is focusing on my loss helping me to feel better?** No, focusing on these negative things only makes me feel worse.

- **Are my sad feelings intensified because I'm ruminating?** No, the fact that I'm doing this thought-shifting exercise shows that I'm ready to do something about this feeling.

- **Is there anything I can learn from this situation?** Yes, I learned that I need more balance in my life.

- **Is there anything at all that is good about this situation?**
  Although I felt sad after my conversation with Ellen, it was a
  wake-up call for me. It just pointed out something I was
  trying to ignore. Now that I've acknowledged it, I can deal
  with it.

3. GENERATE NEW AND REALISTIC MESSAGES THAT YOU CREATE.

Louise realized how her thinking style was making her feel
sadder. She thought about her situation and what realistic statement she could say to herself to feel better. Here's what she created: "The choices I made were right for me when I made them.
Now I'm in a new stage of my life, and I get to create new
choices."

4. DEVELOP AN ACTION PLAN.

Louise's sadness was created by a situation that she does have
some control over. Here's how she used the action plan questions
to help her figure out how to reduce her sad feelings:

- **Am I ready to start feeling better?** Yes, I don't feel the
  need to grieve over my past decisions. I'll feel better if I do
  something about my situation.

- **Am I judging myself harshly? If so, how can I let go of
  that?** Whenever I judge myself negatively, I'll repeat the
  positive self-statement I created: "The choices I made were
  right for me when I made them. Now I'm in a new stage of
  my life, and I get to create new choices." I'll tell my
  statement to my friends so they can say it to me too.

- **What do I need to feel better—support? time alone? a
  plan?** To feel better, I need to create a plan to reduce my
  hours at work. I'll have to talk with my supervisor about
  this. I want to spend more time with friends and family.
  I'm also going to tell my friends that I'm interested in

dating, so if they know of any nice guys they can send them my way.

- **Whom do I know who can support me in feeling better? When will I talk with them?** I have great friends, even though I don't see them much. I'm going to start by talking with Ellen. I'll call her tomorrow.

- **Are there any actions I can take to make this situation better?** Yes, see above answer.

- **If I can't change this situation, how can I accept it?** I do have some control over this situation, so I don't need to just accept it.

- **What resources do I need to feel better? Family, friends, skills, time, etc.?** I need more personal time, and I'm working on that. I would also like my colleagues not to judge me negatively for working fewer hours. But even if they do, I need to do what's right for me.

Louise's decision to begin changing the structure and focus of her life created a dramatic reduction in her sadness. This doesn't mean that she never felt sad again. There were times in the middle of the night when she still longed for a partner, but she felt good that she was taking active steps to create a space in her life for love and friendship—a space that didn't exist before.

Anger and Self-Talk

One day I was walking to my office at UCLA with my colleague Michael. Along the way he spotted a coworker and stopped to say hello. "Dr. Miller," he said, "I'd like you to meet Dr. Darlene Mininni. We've been working on a project together."

I extended my hand to greet him. "It's nice to meet you," I said. With his hands glued in his pockets, he silently looked at me, then turned to Michael and started talking. I stood there in disbelief as my outstretched hand dangled in the air.

As they conversed, my blood was boiling. "How rude," I thought. "I can't believe he would completely ignore me! I'm going to give him a piece of my mind!" Just as I was about to speak, an odd thought popped into my head.

What if Dr. Miller has no hands? I wondered. Maybe he kept his arms in his pockets because he was embarrassed that I would reach out to shake his hand, only to find a stump. He must have been flustered and not known what to say, so out of sheer panic he awkwardly focused his attention on Michael.

Suddenly my anger was gone. My pounding heart slowed as a wave of compassion washed over me. When the two men were finished talking, Dr. Miller walked away, hands still in pockets.

"Michael," I asked, "does Dr. Miller have any hands?"

"What kind of crazy question is that? Of course he has hands," he replied. And with those words, my blood was boiling again.

ANGRY THOUGHTS

This story about Dr. Miller illustrates the power our thoughts have to create and diminish anger. Many of us ruminate on our angry thoughts, replaying the offending situation over and over in our minds.

According to psychologist and science writer Daniel Goleman, "The longer we ruminate about what has made us angry, the more 'good reasons' and self-justifications for being angry we can invent. Brooding fuels anger's flames. But seeing things differently douses those flames."

Although I was angry with Dr. Miller's behavior, I ultimately laughed at the absurdity of my strange thoughts and was able to let go of my ill will. Nothing about the situation had changed. I had changed. I let go of the "who does he think he is!" thinking I kept replaying in my mind.

Anger can be a powerful feeling. Research has shown that it can be controlled and channeled, but it can't be eliminated. Anger shouldn't be eliminated because the energy of anger can help us take action when action is needed. With anger, you need to find either a way to address it or to let go of it. Working with your thoughts is one way to reduce anger's intensity. Let's look at how to do that using the thought-shifting tool.

Tool 1: Thought-Shifting for Anger

1. BECOME AWARE OF YOUR NEGATIVE SELF-TALK.

Since anger-producing self-talk is usually not subtle, it's fairly easy to become aware of it. As mentioned earlier, this type of self-talk is usually negatively focused on a person or situation you feel has wronged you. You may obsess on these thoughts, reviewing and replaying them over and over again. Your thoughts often focus on how you have been violated.

2. DIRECTLY EXAMINE AND CHALLENGE YOUR NEGATIVE ASSUMPTIONS.

Although anger may be difficult to prevent, it is possible to defuse it with *reframing,* looking at a situation from another perspective. If a man cuts you off in traffic, rather than repeatedly thinking, "What a %&#!" try reframing. When your anger hits, take a deep breath and look at the situation in a different way. Maybe the fellow just found out his wife is in labor, and he needs to get home quickly. Maybe he'll run out of gas if he doesn't get to his destination soon. Either way, what does it matter if he's one car in front of you? Take a deep breath. You'll still get to where you're going.

Of course, being able to reframe or challenge your thoughts in the heat of anger is not easy. Sometimes you will need to step away from a situation in order to gain composure. Sometimes, you'll have to use a calming technique (Tool 2) to turn off the switch to your sympathetic nervous system. Other times, a distraction like watching TV or taking a walk can help you shift your thoughts more easily. And sometimes just taking a deep breath will be enough to allow you to shift your thoughts.

Challenge Questions

Challenging the thoughts that trigger your anger can help defuse the intensity of your feelings. Also, ask yourself whether fear or loss may be fueling your ire. If that's the case, use the thought-shifting steps for anxiety or sadness discussed above.

You can ask yourself the following questions to challenge your anger-sustaining self-talk.

- Do I have all the facts?
- Is there another way to look at this situation?
- Is my anger in proportion to the situation?
- Am I really afraid or sad about something?
- What message is my anger trying to give me?
- Is this the way I usually respond to things I don't like?
- Am I angry because this situation is triggering one of my schemas?
- Is there anything at all that is good about this situation?
- Am I hurting myself by staying angry?

3. GENERATE NEW AND REALISTIC MESSAGES THAT YOU CREATE.

After you have challenged your anger-producing self-talk, create a new message to calm yourself. As always, it should be something you believe. Here are some examples. Use these only if they resonate with you.

- Maybe I don't know the whole story.
- It's funny (or sad) if you think about it.
- Just because I think it, that doesn't make it true.

- It's not worth my anger.
- I can do something positive about this.
- This is not my problem; it's his (or hers).

4. DEVELOP AN ACTION PLAN.

Keeping your anger self-statements going, recycling them over and over in your head, or talking to others incessantly about how you've been wronged is a recipe to sustain your anger. In order to let go of it, take some action.

Action Plan Questions

Here are some questions to help you figure out your action plan:

- Am I focused on "why" questions—for example, "Why did he do that to me?" If so, change them to "how" questions ("How can I get past this?").
- What else can I do besides be angry?
- What can I do to feel better? Go for a walk, see a movie, talk with the person I'm upset with, organize a group to change the way things are done?
- Will it be helpful or destructive to express my anger? If helpful, see Tool 3, communication.

Freda's Thought-Shifting for Anger

Freda and her husband bought tickets to a fancy fund-raiser for their church. Freda decided to go all-out. She had her hair done, got a manicure, and bought an especially pretty dress for the occasion. She spent all day primping.

When it was time to go, her husband Henry sat on the couch in the living room waiting for her. Freda descended the stairs feeling like a princess.

"Get your coat, Freda. We don't want to be late," said Henry. He walked out to the car.

Freda was crushed. She had envisioned a wide-eyed Henry paying her glowing compliments. But instead of, "Freda, you look beautiful," he spoke not a word. He didn't even walk her outside.

As she opened the car door, she hoped he'd say then how lovely she looked. Instead, he told her that she shouldn't let the gas tank get so low.

Freda was hurt. She started to get angry, but she said nothing. After all, this was such a petty thing. She knew she looked great. She should just let it go. But she couldn't let it go. The whole night she kept thinking about it. The more she thought about it, the madder she got. Here's how Freda used thought-shifting to make sense of her anger.

1. BECOME AWARE OF YOUR NEGATIVE SELF-TALK.

Freda asked herself, "What thoughts was I having just before the anger started?" Here's what she found:

- I've worked so hard to look pretty, and he doesn't even notice me. He's so self-absorbed.
- He doesn't think I'm attractive anymore.
- He doesn't care about me.
- I feel very alone.

2. DIRECTLY EXAMINE AND CHALLENGE YOUR NEGATIVE ASSUMPTIONS.

To pick apart her angry thoughts, Freda used the challenge questions.

- **Do I have all the facts?** It seems I do, but maybe something is going on with Henry that I don't know about.

- **Is there another way to look at this situation?** Maybe Henry thought that I looked nice, but felt he didn't need to say it out loud.

- **Is my anger in proportion to the situation?** It isn't the end of the world that he didn't compliment me, but it really upsets me.

- **Am I really afraid or sad about something?** Yes, I feel hurt by his lack of attention. Maybe he doesn't find me attractive anymore. I feel terrible when I think about this.

- **What message is my anger trying to give me?** Maybe it's trying to tell me that after all these years, I still need Henry's affection.

- **Is this the way I usually respond to things I don't like?** No, I'm usually pretty slow to anger.

- **Am I angry because this situation is triggering one of my schemas?** No, I don't see any connections.

- **Is there anything at all that is good about this situation?** Maybe it makes me see that I love Henry so much that I want his attention.

- **Am I hurting myself by staying angry?** If I don't stop thinking about this, I will. It certainly ruined the dinner party for me.

3. GENERATE NEW AND REALISTIC MESSAGES THAT YOU CREATE.

I know Henry loves me. He just doesn't always know what I need to feel loved.

4. DEVELOP AN ACTION PLAN.

Freda realized that her anger resulted from being hurt and sad. She could have moved to the action plan for anxiety or sadness, but

she decided to stay with the action questions for anger to shift her
distressing feelings.

- **Am I focused on "why" questions? If so, change them
  to "how" questions.** Yes, I'm thinking things like "Why
  doesn't he notice me?" instead of "How can I resolve this
  problem?"

- **What else can I do besides be angry?** I can tell Henry
  how I feel instead of ruminating on it, which will just make
  me more upset. I know he would not want me to be upset.

- **What can I do to feel better?** I think talking with him
  would be best. I just hope it doesn't seem nitpicky.

- **Will it be helpful or destructive to express my anger? If
  helpful, see Tool 3, communication.** I think it will be
  helpful, but I don't know how to begin. I'll look at the
  communication tools for help.

Although Freda's anger about Henry's indifference was not
based on her schema, her difficulty talking to him about it was. She
grew up believing that she should be nice and not talk about "bad"
feelings. Using the Emotional Tools for communication helped
her understand how this schema prevented her from expressing
herself more fully with Henry, a man who was open to hearing her
feelings.

Freda explained to Henry how hurt she was when he did not
notice how nice she looked for the church dinner. This was a difficult conversation for her, and she told him that too. Henry apologized profusely for his lack of attention. He didn't really want to
attend the dinner, he said, and he now realized he was taking that
out on her. In the end, Henry said, "You are as beautiful to me now
as you were the day we married. Why don't you put your pretty
dress on again, and we can go out to dinner, just the two of us."
And with that conversation, Freda felt loved again.

Some Advice

Negative self-talk can be difficult to shake, for all the reasons we've discussed. Your thinking style did not develop overnight, and it won't vanish overnight. Be prepared for old thinking patterns to resurface as you attempt to shift your thoughts. If this happens, simply observe your thoughts without judgment. Say something like, "Oh, there's that old thinking of mine—how interesting," and return to your new thinking pattern. As Joan Borysenko, former director of the Mind/Body Clinic at New England Deaconess Hospital, Harvard Medical School, writes, "No one can undo the habits of a lifetime without wrestling with those habits again and again and again." This is particularly true when the patterns are the result of ingrained habits, temperaments, or schemas.

In addition to thought-shifting, there is another way to reduce your negative thought patterns. We'll look at the emotional benefits of Tool 2, the meditative arts, in the next chapter.

10

The Power of Quiet

Tool 2: The Meditative Arts

How can you be happy?
Come, return to the root of the root of yourself.

—Rumi, thirteenth-century poet

When Ruby's marriage fell apart, her friend Gina was there to support her. Gina helped her through the early days of disbelief and was available to listen to Ruby's concerns and fears. Every Wednesday, Gina and Ruby went to a local restaurant for dinner and conversation.

Gina's life quickly changed when her mother was diagnosed with Alzheimer's. Now her mother needed her too. Gina had two teenage children relying on her and her husband, as well as a full-time job and a home to take care of. It was overwhelming. She knew something had to give.

Gina decided to tell Ruby that she could no longer meet her for Wednesday dinners. As she pulled into the restaurant parking lot, she could feel herself getting anxious. With a schema that dictated, "I should never disappoint others" and "It is important that everyone like me," Gina often felt nervous about the possibility of hurting people. She thought, "What if Ruby thinks I'm being an un-caring friend?"

As is common with anxiety, Gina's mind raced with what-if thinking, and her shoulders were tense. Before going into the restaurant, she decided to sit in her car and calm herself by breathing slowly and rhythmically.

With her deep inhalations, Gina provided more oxygen to her brain. This oxygen, which had been restricted by her shallow anxiety breathing, helped relax her. Her long exhalations helped calm her racing mind. After a few minutes of deep breathing, Gina could feel a shift. The impact it had on her emotional state was powerful. Her anxiety wasn't completely gone, but she was calmer than before and better able to discuss her situation with Ruby. After listening to Gina, Ruby assured her that she supported her decision to suspend their Wednesday dinners, and that she would do whatever she could to help Gina during her own time of need.

What worked for Gina was Tool 2, the meditative arts. This Emotional Tool is not one specific strategy, but rather a collection of techniques that are used to calm your body and focus your mind. These techniques include mindfulness meditation, meditation-in-action, and the one Gina used to reduce her anxiety, belly breathing.

Belly Breathing

Take a deep breath right now. As you do, notice whether your chest or your belly is expanding. If you're like most people, it's your chest. With belly breathing you breathe into your abdomen. Relaxation is associated with abdominal breathing. Although women are often told to suck their stomachs in, it is belly breathing that can provide your body with more oxygen—as much as ten times more oxygen than chest breathing can. This extra oxygen can help shift your emotions.

Belly breathing consists of three parts:

1. Breathe in.
2. Hold.
3. Breath out.

Slow deep breaths slow your heart rate and move your body into a relaxed state. Neuroscientist James H. Austin, M.D., theorizes that expelling your breath slowly reduces the firing activity of your brain's nerve cells, which in turn helps to quiet your mind.

Belly-Breathing Exercise

Begin by placing your hand on your stomach. As you breathe in, you should feel your belly rise. As you exhale, your belly should fall. Slowly count your breaths. If you find breathing in and out to the counts given here too difficult, you can reduce the numbers. Try to keep your out-breaths longer than your in-breaths.

1. Slowly breathe in, counting 1-2-3-4.
2. Hold your breath in your belly, and count 1-2-3-4.
3. Slowly exhale, counting 1-2-3-4-5-6-7-8.

Count slowly, but maintain a pace that is comfortable for you. Continue this exercise for a few minutes.

The beauty of belly breathing is that it can be done anywhere, anytime. Use it during a break at work, before heading into a stressful situation, or to calm yourself during an angry exchange.

How a Distressed Body Can Foster a Distressed Mind

Beth noticed the impact her distressed body had on her thinking patterns. Her doctor advised her that she would need to undergo a simple medical procedure. Immediately, her jaw clenched, and her breathing sped up. As her bodily reactions intensified, she felt she was in a state of emergency. She began to think about all the things that could go wrong. What if it hurts? What if they make a mistake? Her body signs and thinking patterns fed each other, intensifying her distress.

To slow the cycle, Beth used belly breathing. As her body reactions began to slow and soften, Beth was able to catch her runaway thoughts and calm herself. She was then able to ask her doctor helpful questions that allayed her fears.

Being able to slow and relax your body can be particularly helpful when you're feeling overwhelmed with anger. This is especially true for romantic partners. Researcher John Gottman observed couples having arguments. As their anger increased, so did their heart rates. He found that when one partner's heartbeat exceeded a hundred beats per minute, that person was unable to hear what the other was trying to say, no matter how hard the person tried. Their nervous system reactions created an emotional block for the couple.

So what is Gottman's advice to couples seeking a happy relationship? Find ways to calm your body during anger by turning on the switch to the soothing qualities of your parasympathetic nervous system. Your meditative emotional tools are an excellent way to do that. Take time out from an argument to use the slow, calming breaths of belly breathing, or use the meditative techniques in the next section. Both will slow your heartbeat so that you can communicate more effectively with your partner.

How Does Meditation Reduce Emotional Distress?

Feelings are created by both your mind and body. As we've discussed, anxiety, sadness, and anger are characterized by specific thought patterns and body responses. Meditation can help reduce distressing emotions by shifting your thinking patterns and physical reactions.

The type of meditation we'll discuss is a form of mindfulness meditation with which you simply observe your thoughts or breath or body sensations without judgment. Jon Kabat-Zinn and his colleagues at the University of Massachusetts Medical School taught this type of mindfulness meditation to men and women who were diagnosed with generalized anxiety or panic disorder. The participants, aged twenty-six to sixty-four, learned how to meditate during an eight-week course. At its conclusion, they showed a 65 percent decrease in their anxiety levels and a 49 percent decrease in their depression. Three months after the program ended, these decreases had been maintained. In some cases, they were reduced even further because most participants continued with some form of meditation.

These dramatic results are not limited to Kabat-Zinn's research subjects. Shauna Shapiro and her colleagues at the University of Arizona taught mindfulness meditation to overwhelmed medical students. After eight weeks of practice, the students reported a nearly 50 percent drop in their anxiety and depression levels, while medical students who hadn't learned to meditate experienced no decrease. The meditating medical students were happier than the nonmeditating ones, even though their demanding schedules were the same.

How can simply focusing on your breath or your body sensations reduce your anxiety, sadness, and anger? The answer lies in the way meditation affects your body and your mind.

The Meditating Body

When you meditate, several things happen in your body that help decrease and shift your distressing emotions. Richard Davidson, professor of psychology and psychiatry at the University of Wisconsin, and his colleagues taught twenty-five stressed-out biotech workers to meditate over a two-month period. The researchers measured their brain activity before and after the meditation program. They found that these novice meditators changed their brain function in positive ways. Through meditation, they increased the activity in their left prefrontal cortex, an area of the brain associated with upbeat and happy moods. In other words, because of their meditation, these parts of their brains were activated more often than were the regions associated with sadness, anxiety, or anger, so they felt happier.

When scanning the brains of people who are meditating, other research has shown that certain parts of the brain are activated in response to the focused concentration of meditation. From this information, scientists have theorized that the cortex sends a message to the emotional center of your brain that it's time to activate the calming powers of your parasympathetic nervous system.

As discussed in Chapter 2, when the switch to your parasympathetic nervous system is turned on, your body is flooded with the calming chemical acetylcholine. This surge is responsible for setting in motion a series of biological changes—including reducing your heart rate, lowering your blood pressure, and easing your muscle tension—all leading to a sense of relaxation.

These physical changes are particularly important when you're anxious or angry. With both of these emotions, your body reactions are fast (rapid heartbeat) and tight (tense muscles). Turning on your parasympathetic nervous system can reverse the speed and tension you feel, helping to reduce your distressing emotions.

DID I REALLY DO THAT?

When I taught women at UCLA how to meditate, I used small biofeedback monitors so they could see how meditating changed their body reactions. Each woman received a monitor and was instructed to tape a sensor to her finger. Once it was in place for a few seconds, the monitor provided a reading of skin temperature. Skin temperature, which is different from body temperature (normally 98.6 degrees Fahrenheit), can range from 60 to 100 degrees.

Once everyone was hooked up, we began a ten-minute mindfulness meditation. When we finished, I asked the students to look at their temperature readings. Many were shocked to see the changes.

For some women, skin temperatures jumped as much as 15 degrees. Why? When you turn on the switch to your parasympathetic nervous system, your blood vessels open. When they open, more blood travels to your body's extremities. When the blood arrives to these areas, your skin warms and your temperature goes up.

"Did I really do that?" students often asked me. The women, through focus and concentration, took a process that they previously considered impossible to control—the internal workings of their bodies—and made their physiology change. When the students realized they were controlling their body chemistry—actually making their bodies produce the calming chemical acetylcholine on demand—they were stunned.

Here is what one woman told me about her meditating experience: "When we first learned to meditate, I was skeptical. I didn't really see how sitting down and thinking about my breathing was going to do anything for my life. Then we hooked up to the biofeedback monitors. After meditating for ten minutes, my skin temperature rose twelve degrees. From then on, I was convinced I should give it a try. Since meditating, I've noticed I'm a lot less irritable than I used to be. Upsetting events roll off my shoulders more easily now, and that in turn has made me a happier person."

There are other physical changes that occur in your body during meditation that can reduce your feelings of anxiety, sadness, and anger. Here are three of them:

• **Meditation Reduces the Anxiety Chemicals in Your Blood.** Individuals who feel anxious tend to have more of the chemical lactate in their blood. Meditation can help reduce the presence of this anxiety-associated chemical. Within the first ten minutes of meditating, blood lactate levels fall dramatically, and they stay lower, even when you are no longer meditating. This, in part, helps explain why people who meditate say they feel less nervous and edgy than they did before they learned to meditate.

• **Meditation Increases Your Feel-Good Brain Waves.** Meditation can affect the electrical activity in your brain. Your brain produces electrical currents, or brain waves, from the activity of your brain cells.

When you are alert and thinking, you produce *beta* brain waves. This is normal. If you're nervous or sad and ruminating about negative things, you may be producing an overabundance of beta waves. Meditation can help shift the activity of your brain cells so you produce more *alpha* waves. When your brain produces alpha waves, you are likely to experience feelings of well-being, calmness, and peacefulness.

• **Meditation Recharges Your Body.** When you meditate, there is a dramatic drop in your body's oxygen consumption. Oxygen is needed to run all the functions of your body, including making your heart beat and your blood pump. Meditation slows these systems down so they require less oxygen to run. This drop allows your body to reserve its energy and restore itself. It's like giving your body a break in the middle of its hectic schedule. Herbert Benson, M.D., describes this reduced oxygen consumption as akin to "giving a hyperenergetic kindergartner an afternoon nap." That explains why many people who meditate report feeling

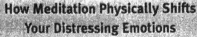

**How Meditation Physically Shifts
Your Distressing Emotions**

- Reduces muscle tension

- Reduces heart rate

- Reduces oxygen
  consumption

- Reduces blood lactate
  levels

- Decreases blood pressure

- Increases the production
  of alpha waves

- Increases activity in the
  brain's left prefrontal
  cortex, an area associated
  with pleasant moods

rested, rejuvenated, and even more energetic. This can be particularly helpful if you're feeling sad, since sadness can zap your energy.

Your Monkey Mind

In order to understand how meditation can soothe your psyche, it helps to know about the monkey mind. If you pay attention to your thoughts, you'll see that they are like little monkeys, hopping from branch to branch, tree to tree, in an endless array of motion. When I talk about the monkey mind, people often think it's a silly phrase I invented. Actually, it's a Buddhist term that describes the natural tendency of your mind to be continually engaged in thought. Often people are not aware of their nonstop thinking until they sit down and try to quiet their minds.

THE MONKEYS ARE JUMPING

When my client Dorothy first tried mindfulness meditation, she became acutely aware of her monkey mind. With the aim of focusing on her breath for five minutes, I gave her the following instructions: Simply be aware of your breathing. When a thought comes to your mind, silently say, "A thought," and then gently bring your attention back to your breathing.

Dorothy went home and gave it a try. Setting an egg timer for five minutes, she then sat comfortably and closed her eyes. Here's how her meditation went:

Okay, I need to relax and focus on my breath. I can do this. Five minutes isn't so long. Now that was a thought, right? I just noticed it. A thought. See, look how good I'm doing already. Like when I took that aerobics class, and I was so worried because I'm not very co-ordinated. But I tried really hard, and I did well. I remember that time. That was just before I was laid off. That was a terrible time in my life. I was so miserable, and it took so long to find a new job. And now look how things have changed. I have a good job and a nice home. And speaking of my home, I really need to vacuum this rug. And I have to go food shopping too. We'll be out of orange juice by tomorrow. Maybe I can go after work. I need to write that report for work. That's due on Friday, and, I . . . Ding.

Those five minutes quickly came and went. Dorothy's monkey mind was racing, and she only focused on her breath once. Dorothy told me she felt like a total failure at her first attempt to meditate, but that's not the way I saw it. To me, she was learning something very important about herself: that her mind is always running, end-lessly jumping from thought to thought, and quietly influencing her emotions. It was something she had never noticed before. This is the nature of the everyday mind. If you observe your own thoughts, you'll see that it's the nature of your mind too.

Mindfulness Meditation

Find a quiet place. Finding a quiet place to meditate sounds like a simple thing to do, but it isn't always so easy. If you meditate with the expectation that you'll be interrupted, you'll have a difficult time relaxing your body and focusing your mind. Many people say that finding a quiet place in their noisy lives is a major obstacle to starting a meditation practice. Here's what some women who meditate have told me they do to find that quiet place:

- "I meditate after everyone else goes to bed."
- "I meditate before everyone else wakes up."
- "I meditate in my backyard or on my balcony or in my basement."
- "I meditate while I'm lying in bed at night, just before going to sleep."
- "I tell my family I'm taking some quiet time to meditate and do not want to be disturbed unless there is a fire or the Prize Patrol rings our doorbell."

Sit any way you want. It doesn't matter. Some suggest that you must sit a certain way to benefit from meditation. I believe you should sit in any position in which you can be comfortable for the duration of your meditation. For example, you can sit in a chair, on your bed, or on the floor. Sometimes when people meditate lying down, they have a hard time staying awake during the meditation—particularly if they lie in their beds, since beds are associated with sleeping. If this is not the case for you, or if you have a physical condition that prevents you from sitting, then by all means lie down if you'd like.

How to Meditate

I'm going to teach you two different mindfulness meditations. With each meditation, you'll follow a similar format: relax your body, and then bring your attention to your focus.

Your focus—the object you bring all your attention to—will be either your breath or your body. As you focus in each meditation, expect to have moments when you start thinking about other things. That's perfectly normal; it's just your monkey mind. When that happens, simply notice that you're thinking. Silently say, "A thought" to yourself to become more aware that you're thinking. Then go back to your focus. If your mind wanders again, bring it back to your focus again and again until the meditation is over.

Many people have the impression that the purpose of meditation is to stop all of their thoughts. This is not true. In fact, the more you try to stop the natural flow of your thoughts, the more tense you'll become. This is the same notion as trying to will yourself to stop negative self-talk that we mentioned earlier. It's not a good idea.

The point of meditation is simply to notice your thoughts as they arise. Once you've noticed them, gently return to the focus of your breath or your body.

Try not to judge your wandering mind with comments like "I'll never be able to do this" or "I'm not good at meditating." The more you practice, the better you'll get at noticing when you have a thought and returning to your focus. That simple process in itself will produce significant benefits for you.

In the beginning, it might seem that all you're doing is bringing your mind back to your focus again and again, but remember, these techniques are skills that must be developed. The more you use them, the better you'll get. In a way it's similar to learning penmanship or how to drive a car. You weren't very good when you started and you may even have been frustrated by the experience, but the more you practiced, the better you got.

Noticing Your Thoughts

Carmen was so busy thinking her thoughts, she wasn't even able to notice she was having them. With practice, she got to the point where she could separate herself from her thinking. Following is

an example of Carmen noticing her thoughts during her meditation in a nonjudgmental way and returning to her focus. In this
case the focus is her breath.

> Breathing in . . . 1-2-3-4 . . . Hold . . . 1-2-3-4 . . .
> Breathing out . . . 1-2-3-4-5-6-7-8 . . .
>
> "I think I'm doing it! . . . A thought."
>
> Breathing in . . . 1-2-3-4 . . . "I need to go to the bank after
> this . . . A thought."
>
> Breathing in . . . 1-2-3-4 . . . Hold . . . 1-2-3-4 . . .
> Breathing out . . . 1-2-3-4-5-6-7-8 . . .
>
> Breathing in . . . 1-2-3-4 . . . "I need to get Angie a birthday
> card . . . A thought."
>
> Breathing in . . . 1-2-3-4 . . . Hold . . . 1-2-3-4 . . .
> Breathing out . . . 1-2-3-4-5-6-7-8 . . .
>
> "What should I make for dinner? . . . A thought."
>
> Breathing in . . . 1-2-3-4 . . . Hold . . . 1-2-3-4 . . . "I don't
> like my job, but I don't know what I really want to do . . .
> A thought."
>
> "What if I don't figure out what I want to do next with my
> life? . . . A thought."
>
> Breathing in . . . 1-2-3-4 . . . . "I don't like feeling this way . . .
> A thought."

In this meditation, Carmen simply observed her thoughts and
feelings, as if she were watching a television show. That's what you
should do: just observe what you find. Even if you don't like what
you find, don't try to change the channel. As Jon Kabat-Zinn
notes, "Meditation is not about feeling a certain way. It's about
feeling the way you feel."

In the next section, you'll find two mindfulness meditations: (1)

relaxation and breath focus and (2) relaxation and body focus. You can try either one or both. Read through the meditation instructions before you try to meditate. Once you feel you understand the process, you can begin. You might even consider reading these instructions into a tape recorder so you can play them back as a meditation guide.

Mindfulness Meditation 1: Relaxation and Breath Focus

Let's begin by getting relaxed. Start by sitting in a comfortable position and closing your eyes. Feel your body settling into the chair or floor. Take a deep breath in through your nose; then, as slowly as you can, let it out. Take another breath in, and this time as you let it out, feel your shoulders melting and getting heavy. Take a slow breath in, and on the out-breath, feel your whole body getting heavier and relaxed. Continue to slowly breathe in and out. As you do, feel all the tension leave your body. Think of your spine as a clothes hanger, strong and erect, and your body is just hanging off the hanger like a rag doll. Your whole body is heavy and limp.

Now bring your attention to your breathing. Notice the way your breath feels in your nose as you breathe in and out. What sensations do you feel? Maybe the warmth of the air in your nose? A tingling? Become aware of how your belly moves with each breath. It expands with the in-breath and retracts with the out-breath. Just as ocean waves ebb and flow, so too does your breath. In and out. Slowly, like the waves.

Now we are going to count the breaths. Slowly breathing in, count 1-2-3-4. Now hold the breath in your belly, and count 1-2-3-4. Now slowly exhale: 1-2-3-4-5-6-7-8. Count slowly, but maintain a pace that is comfortable for you. Continue. Slowly breathing in, count 1-2-3-4. Now hold the breath in your belly, and count 1-2-3-4. Now slowly exhale, 1-2-3-4-5-6-7-8. Continue this exercise for ten minutes. When your mind wanders, silently say, "A thought," and bring your focus back to your breath and your counting.

Mindfulness Meditation 1: Relaxation and Breath Focus

Quick Guide

- Relax your body.
- Breathe in, counting 1-2-3-4.
- Hold your breath in your belly, counting 1-2-3-4.
- Exhale, counting 1-2-3-4-5-6-7-8.
- Bring your attention to your breath.
- When your mind wanders, silently say, "A thought," and return to your focus.

Mindfulness Meditation 2: Relaxation and Body Focus

First, relax by following the same instructions as you did in meditation 1 until your body feels heavy and limp. Now you'll shift your attention away from your breathing and focus on your body.

Bring your awareness to your feet. Notice your left foot. How does it feel? Maybe it's itchy or cold or tingly. Just observe your left foot as if you were watching television. Don't try to change anything you feel; just pay attention to it.

Now notice your right foot. What sensations do you notice in your right foot? What about each one of your toes? Just observe it.

Next, notice your legs and how they feel against the chair or floor. Feel all the sensations of your legs as they meet the surface.

Do they feel warm or cold? Are your legs bent at the knees? If so, what does that feel like? Observe all the details of sensation in your legs.

Now we're going to move up the body to the hands. Notice your left hand. How does it feel? What do you observe? Is it sweaty? Is it hot? Is there any pain? Observe these various sensations without judging them as good or bad. Just watch what you find. Notice each finger. What physical sensations are in your thumb? Or your pinkie?

Now move to your right hand, and do the same thing. How does it feel? Is it resting on your leg or a chair? If so, what does that feel like? Notice each finger. What physical sensations are in your thumb? Your pinkie?

Now let's move to your stomach. Notice any sensation there. Maybe it's tight or rigid. What feelings are in your stomach? Notice how it slowly moves in and out as you breathe.

Now move your awareness up to your shoulders. Observe your right shoulder. Is it rigid and up high, or is it loose and hanging down? What sensations do you notice in your shoulder? Don't judge what you experience. Move to your left shoulder, and examine it too. Maybe it's rigid or heavy. Is it throbbing?

Let's move now to where your jawbones meet on the right side of your face. What does that feel like? Is it clenched tight or loose? Is it throbbing? What about the left side? What sensations do you feel there?

Now take a very slow deep breath in through your nose. Release it very slowly, and as you do, feel your whole body get heavy and loose, just like the clothes draped on the hanger. Your whole body is limp. Continue to breathe slowly. You are here in this moment. All you have to do is breathe and be here right now. Continue to breathe slowly, and when you feel ready, slowly open your eyes.

Once you've opened your eyes, stretch your arms in any direction—over your head, to the side, or behind your back. No-

tice the feeling of your muscles as you stretch them. Breathe deeply
in through your nose, and then slowly let it out.

Mindfulness Meditation 2: Relaxation and Body Focus

Quick Guide

- Relax your body.
- Focus on your feet (left and right).
- Focus on your legs.
- Focus on your hands (left and right).
- Focus on your stomach.
- Focus on your shoulders (left and right).
- Focus on your jawbones (left and right).
- When your mind wanders, silently say, "A thought," and
  return to your focus.

The Mind of Meditation

These deceptively simple mindfulness meditations can actually
change the quality of the thoughts you have. They can shift your
thinking away from fearful, negative, or hostile thoughts to
thoughts that are less affected by the outside events of your life.
One way meditation does this is by helping you break the negative
thought patterns we talked about earlier.

Meditation Can Help Break
Your Negative Thought Patterns

As I said earlier, when I ask women to close their eyes and relax, all
kinds of thoughts pop into their heads during the silence. For Rita,

one thought was, "I'll always be alone." This is a thought that's likely to lead her to sadness. Many women find themselves unconsciously ruminating on distressing thoughts. Or conversely, they may try to push distressing thoughts away and allow only happy thoughts. With meditation, when you become aware you're thinking a thought, you simply notice your thought and silently say to yourself, "A thought." Then come back to your focus, which is your breath or your body. This serves a critical function.

Each time Rita shifts from her thoughts of loneliness to her breathing focus, she is slowly breaking her negative thought patterns. By preventing her mind from jumping further into her network of sad thoughts, meditation reduces those thoughts. In other words, she's training her mind to think in a new way. Slowly over time, she may notice that she has fewer sad thoughts than she used to. Or the sad thoughts she does have may not affect her as strongly as they did before. As a result, she's happier. The same thing will happen with your anxiety or anger-producing thoughts.

Why Is Coming Back to My Focus So Important?

I'm often asked the question, "Why is coming back to my focus, like my breath or my body, so important to shifting my emotions?" There are two main reasons. First, many of our thoughts include constant worrying, negative thinking, or self-criticism. Clearly, these types of thoughts will lead to distressing emotions. Staying with your focus allows you to take a break from this, if only for five minutes. It provides a rest away from the endless directives of an unsupportive schema or judgmental self-talk.

The second reason returning over and over to your focus is so important is that it trains your mind to pay attention to the present. Since each breath you take exists only in the present moment, it is difficult to focus on your breath and be consumed by the past or

Distressing Thinking Patterns	
PAST (Sadness)	FUTURE (Anxiety)
Why did it have to be that way?	What if I can't do this?
I wish I hadn't done that.	What if it doesn't work out?
I wish I had made a different choice.	What if I'm wrong?
If only things were different.	What if things don't change?

future. This is critical because sadness is often found by dwelling negatively on the past, and anxiety is often found by dwelling negatively on the future.

The key word here is *dwelling*. Thinking about the past or future so you can better understand something, make plans, or change directions in your life is necessary and valuable. This is different from ruminating about the same things repeatedly even though doing so makes you unhappy. Continually returning to the presentness of your breath or your body helps to pull you gently away from the thoughts that can create anxiety, sadness, or anger.

How Noticing Your Thoughts Can Change Them

As you practice noticing your thoughts in mindfulness meditation, you begin to separate yourself from them a bit. Each time you say, "A thought," you loosen the power it has over you, and this can create profound emotional changes. When this separation occurs, even if only for a second, you slowly begin to experience a new level of awareness.

According to Deepak Chopra, M.D., former chief of staff at

New England Memorial Hospital and CEO of the Chopra Center, meditation "detaches the mind from its fixed level and allows it to exist, if only for a moment, without any levels at all. It simply experiences silence, devoid of thoughts, emotions, drives, wishes, fears, or anything at all. Afterward, when the mind returns to its usual . . . level of consciousness, it has acquired a little freedom to move."

This "freedom to move" is a fresh, unforced perspective that positively affects your thinking patterns and emotions. When you are able to separate yourself from your thoughts, you develop a new outlook that reduces your anxiety, sadness, and anger. Of course, this doesn't happen overnight. With continued practice, your thinking patterns will change without your doing anything specific to change them, helping you to see your life differently. Instead of being obsessed that a coworker is always late, you just let it go effortlessly.

Creating New Thought Patterns

During mindfulness meditation, you can also reprogram specific thought patterns that cause you emotional distress. Maybe you question whether you deserve to be happy, to have love, or to be financially well-off. During deep relaxation, your brain is more receptive to accepting new ideas and, in effect, to rewiring itself. According to pioneering researcher Herbert Benson, M.D., "I believe the shift in brain waves . . . [during meditation], is in part responsible for the 'door-opening effect' that so many people experience as a result of eliciting the relaxation response. . . . The brain seems to use the quiet time to wipe the slate clean so that new ideas and beliefs can present themselves."

How can you do this? While you are in a deeply relaxed state, either from belly breathing or mindfulness meditation, silently repeat a sentence or phrase you think will have a positive effect on your thinking patterns and emotions. As with thought-shifting (Tool 1), these statements should be created by you and based on your own needs. Examples include:

- I'm open to good things coming to me.
- I can do this.
- I accept this situation without judgment.
- I will find an answer.

Try to keep these statements positive. Instead of saying, "I'm not dumb," say, "I'm smart." Also, keep in mind that repetition is the key. Just saying your phrase once or twice while you are in a relaxed state will not be as helpful as repeating it every time you meditate.

"But I'm Too Busy to Meditate"

Fitting meditation into their busy life is probably the single biggest challenge for most people. When you first start meditating, do it for five minutes. As your ability to concentrate develops; you can increase your time until you are meditating from twenty to thirty minutes per sitting. Meditating on a consistent basis—three to five times per week—is ideal, but if you're having trouble developing a regular meditation practice, try fitting it in where you can. I've squeezed my sitting meditation in while my daughter was taking a nap, and in the car when I was early for a meeting. Do five minutes here and five minutes there if that's all you can do.

Meditation-in-Action

Don't fall into the trap of believing that if you can't sit down to meditate regularly, you might as well not meditate at all. You can turn your life into a meditation. For example, meditate while you're in the shower. Instead of using your breath as the focus of your meditation, use the sensation of the water. Notice how the water feels as it hits your body or how the shampoo smells as you lather it into your hair. Every time a thought comes into your mind, just notice it in a nonjudgmental way, and return your focus to the sensations of the shower. I call this *meditation-in-action*.

You can use meditation-in-action with many of your daily activities, by bringing your attention to a particular focus in the activity.

Meditation-in-Action	
Activity	**Focus**
Brushing teeth	The feel of the toothbrush in your hand, the sensation of the brushing in your mouth, the smell of the toothpaste.
Eating	The colors and shapes of the food, the smell of the food, the sensation of the food in your mouth, the experience of chewing, the flavor of each bite of food.
Going to bed	The feeling of the pillow on your face, the feeling of the sheets on your body, the sense of your body resting in the bed.

Natalia uses meditation-in-action when she goes to bed at night: "Each night when I would climb into bed, my mind would start racing. All kinds of worries went through my head that kept me from sleeping, including the thought about how tired I was going to be tomorrow if I didn't fall asleep soon. I decided to try a "bed focus." I noticed how my pillow felt against my cheek. I became aware of the feeling of my blanket wrapped around my shoulders.

I sensed the warmth of my body in the bed. When my mind went back to my worries, I would simply notice them and return to my bed focus. Within no time, I drifted off to sleep. This has now become my new bedtime ritual."

CINDY'S STORY

The most creative meditation-in-action story I've heard comes from Cindy, a client of mine. One day she walked into my office with a big smile on her face.

"You look happy," I said.

"I am," she said. "I finally figured out how to use meditation-in-action in a way that really helped me."

"That's great. Let's hear it," I said.

"I find I just can't get into sex lately because I'm thinking about all the things on my to-do list. Then, when I finally do get into it, I'm thinking about the few extra pounds I've gained, and what my husband might be thinking about that. By this point, I just want it to be over. I hate thinking like this, because I really miss the satisfying sex we used to have."

"I've heard the same thing from lots of women," I said.

"You know how we've been talking about meditation-in-action? I decided to try it with sex. When my mind starts wandering to thoughts about my body or my worries, I stop and bring my attention to my focus. With sex, my focus is touch: the feeling of my husband's hand on my skin or the sensation of his lips on mine. Each time my thoughts take me away, I just notice them and return to my touch focus. This keeps me in the present moment, just as you said. It's made a huge difference! Now I look forward to sex, and if my mind does wander, I know exactly how to fix it."

As Cindy described, it is the experience of being "taken away by our thoughts" that can contribute to distressing feelings. Meditation teacher and scholar Shinzen Young has said that meditation can reduce the two thought patterns that contribute most to our unhappiness: aversion and grasping.

What Is Aversion?

Aversion is a thinking style in which you believe that you can only be happy once an unpleasant situation becomes what you want it to be. Common aversion thoughts are:

"When I retire, I'll be happy."

"When I lose five pounds, I'll be happy."

"When I get pregnant, I'll be happy."

"When I get everything on my to-do list finished, I'll be happy."

Aversion thinking is predicated on the notion that everything in your life must be as you want it to be for you to be happy. So you wait for something to change so you can experience happiness. Sometimes you wait for years. Of course, rarely is everything the way you want it to be, and when it is, that state doesn't last forever. In life, change is the name of the game.

A simple example of aversion thinking happened to me one night as I was walking out of the supermarket into the parking lot. The weather was dramatically colder than it had been when I went into the store, and the sky was dark, a sudden change because daylight savings time had kicked in the day before. I immediately felt sad. Not the overwhelming sadness you feel when something terrible happens, but that sense of disappointment and longing for the warm, bright days of summer.

I could feel my mood change and my body getting heavier. Then I remembered to use my Emotional Toolkit. To shift my aversion thinking ("I wish it were summer again. I hate when it gets dark so early"), I purposefully moved my thoughts to the present moment. I noticed the feeling of my body as I walked to my car. I became aware of how my sweater felt on my skin and how the crisp air filled my body with each breath. This is what being mindful means. This is meditation-in-action.

My disappointment faded just as quickly as it appeared. I was experiencing the moment without judgment and without my aversion wishes that it be summer again. I was experiencing the place where happiness lives: in the present.

Did that mean my desire for summer was gone? No. But my experience of winter in this moment had changed. And so had my mood.

What Is Grasping?

Grasping is a thinking pattern in which you clutch onto something that's good and want it never to change. Common grasping thoughts are:

"I don't want to get older."

"I love my children and don't want them to grow up."

"I don't want my body to change."

"I always want to be in love the way I am now."

The nature of life is change. Wishing we could hold on to experiences and freeze them in time can only lead to distress. The more we hold on, the more distress we will feel. Many wonderful experiences are bittersweet, encompassing the joy of having and the sadness of letting go. But let go we must. Each time you experience the changing movements of your breath or the fluctuations of your body sensations in meditation, you are learning to accept change in a quiet way.

How Does Meditation
Reduce Aversion and Grasping?

Meditation can help diminish your aversion and grasping by training you to become focused on present-moment experiences. You bring your concentration to your focus—the present—and when a thought arises, you notice it in a nonjudgmental way: "Ah yes, that's another thought. How interesting." This nonjudgment is key. With practice, you will begin to see events in your life with less judgment as well. Instead of events being unbearable, you take them one step at a time, staying present, not allowing overwhelming thoughts about the future or past to sway you.

Anna understands the power meditation has had in preventing her from lapsing into aversion and grasping. Married since the age of twenty-one, Anna was looking forward to sharing a more stress-free time with her husband now that her youngest child had graduated from college. She was in complete shock when her husband announced one day that he wanted a divorce. He said he was no longer in love with her. Anna immediately suggested they go to counseling, but her husband was not interested. He had already rented an apartment in a nearby town.

Anna could easily have shifted into aversion thinking, saying to herself, "My life is ruined," or even grasping, holding on to an image of happier times and saying to herself, "I don't want it to change." She could have tried to will herself to think positive thoughts, but we know that would probably not work.

Instead, she allowed herself to mourn her loss. Because she had been meditating, this process was expedited and done in a skillful way. She focused on staying in the present. Whenever her mind would wander to catastrophic thoughts such as, "My life is ruined," she would simply notice those thoughts by silently saying, "A thought." By doing this, she dismantled the judging nature of her mind, and slowly reduced its power to affect her moods.

Although thinking about the past helped her make sense of her current situation, dwelling on it made her feel overwhelmed with grief. When this happened, she focused on her breathing, which acted as an anchor to bring her back to the present. Through meditation, she was chipping away at her aversion and grasping. She was putting herself in the only place where she had control—the present.

11

Finding Your Voice

Tool 3: Communication

Each person's life is lived as a series of conversations.

—Deborah Tannen, linguist

Most women have never learned how to communicate in a way that allows us to maintain our connections with others and get our needs met at the same time. The two are not necessarily at odds with each other, although many women think they are.

Becoming an effective communicator does not guarantee you'll always get what you want, but it does offer your best shot at it. To strengthen your skills as an effective communicator, this chapter presents seven communication strategies that will help you move from the passive, passive-aggressive, or attacking communication styles discussed previously to an effective style.

1. Begin Difficult Conversations Without Criticism

Naomi wanted to tell Steve that she was upset by his phone conversations with his ex-wife. Fearing her anger would harm both their relationship and her identity as a nice person, she instead expressed herself covertly, in a passive-aggressive style. Her goal to express her anger and still be liked was losing ground quickly. If Naomi didn't learn to communicate effectively, it might jeopardize her marriage.

I asked Naomi, "If you could tell Steve how you feel without any negative consequences, what would you say?"

"Steve, you are so inconsiderate. You should know how much your talks with Dolores bother me, yet you still do it. Don't you care about me?"

According to Gottman's research, 96 percent of the time you can predict how a conversation will end based on its first three minutes. Judging from Naomi's approach, this conversation will probably end badly. Why? Because her tone is blaming. Even if she speaks sweetly, the underlying message is, "You're an uncaring person." Steve is likely to spend more time defending himself than attending to Naomi's feelings and needs.

I instructed Naomi to approach her conversation with Steve gently. Instead of criticizing him, she could tell Steve how this situation affects her. For example, "I really have a tough time when you talk on the phone with Dolores. I don't like feeling this way, but it's the way I feel. I'd like us to talk about it."

With a noncritical approach, not only is Steve more likely to attend to Naomi's feelings, but he is also less likely to become physically overwhelmed and to withdraw from her with silence.

2. Use "I" Statements

Because of Malena's desire to please the people she loves, she puts the needs of everyone else before her own. To her, there is no way she can speak up for herself without hurting others or being seen as selfish. As a result, she ignores her own needs until she barely recognizes them.

"If you could tell your family what you want, what would you say?" I asked.

"I don't see how I could do that," she responded. "They would say I'm being selfish or at least that's what they'd think."

"Maybe they would, but they're not here right now. Let's just make believe," I said. "What would you say?"

"I'd say, 'You expect too much of me. You always want me to be there to help you. But you never think about me. Don't I get to have a life too?'"

"Give me an example of a time people expected too much of you," I said.

"My family was throwing a surprise fiftieth anniversary party for my parents. My sister called and said, 'You've been assigned to make the main course.' She didn't even ask; she just assumed I'd make it even though I had a million other things going on that week."

"How did you respond?" I asked.

"What could I say? I made the main course," she said.

To illustrate how effective communication works, I first suggested the ineffective response that I knew Malena thought was her only option besides acquiescing. "What if you responded like this: 'You're always doing this to me. You just assume I'll do it. You don't even ask. I'm not going to make the main course.' How does it feel to hear that?" I asked.

"You see? It sounds terrible," Malena replied. "My sister would probably get mad and not speak to me. Then, of course, the party would be ruined."

Then I proposed a more effective strategy. "What if you said this instead: 'I really want to help out with the party. I can't make the main course, but I can get the cake.' How does it feel when you hear that? Does it sound selfish?"

"No," said Malena, "but she might say, 'Robert is already getting the cake. We need you to make the main course.'"

"Then you'd say, 'I'm really swamped this week, and there's no way I can make the main course. What else can I do to help?'" I said. "Does that sound selfish?"

"No, that sounds okay."

The difference between the two approaches I used is that on the second response I used "I" statements instead of "you" statements. "I" statements are simply a way of phrasing your thoughts and feelings using the word *I*. Instead of saying, "*You* expect too much of me," you say, "I'm really swamped this week, but *I* want to help with the party."

Some people think using "I" statements is selfish, but it is exactly the opposite. With "I" statements you are taking responsibility for your own feelings rather than blaming others, which is a respectful thing to do.

When you first start using "I" statements, it can seem awkward and strange. You'd be amazed how often you use "you" statements, especially when you are angry. It takes practice to get the knack of "I" statements, but it can create a powerful shift in your communication style. And remember, "I think you're a jerk," is not an example of an "I" statement.

3. Disclose Your Feelings to People You Trust

In close relationships, it's easy to feel stymied by feelings of anger, anxiety, or sadness. Sometimes people lash out, withdraw, or try to cover up their true emotions because they are embarrassed by their feelings. There is another communication alternative: disclosure.

Disclosure happens when you reveal something personal about your emotional world. Let's say, for example, you found out your friend's brother died. You felt terrible, but didn't know what to say or how to help, so you offered your condolences and then tried to avoid her—not out of meanness, but rather out of awkwardness. Now your friend is angry at you, and your relationship suffers.

Instead of avoiding her, you could disclose your awkward feelings to her: "I feel so bad about your brother's death. But I don't know what to do. I'm afraid I'll say the wrong thing and make you feel worse."

Chances are your friend will greatly appreciate your honesty, and ironically, your expression of doubt, confusion, or fear will help create more intimacy between the two of you.

This is something Lynn could try. With a schema that dictates, "the people who love you will try to control you," she is ever-vigilant for signs that the people she cares about are out to dominate her. This has created a problem for Lynn. When she experiences that familiar fear, she reacts with an explosive outburst like, "I don't have to report to you like a servant." This expression serves its temporary purpose—to push the other person away—but it ends up with the unintended consequence of harming the relationship. In those moments of fear, Lynn could instead opt to disclose her vulnerability rather than her anger. For example, "When I hear comments like, 'What are you doing this weekend?' I get scared. I know it sounds crazy, but I feel like I'm being told what to do. I know that's not what you meant, but I just feel that way."

Of course, if Lynn's boyfriend really did show signs that he was trying to control her, that would be a different story. In this case, Lynn's worries are more a projection of her fears rather than reality.

Robin, like many people who view themselves as strong, has difficulty showing her vulnerable side. Her schema, molded from her mother's early death, dictated that she should be strong. This allowed her to feel some sense of control in a frightening situation and, in her ten-year-old mind, to be a good daughter to her grief-stricken father.

Over time, people began to expect this type of stoicism from her, and Robin became a prisoner of her own creation. She felt lonely and isolated because others couldn't see the pain behind her mask. Robin's fear of her "weakness" was harming her relationship with her husband and children.

For Robin, disclosing her feelings was scary. She was afraid others wouldn't accept her vulnerable side. I advised her to start with baby steps by slowly revealing more of her true self to her family and seeing how they responded. Some of the disclosures Robin came up with were:

- I'm having trouble carrying this box. Could you help me?
- Can you give me some advice on how to deal with my boss?
- I worry when you're late and I don't hear from you.
- I'm feeling overwhelmed trying to plan this holiday party.

Robin was surprised and relieved by the results of her experiment. Her family reacted with gratitude that Robin respected them enough to ask for help. They were touched that she cared enough about them to worry when they didn't call. As Robin showed more of her vulnerabilities, her family showed more of their strength. The success of Robin's disclosures prompted her to reveal more of herself. As a result, she is enjoying a level of closeness in her relationships that she never knew before.

Some people resist disclosure because they fear the other person will take advantage of their vulnerability and use that as an opportunity to pounce. But, according to Gerald Goodman, professor emeritus in clinical psychology at UCLA, "These riskier revelations that give away power and leave us vulnerable can paradoxically bring us the strength and protection of intimacy." In other words, if you can overcome your fear of disclosing your true self to the people you trust, you may be surprised to find you have a stronger and richer relationship than before.

4. Be Specific About What You Want

Many of us think the people in our lives are psychic. We expect them to know exactly what we need even though we state those needs in the vaguest of terms, if at all.

Some women say, "If my (husband/mother/children/friend) really loved me, he or she would know what I want." It's true that people who are close can sometimes finish each other's sentences, but this is not the same as knowing the other person's every need.

This type of thinking is often a by-product of women's connection orientation. Earlier I described women's connection orientation as a core identity that is based on relating to and connecting with others. This is in contrast to men's separation orientation, a disposition toward maintaining independence and separateness from others. As I previously mentioned, this does not mean that men don't care about relationships. They do, but connecting with others is not woven into their identity in the same way it is for women. A woman's connection orientation may affect the way she communicates. For example, the desire for emotional closeness can sometimes extend to a belief that we should be able to read each other's minds.

Look at Peggy. She was upset that Neil didn't talk with her about having his friends at the house. She felt comfortable telling him about her concerns, which is good, but she did it in a way that was not only attacking, but also terribly unclear.

"You're always inviting people over without consulting me. It's as if I don't even live here," she says. "Don't I matter to you?"

So what exactly does Peggy want? Does she want Neil not to invite people over? Or does she just want to know ahead of time that people will be coming? She never says.

Instead, Peggy could have stated her needs in a much clearer way: "I know you like having your friends over, and that's fine with me, honey. But when I don't know about it in advance, it messes up my whole day. Could you please tell me ahead of time when they're coming over so I can make other plans?"

Now Neil knows exactly what to do to make Peggy happy. Given her clear and specific request, he'll be more able to meet her needs than he would be with a vague request.

This is something Sheila could have done with Gail. Instead of her silent simmering about Gail's lateness in picking her up for work, she could have told Gail about her desire to call their carpooling quits. Looking to be clear and nonattacking, Sheila came up with the following words. She could have said, "I think driving to the restaurant together was a great idea, but I don't think it's working. My style is to get to the restaurant early so I can get everything in my station organized. Your style is to come in and just get started. So let's just go back to driving our own cars. But if you ever need a ride, feel free to call me, okay?"

There is more than one way to say things. Given Sheila's need to be liked, these words seemed most comfortable to her. Choose whatever feels right for you as long as you are specific about what you want.

5. Don't Try to Convince Others You Are Right

It's a natural tendency to want to be right. When you feel attacked, either by a person's actions or words, it's normal to want to defend yourself. So when you have a disagreement with someone, your reaction is often to explain all the reasons you are right and the other person is wrong. Whether your tone is sweet or combative, the underlying thinking is the same: "Once Charlie realizes how wrong he really is, he'll change." If only it were that easy.

Tamika was stuck in her need to be right. She held a belief I see among many women: "If only he'd change, things would be perfect." Tamika wanted Gerald to strive for a high-level position in his company, but Gerald was happy where he was. He didn't want the pressure an upper-management position would bring.

To his rational explanations Tamika finally responded, "Are you crazy or just lazy?" Her remark is designed, of course, to help Gerald see that he is really wrong about his choices. Once she lays out her logical arguments for him, Gerald will want that promotion, right? It is unlikely Gerald will ever say, "When I think about it, honey, you're right. I am lazy. I'm going to apply for that position tomorrow." Instead, he'll argue about all the reasons he's right. Now they're stuck in a gridlock. And each time they revisit this topic, they will continue to be stuck. So how do they get unstuck?

When you're in a disagreement, your best bet is to go back to your "I" statements and, if you're with someone you trust, disclose. Forget about being right. Forget about facts. Go to your feelings. Why is it so important to Tamika that Gerald gets promoted? She could reveal those feelings to him. Here is what Tamika told Gerald: "My dad could never keep a steady job. As a result, we were always living hand-to-mouth. That's why I work so hard. When I see you decline an opportunity for advancement, I get scared that we'll have the same life I had when I was little. I know you're nothing like my Dad, but I still get worried."

This disclosure is more likely to lead to a fruitful discussion about this couple's values and dreams than will fights to be right, because they are getting to the real issues that are driving their feelings and actions. This is the place where resolution is possible. Through Gerald's disclosure, Tamika learned that his father was an overachiever who was never home while Gerald was growing up. His reaction to this early experience makes Gerald more interested in family time than career strivings.

Communicating in this way probably won't result in Gerald changing his career plans, but it does mean that the couple can now find ways to take care of each other's needs without either of them having to win.

6. When You're Angry, Calm Yourself Before You Begin Communicating

Peggy was upset that Neil had a habit of inviting people over without asking her. She'd had it and was going to give him a piece of her mind. As she accused and badgered Neil, the harsh words flew fast and furious out of her mouth. Given her level of anger, Peggy would likely have gotten a much better outcome if she calmed herself before talking with Neil.

What about the idea that it's good to yell and get it all out? Isn't that cathartic? Isn't that the way to reduce angry feelings? Research shows that yelling in an attacking way does not diminish anger; instead, it increases it. Studies show that when people rant about the shortcomings of the other person or the unfairness of the situation, they feel angrier. The strategy that proved most effective was when both parties waited until they calmed down and then discussed their concerns with each other or worked them out on their own.

If you want to be an effective communicator, there are good reasons to calm yourself before attempting to talk. As mentioned earlier, when one person's heartbeat is higher than 100 beats per minute during an argument, that person will be unable to hear what the other is saying. This physical reaction will stymie your attempts to communicate effectively and probably frustrate you more.

A strong emotion like anger can interfere with your thinking process. When you're worked up, it's more difficult to solve problems and express yourself clearly. Plus you're more likely to say things that will inflame the situation. Once you've calmed down, though, you'll be better able to discuss the problem rationally.

If you're angry and about to give your mate, children, or family members a piece of your mind, consider looking for ways to calm yourself first. Do the same if you're already in an argument and are getting overwhelmed by your emotions. Calming activities can include taking a walk around the block; doing belly breathing; or even watching television. During these calming activities, try to bring your attention to the activity rather than ruminating on your angry thoughts. Ruminating will only serve to maintain the intensity of your anger.

When it's time to talk, start the conversation gently by focusing on what the person has done to upset you rather than by attacking the person's character. Use "I" statements, talk about your feelings, and be clear about what you want from the other person.

7. Recognize Differences in Gender Communication Styles

Misunderstandings can arise from the differing orientation styles of women and men. Look at the following conversation between a wife and husband. Notice how their respective connection and separation orientations play into the way they talk to each other:

Doreen: *I'm going out, honey.*

Jack: *Okay, I'll see you later.*

Doreen: *Don't you want to know where I'm going?*

Jack: *That's okay. You don't have to tell me everything.*

Doreen: *Don't you care?*

Jack: *Of course I care. Where are you going?*

Doreen: *Forget it.*

In this conversation, when Doreen tells Jack she's going out, she is inviting him to ask her more questions about her activities for the day. To her, this conversation is a way to connect with him, not just to impart information. Jack, on the other hand, is content to give Doreen something he values: independence. Doreen interprets this as uncaring. Their conversation leaves Doreen feeling alone, and Jack feeling confused about why Doreen is so upset.

To lessen misunderstandings between the sexes, there are several strategies you can try. First, realize that the way people communicate may be influenced more by their sex than by how they feel about the circumstances at hand.

If your differing communication styles are causing you distress, you may need to educate the other person about your style. This would have helped Virginia, whose husband, Kevin, saw her as a nag when she repeated a request to take out the trash several times. Virginia could have accepted that Kevin would do it when he felt like it and just let it go. Or she could have educated him on the meaning behind her words: "When I ask you to take out the trash and you don't do it, I feel like you don't care about me. I know it's just trash to you, but to me it's a sign that you're doing your share in taking care of our house, and that makes me feel loved. I know that might sound silly to you, but that's how I feel. I'm really not trying to be a drill sergeant. I just want to know we're a team."

Now Kevin understands the meaning that sharing the house-work holds for Virginia and why she repeats her request when he doesn't do it. Given his separation orientation, he might say, "Okay, I'll do it as soon as I finish putting these boxes in the garage." Now he's not feeling bossed, and Virginia is feeling loved.

Another difference in communication styles between connection and separation orientations is the way the sexes listen to another person talk about a problem. When a man listens to someone's problem, he immediately tries to figure it out and come up with a solution. A woman, on the other hand, is more likely to empathize with the other person's feelings. This doesn't mean she doesn't look for solutions as well, but that usually comes after the feeling talk.

Mary, one of my clients, described this scenario perfectly when she told me about a conversation she had with her husband. She told him about a problem she was having with a colleague in her office. Before she could finish her story, her husband said, "If I were you, I'd set her straight. Don't let her push you around like that."

"But I don't want her to dislike me. I have to work with her," Mary said.

"Don't worry about what she thinks of you. What matters is what you think of you, right?" he said.

After the conversation, Mary felt disconnected from her husband, not because he doesn't care about her, but because his communication style is based on a different orientation. She just needed him to listen to her feelings. He needed to fix her problem.

I can relate to this. My husband has a male-oriented, "fix-it" approach to communication, while I have a more female-oriented, "feelings" approach. Knowing this, I once prefaced a conversation to him with this request: "I want to talk to you about something. All I want you to do is listen. You don't have to give me advice or do anything to make it better; just listen to me."

I then proceeded to describe a difficult situation I was having. He carefully listened, nodding here and there to signify that he was paying attention. At the end of our conversation, I felt much better, because I felt connected. And he was happy too—although a bit confused over exactly what he had done to help me.

Communication Tools

Quick Guide

- Begin difficult conversations without criticism.
- Use "I" statements.
- Disclose your feelings to people you trust.
- Be specific about what you want.
- Don't try to convince others you are right.
- When you're angry, calm yourself before you begin communicating, or take a break from a heated discussion if you're feeling overwhelmed.
- Recognize differences in gender communication styles.

12

Putting It on Paper

Tool 4: Emotional Writing

Worrying about the job, the laundry,
the funny knock in the car,
the weird look in your lover's eye—
this stuff eddies through our
subconscious and muddies our days. Get it on the page.

—Julia Cameron, writer

Grace was struggling with the complex emotions she felt after a difficult breakup with Elliott. Although things had seemed a bit tense between them, she was caught completely off guard when Elliott told her he wanted to date other women.

"I was stunned and hurt," she told me. "I didn't know whether to cry or yell. As the days went on, I couldn't stop thinking about him and our relationship. Over and over, I asked myself, 'What went wrong? Was it my fault? Did he ever really love me?'"

Tormented by her emotions, Grace knew she needed to find a way to make sense of them. She decided to write about her experience. In an old spiral notebook she normally used for grocery lists, she wrote about how sad and abandoned she felt. She tried to process what had happened and figure out what to do. Here is what she told me a few days later: "After writing, I felt like a heavy weight had been lifted off my shoulders. In a sense I felt free—free from my own burdening feelings. I knew the feelings had not gone away—I still felt hurt and abandoned—but just getting my emotions out, even if no one else heard them, made me feel liberated. What made the difference was staring my feelings in the face and seeing them stare back at me. Since I wrote about this experience, I have not had a single dream about Elliott. I still think about the situation, but I feel at peace with it now."

That Grace's writing helped shift her emotions did not surprise me. Many women have told me how much emotional writing has helped them cope with their distress. I wondered why. How could the simple act of writing about your thoughts and feelings cause them to change? My research to answer this question and my conversations with numerous women who use it as a coping tool convinced me that emotional writing is an important part of the Emotional Toolkit.

The Healing Power of the Pen

In 1983, James Pennebaker, a pioneer in the field of emotional writing, recruited forty-three college students to participate in a groundbreaking study assessing the impact of writing on physical and emotional health. He divided the participants into two groups and asked them to write for just fifteen minutes a day for four straight days while sitting alone in a room. All participants were assured of complete anonymity.

One group was asked to write about what their shoes or bedrooms looked like. The other group was given the following instructions: "For the next four days, I would like you to write about the most upsetting or traumatic experience of your life. In your writing, I'd like you to really let go and explore your very deepest emotions and thoughts. Write about what happened, how you felt about it, and how you feel about it now."

The participants opened up and wrote about intimate and terrible experiences. One young woman recalled that when she was a little girl, her mother asked her to pick up her toys, because her grandmother was coming to visit. She didn't do as her mother had asked. That evening, as her grandmother walked into the house, she slipped on one of the girl's toys and broke her hip. A week later, her grandmother died during hip surgery. Years later, this woman was still tortured by her guilt.

The intensity of the feelings recounted by many of the participants led Pennebaker and his staff to fear that delving into these difficult emotions would only make people feel worse. They were wrong. Although some students reported feeling worse after their emotional writing, those feelings usually went away within a few hours. Emotionally, they felt better. Up to four months later, those who wrote about their deepest feelings were less depressed, less anxious, and more positive about life than the other group. They even had better grades.

Pennebaker's study has been replicated with all types of people, including women who have recently given birth, crime victims, medical students, chronic pain sufferers, and nursing-home residents. All have shown the same impressive results. It appears that emotional writing is an equal-opportunity coping tool. However, there is a specific style your writing needs to take to get the greatest benefit, which I'll explain as we go on.

Audrey's Writing

Although Audrey often relies on her family and close friends for support, she doesn't share everything with others. "There are times when I don't want to tell everyone what's happening in my life," she said. One time Audrey was facing several challenges. She tried to figure things out in her head, but the more she pondered, the more her mind became cluttered with an endless loop of negative thoughts. Looking for a way to free her mind from its constant chatter, Audrey returned to something she had done as a young girl—writing: "I have so much going on in my life right now—so much on my mind. My daughter is having trouble in school, my widowed father is ill, and my husband's company may be relocating to another state. My release is writing. When I write, it's a chance to get everything that's swirling in my head out of my mind and onto paper. It's like taking out the trash. All the thoughts and feelings get put in the can and the garbage is taken away. Afterward, I feel relieved and calmer. I'm able to focus on my day."

Why Does Writing Make You Feel Better?

Writing and Your Body

As you write, subtle changes occur in your body—changes that can shift your emotions. When you hold your upsetting feelings in and allow them to exist only as unpleasant recurring thoughts in your head, it's hard work for your body. Keeping your emotions bottled up is associated with the activation of your sympathetic nervous system. If you recall, when the switch to this system is turned on, your internal organs work overtime and your body is in a state of tension.

The deceptively simple act of releasing your deepest thoughts and feelings onto paper can flip off this switch. Studies have shown that after people used emotional writing to confront distressing experiences, they had lower blood pressure and less moisture on their hands, signs that their sympathetic nervous systems were now turned off. This shift to a calmer physical state leads to a calmer emotional state. As your body releases the tension associated with holding in your feelings, your emotions soften, and you feel lighter and less troubled.

The Dilemma of Caring for Others

Natalie's need to take care of other people's feelings often resulted in her bottling up the "bad feelings" she sometimes felt toward them. This holding-in contributed to her overthinking—she just couldn't stop rehashing her distressing thoughts.

Earlier I explained how women, on account of their early mother-daughter bond and cultural messages, often develop an identity based on connection with others; this is why women are more likely than men to care about how their words and actions affect other people. Emotional writing was a way for Natalie to express herself when she was consumed by upsetting emotions. After writing, she could then decide whether to talk with the other person or just let it go: "Sometimes when I say my true feelings to people I love, they feel bad; then I feel bad. When I write, I don't have to worry about being nice or using the right words. I write things I'd never really say, because they would hurt people's feelings. Once I write things down, I usually feel better and less intense, as if I took my emotions down a notch."

Emotional writing helped Ronnie in this way too: "When people ask how I'm dealing with my loss, I just say fine. If I told them how I was really feeling about everything, I know they'd feel bad. Then I'd feel the need to take care of their feelings, and I'd be worrying about them, and if they're okay. When I write, I can write about my feelings without having to take care of anybody but me."

Ramona's Anger Repository

Unlike Natalie and Ronnie, Ramona said too much about her distressing feelings, impulsively expressing whatever popped into her head without thinking much about its effect on the other person. Her concern for her relationship with her husband led her to emotional writing.

In assessing Ramona's temperament style, I found that she doesn't enjoy change and is emotionally intense. The strength of her temperament is that she is a passionate and loving woman. She's also the person everyone depends on in a crisis because of her stability.

Ramona married Manny, a person who is highly sensitive and likes to do things spontaneously—for example, changing his mind at the last minute about long-held plans. This drives Ramona—with her need for predictability—crazy. Given her emotional intensity, she reacts by blowing up. Given his sensitivity, Manny withdraws in silence.

Their differing temperament styles have led to numerous fights. Frightened that their constant arguments were jeopardizing their marriage, Ramona decided to try emotional writing. She went into her bedroom whenever she felt the urge to yell and instead "yelled" at her journal. By writing, she was able to release her intense emotions into what she called her "anger repository." This helped her calm down so that she could summarize her feelings and present them to Manny in a more concise and respectful way. She says the changes in their relationship have been dramatic: "I know I'm quick to anger. That's just the way I am. When Manny does things like decide on a whim that he's going to build a patio, it makes me nuts. I like to know what I'm doing each day, and his carefree nature throws all my plans out the window. Emotional writing has been a blessing. When I feel the need to scream at him, I go into the bedroom and grab my journal. Sometimes I write in big block letters almost like I'm screaming at the page. Then I feel calmer. After I read what I've written a few times, I realize what I need to say to him and how to say it without attacking him. I think it's saved our marriage. Manny said, 'I don't know what you write in that little notebook, but keep doing it.' "

The Biology of Making Sense

Being able to translate raw or unprocessed feelings into language can help people make sense of them, and making sense can be the powerful key to shifting your feelings. Eighty percent of those who wrote about their deepest feelings in emotional-writing studies said they had more insight and understanding of their problems after writing about them.

One explanation for this new perspective might have to do with the way the brain works. Some emotional information is processed in the right frontal lobe of the brain, while some linguistic information is processed in the left frontal lobe. When people translate their feelings into words through writing, it appears to integrate these separate areas of the brain, perhaps helping people make sense of their experiences more effectively.

This integration after emotional writing was evident in the women I talked with. Jill said, "When I write, everything becomes clearer." Kim told me, "After I write, I look at it, and it makes sense." "I can't explain it," said Elba, "but writing just helps me realize things."

The Mind of Emotional Writing

Although using your journal as a place to vent all your distressing feelings can be helpful, it's the combination of expressing and then questioning your thoughts and feelings that can bring about the most powerful change in your emotions. Just as ruminating thoughts can keep your distressing feelings going, so can ruminative writing. When people write exclusively about their unhappy feelings or their terrible circumstances, they tend to stay stuck in those emotions. The key word here is *exclusively*. Expressing upsetting feelings can be helpful, but to gain therapeutic benefit, you need to examine those feelings and explore ways to resolve them.

Psychologists Linda Cameron of the University of Auckland and Greg Nicholls of St. Joseph's University found that individuals who wrote solely about the negative aspects of their situations continued to feel sad, anxious, or angry. When they were guided to include probing questions and alternate ways of looking at their problems in their emotional writing, they felt better.

Once you've written about your distressing feelings, it's important to examine what those feelings mean. What is underneath your emotions? Instead of ranting about how horrible your sister is, ask yourself why she bothers you so much. What specific things can you do to feel better? Writing in this way can help shift your perspective and reduce your sadness, anxiety, and anger.

This type of written self-examination is key. Moira found that exploring a variety of questions about herself and her situation helped her resolve her dilemmas: "When I write, I ask myself a lot of questions: Why do I feel this way? What do I really want? I start answering my own questions. It's like my therapy. My answers help me understand my personal philosophy. It's also evidence that I have to face. I can't just dismiss what I've written the way I can dismiss my thoughts."

The Importance of Processing Your Feelings

When Vera was fifty-two, she was diagnosed with uterine cancer. She was frightened, because her own mother died of cancer when Vera was just a girl. She had no one to talk with who had survived the disease. Feeling overwhelmed, she turned to writing: "I knew I had to fight it. My goal was to survive. But to do that, I had to change my mindset. I hated the doctors, the nurses, the chemo, and the radiation. I had to find a way to calm myself and concentrate on what I needed to do to get through this, so I picked up a book and started writing."

Writing in this way allowed Vera to take an overwhelming ex-

perience and somehow contain it on a piece of paper. Writing allowed her to feel some control over it. On a yellow legal pad, she
wrote about her feelings and her plan to manage her experience:
"Writing gave me a chance to express myself in a way I couldn't
with anyone else. I explored my whole thought process. This
opened me to the possibility of seeing myself in a better place. The
first day I started journaling, I set my goals. They seemed so far-
fetched when I wrote them, but something in me knew I could do
them, even if I didn't feel that way at the moment."

When she's upset, Vera uses probing questions and alternate
ways of looking at her situation to help her make sense of it all: "I
start out with how I'm feeling, why I'm feeling this way, how it affects me and others, what I can do to change the situation, and
what would happen if I did this or that. I'm cancer-free now, and I
work with women who are coping with the disease. When we talk,
I tell them about writing. I say, 'Write whatever you're feeling, set
goals for yourself, write about it.' "

The Unemployed Engineer

Few tales about the value of emotional writing are more compelling than the story of the unemployed engineers. With hard
times looming, a Dallas computer company laid off a large number
of engineers. Most of them were men in their fifties who had
worked at the company for thirty years. With no warning, each
man was called into his supervisor's office, told of his immediate
layoff, escorted by a security guard to clean out his desk, and shown
the door.

Five months later, not one of these highly experienced engineers
had a job, although they were actively searching and going on job
interviews. Psychologist Stefanie Spera and her colleagues wondered if emotional writing might help these unemployed workers.

Spera and her team recruited volunteers from the group of unemployed men. One group went about their job search as usual without writing at all. Another group wrote twenty minutes a day for five consecutive days about their deepest thoughts and feelings related to the layoff and how it affected them personally and professionally. Many of their essays described not only the humiliation and bitterness they felt about the way they had been treated, but also the ripple effect this event had on their home lives.

The results of the experiment were astonishing. Eight months after the writing exercise, 53 percent of the writing group had found full-time employment compared to 14 percent of the non-writing group, even though both groups had gone on the same number of job interviews. How can this be explained?

Before the writing exercise, both groups were filled with anger and resentment, ruminating obsessively over what had happened. These emotions probably affected the way they came across on job interviews and their attitude toward prospective employers.

Putting their distressing feelings into words helped the engineers in the writing group come to terms with what happened. They were able to make sense of their feelings, and they could move on and present their best self to potential employers.

What About the Future?

What if your distress isn't about something that's happening right now, like a job loss or illness, but rather something you expect to happen in the future? Maybe you're anticipating surgery or a first baby or having a difficult conversation. Emotional writing can help in these situations as well.

Rebecca was scheduled to take her medical-school entrance exams. Her score on this competitive and difficult test would determine whether she could fulfill her lifelong dream of becoming a doctor. Given the importance of the exam, it's no surprise that Rebecca was plagued by negative thoughts: "Am I really smart enough to do this? What if I get a low score, and I can't get into medical school?" Slowly, she began to doubt herself, feeling sad and hopeless.

Ten days before the test, Brooklyn College psychology professor Stephen Lepore asked half the students poised to take the exam to write their deepest thoughts and feelings about it. He asked the other group simply to write about the things they had done in the last day.

He found that those who wrote about their feelings were less depressed in the days prior to the exam than were those who wrote about mundane things. Those who wrote about feelings had not stopped worrying, but their worries no longer affected them in the same way. Their writing helped them make sense of their emotions and put their worrisome thoughts into perspective.

Faye's Big Decision

All her life, Faye lived in Miami. She enjoyed the comfort and familiarity of her hometown. She still socialized with her friends from elementary school and shopped at the same supermarket her mother went to when Faye was a little girl.

After her divorce, however, Faye felt the need to pick up stakes and create a new life. For some reason she felt drawn to Vermont: "Maybe it's because things don't seem so harried there, or maybe it's the chance to see the seasons change in a way we don't in Miami," she said. Whatever the attraction, Faye wanted to go.

She sent out resumes and landed a job teaching high-school biology. But Faye soon realized that taking care of the details of packing were easy compared to managing her fear of the unknown. So Faye used emotional writing to help her cope with her anxiety about the move: "I had a lot of fear about leaving my home, even though it was something I really wanted to do. I wrote in my journal a ton. I wrote almost the same exact thing every day:

'What if I've made a mistake? What if I don't like the job? What if I get lonely?' I just let myself vent all my fears. And then I would address them one by one. How realistic were my fears? What was the worst that could happen? I decided I needed to make my future feel as familiar as possible, so I wrote about what my new apartment would look like; how I would decorate it; what my classroom would be like. This gave me a feeling that the unknown was known. It helped me tremendously."

Writing and Your Unconscious

Many women have told me that emotional writing takes them to a deeper understanding of themselves and their needs, or of how to approach difficult situations. Sometimes when you write about your deepest feelings and thoughts, you find yourself writing about things you didn't even know you knew.

Writing can open up hidden parts of yourself to reveal your deeper thoughts, emotions, and needs. Sigmund Freud called these deep places that are outside of your awareness "the unconscious." Carl Jung described the unconscious as "everything of which I know, but of which I am not at the moment thinking . . . everything perceived by my senses, but not noted by my conscious mind."

Gwyn recalls how journal writing helped her tap into this deeper part of herself. The process helped her end a relationship with which she was struggling. Gwyn wrote, "I shouldn't have been with Louis, and I knew it. The relationship wasn't good for me. I had to end it, but I didn't think I was strong enough to break it off. I wrote about it over and over in my journal. Then as I was writing one day, something different happened. It was as if an angel were writing through me. I wrote, 'He serves no purpose in my life.' I put my pen down and read what I had just written. In that instant, something shifted in me. I was able to end the relationship."

Sally experienced a revelation in her writing similar to Gwyn's. A stay-at-home mom with three young children and a household to run, she found herself emotionally overloaded. Sally was often short with her family and frequently cried for what she described as "no good reason." She couldn't make sense of her feelings until she reached a deeper place through her writing: "I found myself just writing pages and pages of feelings and thoughts. They just flowed out of me. I was sad and angry, and I couldn't make sense of it. Then I had an epiphany. I wrote the sentence, 'I feel like I'm in this all alone.' That was the key that unlocked everything. I didn't know that's what I was feeling, but it was exactly right. I shared this feeling with my husband. He was upset to know I felt so lonely and was eager to make things better between us. From there, we were able to work out more balance in our day-to-day life so I didn't feel like the person in charge of everything."

In a study conducted by Carolyn Schwartz, professor of medicine at University of Massachusetts Medical School, and Elizabeth David terminally ill women met for six sessions to write about a variety of issues related to their lives and their illness. The women were often surprised by what they wrote about: "Some participants expressed . . . having encountered an 'inner guide' or 'a little person on my shoulder' who prompted them in ways they would not have expected."

Accessing this deeper knowledge—whether viewed as your unconscious, an epiphany, or an inner guide—can provide people with clarity during difficult times. To increase the likelihood of accessing your deeper knowledge, try the belly breathing or meditation exercises you learned from Tool 2 before you begin writing. Being in a state of relaxation helps to clear your mind and allows you to become more receptive to your unconscious thoughts. This is what Isabelle does: "When I meditate before I write, it helps me get at something in my unconscious mind. I find I can pull things out that I normally wouldn't be able to. Sometimes I don't get immediate insights as I'm writing, but then a day or two later I get clarity about what I need to do. It's as if my writing causes something to percolate, and the answer I need comes to me."

How to Write to Reduce Your Anxiety, Sadness, and Anger

Stick with it. Write for fifteen to twenty minutes for three or four consecutive days about whatever is upsetting you. If you run out of things to say, just write the same things over again.

Write for yourself. As one woman told me, "Once I realized I didn't have to write as if my journal was a listening person, I was able to be more open about my feelings and thoughts." The beauty of your journal, as I often heard women say, is, "My journal doesn't judge me." Allow yourself to open up to your deepest feelings and thoughts to get the most benefit for your emotional writing. To help with this, don't show your writing to others.

Don't worry about grammar, spelling, or penmanship.

Use your emotional writing to express and explore your feelings. If you simply use it as a place for uncensored complaining, you'll feel worse. Here are some questions you can consider:

- How do I feel?
- Why does this upset me so much?
- What's the worst that could happen in this situation?
- How can I handle that?
- What would I like to see happen?
- What things can I do to deal with this challenge? Be specific.
    Vague: "Be more honest about my needs."
    Specific: "Tell Chris I can't join her committee."
- What have I learned from this experience?

Experiment to see what works for you. Although these guidelines are based on research, everyone is different. Do whatever makes you feel better.

Don't use emotional writing as a substitute for action, emotional support, or clinical care.

Using Emotional Writing to Become Happier

You don't have to write about upsetting or traumatic events to benefit from emotional writing. Just as writing about distressing emotions can help reduce them, writing about positive or hopeful thoughts and feelings can increase them.

When Laura King, associate professor of psychology at the University of Missouri, asked people to write for four consecutive days about their hopeful visions for the future, they became happier and more optimistic than did a group who wrote about their plans for the day. Why is this?

First, writing, as opposed to just thinking about your life, forces you to become focused on your desires, values, and priorities. In this sense, a personal philosophy emerges that creates a blueprint for forward movement. This movement may include creating a better relationship with your family, making more time for fun, or looking for opportunities to share your wisdom with others. Being able to see your path clearly makes it more likely you'll walk down it, and that feels good.

The Habit of Pleasure

There's another reason why writing about positive things makes you feel better. Your feelings are influenced by what you focus on. We have so many things calling for our attention in life: family, work, daily chores, and much more. It's difficult to attend to them all at once, so we choose one or two to the exclusion of others.

Often we choose the most worrisome of the bunch, causing the good things in life to go unnoticed. This is called *selective abstraction* (see page 120).

It takes practice for most of us to consistently pay attention to the positive aspects of our lives. The people who wrote about hopeful things in Laura King's study became more positive because they put their attention on hope. Their writing led them to optimism.

The Gratitude Journal

Purposeful focus on the positive is the theory behind the popular use of gratitude journals. A *gratitude journal* is a list of, or essay about, all the things for which a person is thankful. In writing a gratitude journal, you use selective abstraction to your advantage, purposefully noticing the good instead of the bad. Paige has used this strategy for years: "I find it easy to get pulled away by all the 'have-tos' in my life. I have to get the car fixed, take my son to the doctor, and clean the house. I start feeling depressed by it all. This is often the time I write in my gratitude journal. It helps me shift my thinking so I'm thankful that I have a car and a son and a house."

When you choose to find something for which to be grateful, you often feel more grateful. This practice is a habit that needs to be cultivated. Doing so can create dynamic changes in your mind and body.

People who are able to sincerely search for a benefit in difficult situations tend to be happier, more satisfied with their lives, and more hopeful than are people who dwell on the negative. They are also less depressed, anxious, and envious.

Experiencing gratitude is even good for your body. Research shows that when people feel sincere appreciation for what they have in their lives, their heart rate becomes even and smooth, which leads to a more efficient nervous system.

The Scientist and the *Saturday Evening Post*

To illustrate how your selective attention can change your mood and your body, let me tell you an amazing story. In the late 1970s, social psychologist Ellen Langer of Harvard University enlisted a group of healthy men aged seventy-five to eighty years old for a remarkable experiment. Her goal was simple—although some might call it crazy. Langer's goal was to try to create in these men the same mindsets they had when they were fifty-five. She would also attempt to turn back the clock on their physical aging process.

To do this, she sequestered the men in a country retreat for five days, where they lived as if it were 1959. In her instructions Langer said, "We are not asking you to 'act as if it is 1959,' but to let yourself be just who you were in 1959." The men lived and spoke as if 1959 were the present. In each man's bedroom were copies of the *Saturday Evening Post* and *Life* from the same week in 1959. They listened to music on an old radio, watched television shows, discussed politics and sports, and heard a speech from President Eisenhower—all were from 1959.

After only five days, the changes were dramatic. The men's vision and hearing had improved, their memories were sharper, their hand strength and dexterity increased, their joints were more flexible, their scores on intelligence tests were higher, they acted more independently, and as evidenced by before-and-after photographs, their faces looked an average of three years younger.

Nothing was different about these men compared to the previous week except where they placed their attention. By focusing on a mindset that was twenty years younger, they became mentally and physically younger.

This explains how a gratitude journal can help increase your happiness. You train yourself to change where you put your attention, focusing on what you have instead of what you don't have. Note, however, that this strategy should not be a substitute for therapeutic care if you are dealing with clinical depression or clinical anxiety.

Forced Positive Thinking

As you know by now, I'm not a big fan of syrupy positive thinking. But, when the positive thoughts you write are generated by you and have specific meaning for you, they can be powerful agents for changing feelings.

Let's say your house burns down, and you write, "I'm grateful my family and I are alive and well." If this is a spontaneous and genuine statement, stay focused on it. Write about it. If you're writing it because you're trying to force yourself to feel appreciative, it's probably not going to happen. First, you need to grieve or rant or be sad in your writing before you can reframe your situation to find positive things from your upsetting experience.

Let me give you an example. When I was in a counselor-training program during college, my teacher told us the story of her friend Joyce. After learning she had breast cancer, Joyce underwent a single mastectomy. Her close friends came to visit during her recovery period. Many of them tried to help Joyce focus on the positive, saying things like, "You should be grateful you're alive" and "At least it was only one breast; it could've been two." These words did little to lift Joyce's spirits. When my teacher went to visit her, she said, "This is a terrible thing that's happened to you, and I'm very sorry." Joyce's face softened.

Once Joyce acknowledged and wrote about her painful feelings, she was able to answer the question, "How can I face this crisis in a way that will make me stronger?" In other words, she needed to express her sadness before she could write about the positive. This need is not the same for everyone. Some people are genetically prone to optimism and may jump right into looking for the bright side, but most people need to experience their upset feelings before they can find positive meaning in a difficult experience.

How to Write to Increase Your Happiness

Here are two ways your emotional writing can create more happiness in your life; the most compelling of them is gratitude writing.

- **Gratitude writing:** Write about things in your life—no matter how small they are—for which you are thankful. They could include a body that moves, healthy grandchildren, sunlight through your kitchen window, a friend to talk with, a delicious chicken recipe, or a chance to make changes in your life. Do this on a consistent basis.

  I keep a gratitude list in the front of my date book, so I can read it every day. The more you write about or read your list, the more you can create a habit of selecting to notice the positive things in your life. On average it takes twenty-one days of consistent behavior change to create a new habit, so stay with this daily for three weeks and see how it affects you.

- **Visualization writing:** Visualize something you would like in your life. Don't write about it in negative terms ("I don't want a new job with a long commute"). Instead write about it in positive terms ("I want a new job with a short commute"). Write in as much detail as you can, noting the colors, sounds, and sights you find in your visualization.

A Final Note on Privacy

Keeping your journals private is important. Knowing that others won't see your writing will help you reach the level of freedom you need to write honestly. Some women told me they have a lock on their notebooks. Others said they feel safe that no one will read what they have written. And some women live alone and don't give privacy a second thought.

Although many women like to keep what they've written, you will get the same emotional benefit from your writing whether you keep it or throw it away. So if getting rid of it will make you feel more secure, feel free to discard it.

Some women like to do their emotional writing in longhand, and others prefer the privacy of writing on a computer. One of my students, Tracy Baughman, uses a confidential system for her computer journals. This is how she does it:

HOW TO CREATE A PRIVATE COMPUTER JOURNAL

1. Go to Microsoft Word and create a new document.

2. Click Save As and pick a name for your document.

3. Now go to Options. At the bottom of the Options menu it reads Password to open. Fill in a password. You may have to enter it twice. Then save your document.

4. From this point on, the only way you can get into your journal is by typing in your password. Make sure you know what case you typed it in since it may be case sensitive.

5. You now have a private journal on your computer that can be accessed only by you.

13

Your Body of Emotions

Tool 5: Physical Movement

Dance, even if you have nowhere to do it but your living room.

—Kurt Vonnegut, writer

Adrienne remembers the humiliation she felt in gym class. Always the last to be picked for a team, always the first to drop the ball. This image seared in her mind the connection that physical activity and joy were mutually exclusive. That's why, as her weight ballooned in her mid-forties, she dreaded the exercise she knew she needed to do.

She started slowly: "I'm just going to walk to this tree, then to this driveway," Adrienne told herself. "I kept at it, and eventually my walks got longer," she said. "It was hard in the beginning. It took persistence to stick with it, but somewhere along the line, I got hooked."

The hook, according to Adrienne, was the unexpected emotional benefit she got from walking. "After a brisk walk, I felt happier than before. My thoughts were more positive. My mood was improved," she said. "I can't explain it, but I just felt better when I moved my body."

Moving the Body Moves the Mind

To understand how physical movement changed Adrienne's moods, recall what was said in Chapter 2: a feeling is a full-body experience. Since an emotion involves your body as well as your mind, it makes sense that moving your body can change your feelings.

Feelings are created, in part, by specific body states. When you're sad, you're likely to have low energy or heaviness in your chest. Anxiety usually comes with tense muscles or a rapid heart rate. Although you may not be conscious of the physical components of your feelings, any physical movement that can directly change your body states can help shift your moods.

Physical activity does not just mean going to a gym or taking an aerobics class. It includes things you might not ordinarily consider exercise, like walking in the mall, dancing in your living room, or climbing stairs. In order to get an emotional payoff from physical activity, your movement needs to include certain features. These will be described in the following pages.

When done in a specific way, any physical activity can become part of an emotional exercise program. First, let me explain how changes in your body can help you reduce feelings of sadness, anxiety, and anger.

Swimming in Chemicals

Sharon admits she's not a great swimmer, yet she's been swimming several times a week for more than twenty years. "Originally I started out just for fitness," she says. "I wanted to be healthy. Then I realized how much it helped me emotionally. I love how I feel afterward. It elevates my mood. I'm more even-keeled, less prone to sadness."

There's no doubt that Sharon gets a sense of peace from a stolen hour just for herself. But scientists hypothesize that something else may be happening to account for her lifted spirits. Chemical changes are taking place in Sharon's body. Her swimming activates a release of powerful chemical messengers from her brain called *neurotransmitters*. Two neurotransmitters activated by physical movement—serotonin and norepinephrine—are in part responsible for the quality of her moods. People with low amounts of these chemicals are more likely to be depressed. Sharon's exercise helps elevate the levels of these neurotransmitters. The quantity of norepinephrine released as she swims can increase as much as two to six times her normal level. In this way, physical movement is creating an effect in her brain similar to that of antidepressant drugs like Prozac.

Sadness and Exercise

When you are sad, you're apt to feel as if everything in your body is running in slow motion. You may be tired or lethargic. Though this is probably the precise time you don't feel like moving, it might actually be the best time to move. This was the case for Dana. She had just returned home from leaving her youngest daughter at college for her freshman year. Dana was sad. For her, exercise was the emotional tool she knew would help.

"I was miserable when I said good-bye to Corey, although I tried not to let it show," said Dana. "When I returned home, I had no energy. I knew if I didn't move, I'd just sit and watch TV all day, and that would take me down a path that would make me feel worse. I had to force myself to move. I exercised because I knew I'd feel better if I did. I didn't need to go to a gym. I just needed to move my body."

Dana played some upbeat music and started to dance in her living room. She danced for only ten minutes, but that was enough to boost her energy level and help pull her out of the dumps. For most people, the mood boost gained from movement will last from twelve to twenty-six hours. For others, it may last even longer.

Moving and Mood

To test the impact physical exercise has on depression, James Blumenthal, professor of medical psychology at Duke University, and his colleagues asked a group of depressed women and men aged fifty-five to seventy to exercise. Their movement consisted of a ten-minute warm-up followed by thirty minutes of walking or jogging, and ending with a five-minute cooldown. After four months of exercise, the group was compared with a similar group who took antidepressants. Although those who took antidepressants noticed a quicker decrease in their depressive symptoms, at the end of the program the exercise group showed the same emotional benefits as did the group using medication.

I'm not suggesting that people should stop taking antidepressant medication and start walking or jogging instead. Rather, I'm illustrating the powerful effect physical movement can have on your mood. Studies have shown that this mood-boosting effect works for normal feelings of sadness and low energy as well as for clinical depression.

Anxiety and Exercise

For Roberta, who describes herself as "someone who constantly lives in my head," physical movement is the antidote for anxiety. Being able to move her body helps take her away from her thoughts. "I think too much," she says. "Then I get lots of nervous energy. Exercise gets that out, and it feels good. It makes me feel more positive."

For most people, anxiety creates a body state in which everything just seems to go faster (heartbeat, breathing) or feel tighter (muscles, jaw). Physical movement can help reverse those states, leading to feelings of calmness and relaxation.

Andrew Steptoe, professor of psychology at University College London, and his colleagues enlisted volunteers between the ages of

Figure 1. The Effects of Walking on Tension Anxiety

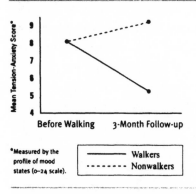

Dr. Steptoe asked people who felt tense to walk for twenty minutes plus perform ten minutes of warm-up and cooldown. They did this four times a week for ten weeks. When compared to a group who felt equal tension but did no exercise, there was a significant difference in their anxiety scores.

twenty and sixty to figure out what effect exercise might have on anxiety. The participants all said they had high levels of anxiety and tension. For two and a half months, the group walked briskly for twenty minutes four times per week. Each walking session included a five-minute warm-up and cooldown. At the end of the program, the walking group had less anxiety and tension than a similar group who didn't exercise at all. They also felt better able to cope with the stress of their lives than the nonwalkers did. (See Figure 1.)

According to Keith Johnsgard, professor emeritus from San Jose State University, mild to moderate exercise produces a relaxation response with an effect on muscle tension "more powerful than those of a minor tranquilizer." This anxiety-tranquilizing effect generally lasts for two to four hours, but as all bodies are different, this may vary for you.

Anxiety and Movement

It seems counterintuitive to think that speeding up your body, as in brisk walking, can actually calm and relax you. If you recall, when you're anxious, the switch to your sympathetic nervous system gets turned on. When this fight-or-flight response kicks in, your body spits out chemicals to help you fight a vicious lion or run like crazy to get away from it. Since your anxiety is more likely to be caused by your worries than by a wild animal, you don't need the extra reserves of energy your body is offering. As this heightened state of muscle tension continues, so do your feelings of anxiety.

One way to release your tension is to do exactly what nature intended you to do: fight or flee. Moving your body briskly with walking, running, or dancing—the same motions you'd use if you were to fight or flee that animal—will reduce the chemicals produced during your body's anxiety reaction. This will help turn off the switch to your sympathetic nervous system more quickly than if you sat around worrying.

This is the effect Brenda, a busy entrepreneur, has noticed. "I find myself obsessing over things like fears about my future in a way that I don't when I'm exercising regularly. When I don't exercise for a week or two, I notice I start to eat more. My anxiety levels get raised. That doesn't happen when I exercise. Those anxiety-provoking thoughts don't even enter my mind."

Easy Does It

You don't have to run to reduce your anxiety. For many people, the slow, deliberate movements of yoga or tai chi help the most. The stretching and bending of these physical activities can release the stored-up muscle tension that contributes to anxiety.

Alicia finds yoga particularly helpful when she's tense or overwhelmed: "Yoga is a relaxing thing. It makes me feel more peaceful. It calms me down. Even five minutes of it releases my tension. It's incredible how much it does that. My favorite series is the sun salutation, or any pose that stretches my back since that's where I hold my tension."

In addition to stretching the tension out of tight muscles, practices like yoga and tai chi can also lower levels of cortisol, a hor-

mone released by your body in response to stress. Cortisol sets in
motion a series of biological changes that prepare your body for
danger. When present for prolonged periods of time, high levels of
cortisol can contribute to ongoing anxiety and depression.

Putai Jin of La Trobe University in Australia explored the impact of tai chi, an ancient Chinese system of slow, coordinated
body movements, on the emotional health of those who practice it.
After practicing tai chi, the participants had a significant drop in
cortisol. They also reported feeling less tension, anxiety, depression,
anger, and fatigue, and having more energy than they had before.

Anger and Exercise

Many women use fast-moving exercise as a way to manage their
anger, and it makes sense. Since you have the same tension and
speed in your body when you're angry as you do when you're anxious, the same brisk movements that can help you with anxiety can
also help reduce anger.

Monica finds the vigorous movements of running are most helpful. "When I'm angry, I run," she said. "The madder I am, the faster
I run. It's almost like a mass exodus of aggressive feeling through
my feet. When I'm done, I feel calmer and better able to think."

One couple found that physical exercise helps when they quar-
rel. "When Charlie and I are not seeing eye-to-eye on something,
we have a hard time talking about it. Either we don't talk, or we say
the wrong things. When this happens, our strategy is to go for a
swim together. Afterward we're able to talk much better. I'm not
sure why, but it seems to work for us."

Slowing Down to Reduce Anger

Not everyone needs to engage in vigorous activity to release the
physical intensity of their anger. Professors Bonnie Berger of Bowl-

ing Green State University and David Owen of Brooklyn College found that people who practiced yoga for an hour a week for three and a half months showed the same decreases in tension and anger as did those who swam for the same amount of time.

The key is to find what works for your body. That's what Marisol discovered when she decided to take a ballet class: "The emotional change I feel after dancing is amazing. It's as if I take all my emotions, put them into motion, and watch them dance away."

The Three Basics of Emotional Exercise

In order to get an emotional boost from physical movement, follow these three basic guidelines:

1. **Pick a noncompetitive activity.** In general, physical movement that includes competition does not provide a mood boost. That's because competition often involves pressure to perform, and for most people, this does not help alleviate sadness, anxiety, or anger, especially if you're on the losing side.

   Nevertheless, if you do choose a competitive activity like tennis or basketball, try to focus on the experience of playing, rather than on the end result. That's what Malika did. "I was going through a difficult time when I lost my job," she said. "Playing tennis really helped me. It was like meditation. All my concentration had to be on the game. I was completely focused on the ball—following it, watching it, hitting it. I couldn't think about my problems even if I wanted to."

2. **Move at a moderate pace.** People often think that if a little is good, a lot is better. That's not necessarily the case when it comes to getting an emotional benefit from physical activity. High-intensity exercise often won't help your mood, and in some cases it can actually make you feel

worse than not exercising at all. This is true whether you're a Sunday stroller or a world-class athlete.

You'll know you're pushing yourself too hard if you are too winded to talk while you're moving, or if it takes you more than an hour to recover from your exercise. Find a pace that feels comfortable for you. This pace may differ from day to day. Listen to your body.

3. **Move for ten minutes or more.** I hesitate to give guidelines for how much movement is best. That's because women often become critical of themselves if they fall short. And some women who can't find the time to move a prescribed amount simply throw in the towel. Before you take my recommendations too seriously, please note that you are the only one who knows how much movement is right for you. That amount will vary based on your mood, temperament, body type, and lifestyle. Experiment to find what's best for you. You are your own expert.

There are two ways you can use the emotional tool of physical movement. First, use it on an as-needed basis. When you feel sad, anxious, or angry, go for a walk. Do some yoga. Dance in your living room. Usually ten minutes is all the time you need to change your mood. If you feel you can go a little longer, twenty minutes will provide maximum benefit.

The second way is to use physical activity as a form of preventive maintenance. In general, twenty to thirty minutes of movement—walking, swimming, dancing, yoga—three times a week will significantly reduce normal sadness or anxiety. Since the antidepressant effects of exercise last twelve to twenty-six hours, and the antianxiety effects of movement last two to four hours, some people may need more than three activities each week to get an emotional benefit.

Boosting the Power of Your Emotional Exercise: The Thinking and Breathing Factor

For exercise to help the most with your distressing feelings, it should integrate both your body and mind into the action. By coordinating your movements and thoughts, you can boost the emotional benefit of any physical activity. You can do this by becoming aware of your thinking and your breathing while you move your body.

Thinking

What do you usually think about when you move your body? Are you ruminating about your fears or problems? Do you recycle your worries? When you do repetitive movements that don't require constant attention—such as walking, yoga, running, or riding a stationary bike—your mind is free to drift. What you think about during those wandering times can make a huge difference in reducing your distressing emotions.

FOCUSED MOVEMENT

Focus is where you put your attention. In the section on mindfulness meditation (Tool 2), two examples of a meditative focus were described: your breath and your body sensations. This same type of concentration can be used while you are moving your body, giving an added bonus to your emotional exercise.

When you exercise with a focus, your alpha brain waves are increased, giving you some of the same emotional benefits as meditation. The presence of these brain waves is associated with feelings of calmness and well-being. Herbert Benson, M.D., discovered that having a focus during movement activates the relaxation response. In other words, the switch to your calming parasympathetic nervous system gets flipped on. That's why Youde Wang and his colleagues at the University of Massachusetts found that focused walking was associated with reduced anxiety and diminished negative thoughts. The two types of movement focus I often suggest to women are *inward* and *outward*.

Inward Focus

"Initially I may think about my problems when I'm walking," said Josie, "but then I'm pulled into the sensations of my body, like the feeling of my muscles or my heart expanding."

Josie's thoughts are an example of an inward focus. With this type of focus, you bring your attention to the sensations of your body as you move. This might include the feeling of your legs as you spin on your bicycle, the sensation of your feet touching the ground as you walk, or the sound of your breath as you run. "I love the feeling I get when I walk my dog," says Amy. "I feel my feet striking the ground, the breeze on my skin, my arms swinging. It makes me feel alive and calm at the same time."

Neela uses an inward focus when she swims. "I focus on my stroke—the feeling of my hand going into the water and the sensation of pressure I feel as I push the water away. There is no sound except my breathing. I'm immersing myself in myself. It gives me a sense of calm and clarity. Even if I've had a terrible day, I feel more relaxed when I get out of the pool."

When concentrating on your inward focus, follow the same concepts you do with meditation. If you find your mind wandering to your distressing thoughts, simply say to yourself "A thought" and then bring your focus back to your body. Try not to label your physical feelings as good or bad. Avoid words like *wonderful* or *painful* to describe your physical feelings since these words imply a judgment. Simply notice how it feels when your body parts stretch, bend, reach, or twirl. Notice the sensations of heat, pressure, or tingling when your body moves. This is what Tamera does.

"When I do yoga, I focus on the sensations in my body," said

Tamera. "I always ask myself, 'What does this pose feel like? Where do I feel this stretch in my body?' And sometimes I'll silently talk to my tension and say, 'Just let it go,' to encourage my body to open up."

Outward Focus

With an outward focus you bring your attention to your surroundings rather than your body. The key again is to notice your environment without judgment. If you are going for a walk, for example, become aware of the world around you as you move. Try to do it without labeling anything you see as good or bad. If you see a beat-up car, don't label it as unsightly. If you see a tree, don't label it as lovely. Rather, notice how many shades of green the leaves have or the shape of the lines in the bark. If your mind wanders to your problems, simply notice your distressing thoughts with the observation "A thought."

With repetition, both the inward and outward focus during movement trains your mind to reduce its judging. Slowly, you'll find that this nonjudgmental perspective begins to transfer into your life. You may notice that you judge yourself or situations less than before. As your judging decreases, so do your feelings of sadness, anxiety, or anger. Here's what Regina told me about her experience of moving with an outward focus.

I usually walk into town during my lunch hour to grab a sandwich. I decided to try walking with an outward focus. My goal: simply to observe the things around me without judgment. It was much more of a challenge than I expected. When I look at a flower I automatically think beautiful, or when I see an old apartment building I immediately think ugly. But eventually I was able to just walk and observe without having a running commentary in my mind. This was a surprisingly nice feeling.

My nonjudgment began to spread, and I found I was becoming less judgmental in other areas of my life. I stopped evaluating myself so harshly. The results of this were phenomenal. It became easier for me to forgive myself. At times I was even able to laugh at myself.

I stopped criticizing those around me too. Others felt more willing to come to me with their problems because they knew I would not judge them critically but would try to understand them. I was able to connect with people on a deeper level. This simple little exercise has changed the way I see everything.

Focus and Flow

Many women have told me about an almost magical state they sometimes enter when they move their bodies and bring their total attention to either an inward or outward focus. "When I run," said Pilar, "I look around at the scenery. I reflect on nature, the birds, the water. It puts me in a trance. Time goes so fast."

Marsha has had similar experiences when she exercises in a focused way: "I experience intense feelings of freedom while moving my body, mostly in things like running, swimming, or biking. Once I get into a rhythm, I feel like I could keep going forever."

Mihaly Csikszentmihalyi, professor of psychology at Claremont Graduate University, calls these states "flow." According to Csikszentmihalyi, "When an activity is thoroughly engrossing, there is not enough attention left over to allow a person to consider either the past or the future." When in this state, he says that people "stop being aware of themselves as separate from the actions they are performing."

Often when you are in a flow experience, you become more open to your intuition, and difficult problems seem to solve themselves without your actively thinking about them. That happened for Florence. "I was grappling with a problem once," she said. "I was confused and unsure how to handle my friend's indifference toward me. I went swimming to take my mind off it. I didn't want to think about it anymore. When I swim it's like meditation.

I feel transported. My body is weightless. It's quiet. All I hear is my breathing. I get into a rhythm. I'm not thinking. As I pushed through the water, focused on each stroke and the sound of my breath, I had a sudden realization: 'You don't need to struggle with things; you already know what to do.' It was true. I did. And in that moment, my confusion disappeared."

By using either an inward or outward focus or a combination of both when you move your body, you will gain added emotional benefits from your physical activity. I often recommend these strategies to women who have trouble sitting to meditate because they are too fidgety to be still. For people with high energy levels, high anxiety, or women who are just busy, this can be a great way to meditate while moving.

Breathing

When you dance, walk, or practice yoga, what is your breathing like? Do you breathe through your mouth? Are your breaths deep or shallow? Have you ever noticed? Studies have shown that the quality of your breathing during movement affects your emotions. One particular type of breathing that has been shown to reduce distressing emotions is called *ujjayi pranayama,* or "the victorious breath."

UJJAYI BREATHING

Ujjayi pranayama is an ancient Indian breathing practice. In Sanskrit, the ancient language of India, *prana* means "breath" or "life force," and *ayama* means "expansion." This technique is said to enhance your mood by creating additional vital energy in your body. According to yoga master and scholar B. D. S. Iyengar, "Pranayama is the connecting link between the body and the soul."

The concept of pranayama is part of a five-thousand-year-old philosophy that differs from the ideas of Western psychology. But modern science is beginning to understand why this method of breathing can be so powerful.

FOLLOW YOUR NOSE

Ujjayi breathing is experienced as a deep and forceful sound coming from your throat. It is practiced only through your nose, not through your mouth. This nose-breathing component is critical. Because breathing deeply through your nose takes longer than breathing through your mouth, it allows air to get deeper into your lungs and gives your lungs more time to absorb oxygen. This deeper penetration turns on the switch to your parasympathetic nervous system, which gives you a feeling of calm and relaxation.

The effect *ujjayi* breathing can have when used with physical movement is particularly striking. John Douillard, Ayurvedic doctor and fitness expert, studied ten athletes riding exercise bicycles. He monitored their brain waves while they were moving and breathing as they normally did. He then assessed them again, using *ujjayi* breathing with their exercise.

He found that during *ujjayi* breathing, the athletes produced alpha brain waves, these same brain waves produced during meditation. Thus, even though their bodies were moving vigorously, they were in a tranquil state. Douillard describes this finding as unprecedented. Although his sample size was small, his initial research demonstrates that with *ujjayi* breathing, it is possible to get the benefits of meditation even if you are dancing in your living room.

HOW TO DO *UJJAYI* BREATHING

The key to *ujjayi* breathing is to tighten the opening of your throat with each breath and inhale deeply into your belly. Here's how to do it:

1. Whisper the sound *haaaa* with your mouth open. This should be a breathy sound. It's similar to the sound you

make when you fog a mirror or your glasses with your breath to clean them. Or the sound of static on the radio. John Douillard cleverly describes it as Darth Vader breathing.

2. Make this sound as you exhale and inhale, using long, slow, deep breaths.

3. Your belly should rise as you inhale and fall as you exhale.

4. Close your mouth, and continue to make this same sound. You should now be breathing the same way as before, but through your nose only.

Continue this breathing pattern throughout your exercise, whether you are walking, dancing, or doing yoga. I've done *ujjayi* breathing while walking on a treadmill. I also bring all my attention to the sound of my breath so I can get the added benefit of an internal focus. I find I feel more centered after exercising when I breathe and focus this way than I do when I read a magazine on the treadmill.

If you're a swimmer, you can modify this breathing technique. Douillard advises you to breathe in deeply through your mouth, filling your belly with air. On the out-breath, exhale through your nose using the *haaa* sound.

The Unique Benefits of Hatha Yoga

In Sanskrit, the word *yoga* means "union." In that sense, *hatha yoga* is designed to unify your mind and body through the practice of specific body poses called *asanas*, as well as certain breathing patterns. Hatha yoga is a physical way to move prana, or life energy, through your body, and it can create significant changes in your emotions, as it did for Eileen.

A Yoga Story

Although Eileen had exercised for many years, she wasn't getting the emotional benefit she was seeking. Then she saw an ad at a local adult education center offering ten sessions of yoga for ten dollars a class. She decided to give it a try.

I know some people say that it takes a while before they begin to notice the benefits, but I noticed them immediately. I was calmer. Little things that usually would get me down seemed to roll off my shoulders.

I think I became most grateful for yoga when my husband and I decided to divorce after four years of marriage. He is a wonderful person, but we both knew we were better as friends than as husband and wife.

Because Randy and I have known each other since we were sixteen, it was important to both of us that we keep our friendship alive. But I could see that it wouldn't be easy. When we started separating our belongings and dealing with the realities of the breakup, I could feel myself getting angry with him and acting petty. It was then that I relied on my yoga practice.

Yoga has transformed the way I handle my difficult feelings. It taught me to let the little things go for the sake of something bigger. It helped me separate from Randy without getting pulled under by negativity. Because of that, we're still good friends today.

How Hatha Yoga Can Change Your Emotions

When practiced with a focus, hatha yoga can become a meditative experience. Many women use an internal focus during yoga—for example, they focus on the feeling of their muscles as they bend or the sensations of a stretch. Others choose spiritual images like prayer or an image of a higher power on which to focus during their practice. When practiced this way, hatha yoga can provide the same emotional benefits as meditation.

There are also physical changes that happen during yoga that can contribute to a shift in your emotions. Certain poses are excellent for reducing the muscular tension associated with anxiety. Some *asanas* can help increase the elasticity of your rib cage. This will allow you to breathe more deeply, resulting in more available oxygen and a calm feeling.

Other yoga poses improve your blood circulation, which in turn provides the cells of your body with the oxygen and nutrients they need. According to Karen Koffler, M.D., director of the Center for Integrative Medicine at Evanston Northwestern Healthcare, "The improved blood flow from hatha yoga poses can facilitate the production of those brain chemicals associated with feelings of well-being, such as norepinephrine and serotonin."

Four Ways to Get the Most Emotional Benefit from Yoga

1. **Do yoga postures slowly for best results.** It is important not to rush through yoga. Allowing yourself to be aware of your body and its sensations as you practice will provide the most emotional benefit. I can't stress this enough. Using an inward focus with your movements will greatly enhance their impact on your emotions.

2. **You don't need to do the poses perfectly to benefit from them.** Leslie Bogart, yoga teacher and registered nurse, says that even if you need to do certain poses with support or a chair, it's still yoga. Adapt the poses to match your level of flexibility. Don't judge your ability to do yoga as good or bad.

3. **Listen to what your body tells you.** Don't force or bounce on any movement. Stop if you feel any pain. Allow your body to guide you.

4. **Find a good teacher.** To understand the proper way to practice yoga, it's helpful to find a teacher with a style and practice that works for you. A teacher will also be able to tailor a program to meet your needs.

Yoga for Emotional Benefit

A classic series of *asanas* is called *sun salutation*. Since this series includes a variety of movements, many teachers and students practice it to shift a range of distressing emotions. I often use sun salutation in the morning as a way to gain energy and clear my thinking. Many women find it helps to reduce the tension of their anxiety, as well as to increase the low energy associated with sadness.

Nischala Joy Devi, former director of stress management for Dean Ornish's Lifestyle and Multicenter Lifestyle Heart Trial and author of *The Healing Path of Yoga,* has modified the movements so individuals of varied abilities can practice these poses. Figures 2 and 3, taken from her handbook, *Yoga of the Heart ® Cardiac and Cancer Certification Training Manual,* illustrate two of her versions of sun salutation: standing with assistance (page 218) and standing alone (page 220).

Start with whatever series of poses feels most comfortable to you. You will benefit from the sun salutation series in whatever form you practice it.

The positions of the sun salutation are not meant to be held for a fixed period of time. Rather, you should flow from one movement to the next. For all these poses, it is important to be aware of your breathing. Use *ujjayi* breathing when you can. Be aware of how your body feels as you move. Don't judge yourself or your practice.

Psychological Perks of Physical Activity

For many women, the emotional benefit that comes from physical movement comes in part from the chance to have some much-needed time away from the demands of others. It's a piece of the day when you are free to do whatever you want. "I'm an extrovert," says Melissa, "but I don't like to exercise with other people. I like to have something that's all mine, something I do just for me."

Many women use this private time as a distraction from their busy lives. Some use it as a time for personal reflection. Experiencing a life crisis in his mid-forties, cardiologist George Sheehan, M.D., turned to running as a way to renew his life. Of this he wrote, "On my solitary run, I am searching for the meaning within my experiences. In that hour devoid of distraction, when the world is on hold . . . I am the closest I will ever come to who I am, what I believe, and what I should do about it."

On the other hand, some women use their physical activity as a social time to stay connected and gain support from others. "I like to be with other people when I exercise," said Camille. "I work out with the girls three times a week. It helps me laugh. It's my social activity."

Physical movement can also enhance your mood simply because you've accomplished something that feels important. That was the case for Alice. "There's a tremendous sense of confidence that exercise gives me. I feel good about myself because I exercise. I feel proud. Because I've accomplished this difficult task, I know I can accomplish other difficult tasks as well, because I've done it before."

Figure 2. Sun Salutation: Standing with Assistance

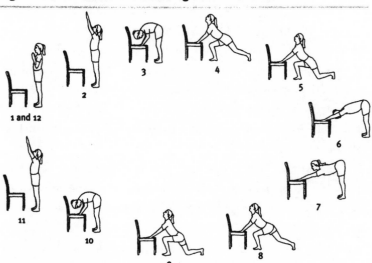

Position 1: Stand erect, feet together but not touching. Bring your palms together in front of your heart area.

Position 2: Lock your thumbs. Stretch your arms out from your heart area. Follow your hands as you slowly raise your arms up beside your head. Stretch up all the way from your feet to the tips of your fingers. Look up at your hands.

Position 3: Keeping your arms alongside your head, look at your hands, and then slowly fold forward from your hips, keeping your knees slightly bent. Place both hands on the seat of your chair, and allow your head to relax.

Position 4: Stretch your left foot back, placing it on the floor a few feet behind you. Keep your left leg straight and your right knee bent. Look up.

Position 5: Keeping both hands on your chair and your right knee bent, lower your left knee to the floor. Arch your back. Look up and back.

Position 6: Bring your right leg back to meet your left. Your feet are together with both knees on the floor. Pushing with your hands, straighten your legs. Look toward your feet. Stretch your heels toward the floor.

Position 7: Leaving your legs and arms in place, look up.

Position 8: Bring your left foot forward, bending your knee. Your right leg remains stretched back with your foot on the floor. Look up.

Position 9: Lower your right knee to the floor. Look up and arch back.

Position 10: Keeping your hands on your chair, straighten both legs as your right leg comes forward to meet your left. Allow your head, neck, and shoulders to relax downward toward the floor.

Position 11: Lock your thumbs. Stretch your arms out, looking at your hands. Raise your arms up toward the ceiling as you straighten your knees, and come to a standing position. Look up.

Position 12: Slowly allow your arms to come down in front. Bring your palms together at your heart area. Relax. Stand quietly for a moment with your hands at your heart center, and be conscious of your breath. When you're ready, sit down and relax. This series can be repeated up to three times.

Figure 3. Sun Salutation: Standing Alone

Position 1: Stand erect with your feet together but not touching. Bring your palms together in front of your heart area.

Position 2: Lock your thumbs. Stretch your arms out from your heart area. Watch your hands as you slowly raise your arms up beside your ears. Looking up at your hands, stretch up all the way from your feet to the tips of your fingers.

Position 3: Keeping your arms alongside your head, look at your hands and slowly fold forward from your hips, keeping your knees slightly bent. Allow your arms and head to relax toward the floor. *Practice position 1 to 3 for a few days until your blood pressure becomes accustomed to your head moving up and down. When that feels comfortable, move on to position 4.*

Position 4: Bend your knees deeply and place your palms alongside the outside of your feet. Stretch your left leg back, placing your left foot and knee on the floor. Place your right foot on the floor between your hands and your right knee close to your chest. Arch your back. Look up and back. (You may skip position 5 if it is too difficult and go directly to 5A).

Position 5: Raise your buttocks up so that your body now forms a triangle. Your hands and feet are on the floor. Stretch your heels toward the floor and look back at your feet.

Position 5A: Place both knees and both hands on the floor. You should now be on all fours. Look up and back.

Position 6: Slowly lower your chest and chin to the floor, and bend your elbows. Leave your hips slightly raised or, if more comfortable, just lower your body flat on the floor.

Position 7: Lower your pelvis to the floor. Place your palms on the floor beneath your shoulders, elbows close to your body and pointing upward. Gently stretch upward with your head, neck, and chest. Keep your elbows slightly bent and in toward your body. Do not push up with your hands. In the next positions, you will repeat the poses going back in the opposite direction. (You may skip position 8 if it is too difficult and go directly to 8A).

Position 8: Press down on your hands and feet to lift your buttocks and form a triangle.

Position 8A: Place your knees and hands on the floor so you are on all fours.

Position 9: Bring your left foot forward between your hands so that your left knee comes close to your chest. Look up. If this is difficult, grasp your left ankle with your left hand and bring it forward. Your right knee remains on the floor.

Position 9A: Return your left knee to the floor so that you are on all fours.

Position 10: Bend your knees as in a squat. Allow your hands to come off the floor as your legs straighten. Keeping your knees slightly bent, allow your head, neck, and shoulders to relax downward toward the floor.

Position 11: With your arms still down, lock your thumbs and look out at your hands. Stretch your arms out and level with your ears. Slowly come up to a standing position. Raise your arms up toward the ceiling. Look up.

Position 12: Slowly bring your arms down in front and bring your palms together at your heart area. Stand very still. Observe your breath. Relax with your arms at your side. As you grow comfortable with this series, it can be repeated up to two or three times.

Finding the Right Emotional Exercise for You

One thing I've learned from teaching and working with clients is that one size doesn't fit everyone. And that includes emotional exercise. Some women find brisk walking helps most with their anxiety, while others find yoga works better. Since all bodies and minds are different, you will need to experiment to find the type of physical movement that gives you the emotional benefit you want. Your preference may be vigorous activity like running or swimming or the slow pace of yoga or tai chi. It's possible you may need to try a few different activities before you find the one that works best for you.

"Many of my friends are runners," says Nora. "They're always going on and on about how much they love it and how it's helped them cope with their stress. After much pressure from them, I finally decided to run with them. I hated it. It was boring and tedious. All I could think about was when I could sit down. Not being a big exercise fan to begin with, I was ready to call it quits. Then I decided to try a tai-chi class at my community center. It had everything that was right for my personality. It was gentle and slow and nondemanding. I felt relaxed and calm after practicing just a few times, and to the amazement of my friends, I've been going ever since."

If you aren't normally active or if you have any health concerns or injuries, it's a good idea to consult with a clinician before you embark upon an exercise program. Finally, don't use physical activity as a substitute for the treatment of emotional disorders. Although movement can help with the symptoms of clinical conditions, it is not a replacement for professional care.

14

The Importance of Others

Tool 6: Connection

Throughout history people have used connections with small groups, with family and kinfolk, with peers and the like-minded, to give themselves anchorage in stormy, shifting seas.

—Alfred Katz, UCLA professor emeritus

Whenever Julie has a problem, she does the same thing—she picks up the phone. And that's just what she did when Doug asked her to marry him. She's been dating Doug for a year. Although she loves him very much, she's not in love with him.

All her life, Julie has dreamed of being married and having children. Now in her late thirties, she feels as though her dream could easily slip away. She is afraid of what might happen if she says no to Doug's proposal—or what might happen if she says yes. To help manage her intense emotions, Julie needed to talk, to vent, to question, to complain, to think out loud. She called Tina.

"I can't describe how Tina helps me. She certainly doesn't tell me what to do. I just know the minute I share something with her, even if she doesn't offer me anything other than listening, I come to a realization I didn't have on my own—no matter how many times

I went through it in my head. When I told her about Doug, she calmed me down. She helped me see the situation for what it was."

Although Tina never told Julie what to do, her calm presence and helpful questions helped Julie decide. She declined Doug's proposal. Although she feels it was the right choice for her, she is still sad about it, but Tina will be there to talk about that too.

Feeling Connected

Social scientists have used all kinds of words to describe this feeling of connection to others: *social support, affiliation,* and *social embeddedness* are just a few. Basically, it's the notion that there are people in your life who know and care about you. It's the feeling that you are a part of something greater than yourself, whether it's a family, marriage, friendship, church, or community organization. It's the knowledge that others will be there for you, and you'll be there for them, whether it's to talk about a difficult problem or recommend a new dentist.

I've included connection to others as one of the seven Emotional Tools for a good reason. Aside from the fact that common sense says being cared for is good for you, the research shows that people who feel supported by others and use that support in times of need are able to reduce the intensity and duration of their distressing emotions.

Social Support and Health

In 1965, researchers Lisa Berkman and Len Syme interviewed 6,928 adult men and women about the connections they had in their lives. They asked three questions:

- How many close friends do you have?
- How many relatives do you have that you feel close to?
- How often do you see these people each month?

What they discovered was astonishing. Nine years after posing their questions, those people who lacked social ties—family, friends, or groups they could turn to for support and help—were up to three times more likely to die than were those with stronger social connections. This was true even when they took into account their original level of health, smoking, income, alcohol use, and physical exercise. Moreover, people who face life's challenges without the support of others age faster than do those with caring connections.

Connection and Emotional Health

Given the profound impact caring connections can have on your physical health, it should come as no surprise that supportive interactions with others can boost your emotional health too. Numerous studies show that feeling connected to others and using that care when needed can decrease sadness, anxiety, loneliness, and feelings of helplessness, and can increase your self-esteem. And you don't need an army of support. It's been shown time and again that people who have an intimate and confiding relationship with one other person are able to deal with life's ups and downs better than those who don't. In one study, women who had major difficulties in their lives and didn't have one close person to confide in were about ten times more likely to be depressed than were those with a confidant.

Mommy Talk

In one study, a trained interviewer visited new mothers in the maternity ward. She asked them to talk about the feelings they had during labor and delivery, such as sadness, joy, fear, euphoria, and panic. They each talked for about forty-five minutes. Six weeks later, this group was compared to a group of new moms who did not talk with the interviewer. The women who talked had fewer obsessive thoughts about their birth experience, and they were less depressed and anxious than were the women who did not talk at all. By simply sharing their feelings with a caring stranger for less than an hour, they were able to reduce their distress.

Holly and Her Husband

For Holly, the relationship with her husband helps keep her emotionally balanced. A scientific researcher for a major university, Holly is one of a handful of women who holds a high-level position in the chemistry department. Although she loves her job, she describes the world of science as "competitive and pressure-filled." To help manage the anxieties she sometimes feels about her work, Holly turns to her husband. She says, "Ed is a great help with my workplace dramas. Every evening we talk about what happened during our day. If there is a particularly stressful thing, it really helps to talk it through with him. He always has a different perspective from mine. I like getting a male viewpoint since I work with mostly men. Sometimes I'll get upset with something at work, and he'll say, 'Hey that's just men. It has nothing to do with you.' Talking with him helps me get past my bad feelings. I know I would stay stuck in my anxiety if it weren't for our conversations."

A Core Feeling

Throughout our life span and across cultures, women often use social support as a way to manage difficult emotions. One reason women turn to others for comfort and help may have to do with the way women's identities are formed. If you recall from Chapter 7, baby Elizabeth—unlike her brother, Luke—learns what it means to be female by identifying with her mother. Because of this, she develops a core identity based on relating to and connecting with others. To her, it is not only natural but sustaining to connect with others during times of stress. As an adult, you can see why social support becomes an important part of Elizabeth's coping strategy: "I don't feel complete until I've talked with my family and friends. Being connected makes me feel whole. It makes me feel loved. It helps me look at myself more clearly."

It May Come Down to Biology

Is women's desire to connect with others during times of stress linked to our ancestors? That's what UCLA professor of psychology Shelley Taylor believes. Forget about "fight or flight"; Taylor says women are more likely to engage in "tend and befriend" when they are upset.

According to Taylor, during prehistoric times, women—who were often pregnant, nursing, or caring for numerous children—were not in a good position to fight an intruder while their mate was out in the brush. Nor would they consider running away and leaving their children behind. As a result, they formed alliances with other women as a form of protection and survival. Since this response worked so well, women may have evolved an innate instinct to connect with other women when they are upset. This instinct is maintained by the beneficial effect it has on women. When you reach for the telephone to call your mother, sister, or girlfriend to talk about a problem, you may be activating a primal survival mechanism that helps you cope more effectively with your distress.

The Phone Call

Jennifer has come to rely on alliances with other women to help manage her distress. When she and her husband planned for three out-of-town relatives to stay at their house, Jennifer was running ninety miles an hour to get ready. There were groceries to buy, the carpet to clean, and the house to dust. The list seemed endless. As

Jennifer describes it, "I was real stressed and getting kind of snippy at my husband. He said, 'Why are you getting stressed out? You don't have to clean the carpet.' Well, I'm not going to have people stay at my house with a dirty carpet! So I called Janie, and I said, 'You know I have to clean the carpet,' and she said, 'Well, of course you do!' I felt so much better." For Jennifer, simply being understood by another woman helped reduce her distress.

How Social Support Changes Your Biochemistry

Having a caring person or a network of people to share things with—whether they are female or male—can affect the chemicals in your body that promote feelings of well-being and happiness. According to Shelly Taylor, our sympathetic nervous system (that's the pounding heart, muscle tension, and rapid breathing) is quieter when supportive people are with us. If that system is already engaged, it will calm down faster with comforting people around. As one woman told me, "When I keep my feelings bottled up, my shoulders get tense, my muscles ache, and I have problems with my stomach. It's a relief when I talk to others, even if all they do is just listen to me and don't have an answer. I just feel so much better."

Even a supportive stranger can help decrease your distress. When psychology professor Stephen Lepore and his colleagues asked college students to give an impromptu six-minute speech while being observed and filmed through a two-way mirror, you can imagine how nervous they might have been.

A supportive stranger stayed in the room with some of the students. The stranger said things like "It will be over in a few minutes" and "That's good." The stranger smiled, nodded, and even offered the speaker a cup of water. Other unfortunate souls were placed in a room with a nonsupportive stranger. This stranger wasn't mean, just indifferent. The person didn't pay much attention to the speaker or responded to the student's questions with comments like "I don't know."

Those students who spoke in front of the disinterested stranger had higher blood-pressure readings than did those in the room with the supportive stranger. Just being in the presence of kind people, even if you don't know them, can make you feel better. In some cases, being in the presence of a friend, even if he or she doesn't say a word, can calm your body's nervous system. When Marie was anxiously sitting in the hospital, waiting to undergo a difficult test, she and her fiancé sat without saying a word. As she describes it, "Just having James sitting there helped me. His presence was comforting. Knowing he was close by made me feel better."

What exactly is happening in these situations? It appears that women's close relationships and talk may stimulate the release of oxytocin and endogenous opiod peptides, hormones that produce feelings of calm and relaxation. Although oxytocin is secreted in men, estrogen magnifies its soothing effects, suggesting in part why women look to others for comfort and help more often than men do.

How Social Support Aids Your Psyche

A BOOST TO YOUR SELF-ESTEEM

When you're upset, you can begin to doubt yourself. When Esther didn't get the promotion she'd hoped for, she thought, "It's all my fault. If I'd only tried harder." Left to her own self-attacking thoughts, Esther's self-esteem began to plummet. Without a support system, people are more likely to blame themselves for their problems since the only source of information they have is themselves. When Esther shared her unhappiness with her brother, he helped Esther see other aspects of the situation and confirmed that Esther was indeed a capable and worthy person. Removed from her self-imposed isolation, Esther began to see the bigger picture, and her mood changed for the better.

BEING UNDERSTOOD IS HEALING

For many women, simply having the opportunity to vent to an empathetic person—even if it doesn't change the problem—is like salve on a wound. Marnie meets her friend Alma every morning before work for coffee. This morning ritual is part of the way Marnie feeds herself emotionally: "When Alma and I talk, we don't spend time chatting about the weather. We cut right to the chase. It's like, 'Hey, listen to this.' We get down to business. We talk about us. We let it all out. Sometimes my husband thinks that when I talk with my friends, it's just chatting, but what he doesn't understand is that it's actually therapeutic for me."

Psychological theory has consistently maintained that joining another person in his or her feelings can be healing. Again and again, women have told me that talking to a supportive person makes them feel as though they are not alone in their problems, and that in itself significantly reduces their feelings of anxiety, sadness, or anger. Here is what Lena said: "I feel better if someone understands why something is so upsetting to me. If someone takes the time to listen, then I feel I'm not totally alone with my problem. If other people have experienced this, and they somehow managed to survive and not crumble and die, then maybe I'll be okay too."

A HELPING HAND

Sometimes the support given by others is just as much practical as it is emotional—what social scientists call *instrumental support*. Maybe your family donates old furniture so your first apartment won't be completely barren, or your cousin baby-sits so you can have a needed day out, or a friend drives you to the doctor when you're too sick to drive yourself. Alexis and her three friends from her college days have the kind of practical and emotional connection that has supported them through difficult times in their lives. According to Alexis, "There are four of us who went to college together. Sometimes we call ourselves the Ya-Ya Sisterhood. They're the ones I call if I have good news or bad news. When Carly went through a divorce, we moved her out in the middle of the night. We stuffed Becky's wedding invitations. The three of us went to visit Joy in South Carolina when she was expecting a baby so we could decorate her nursery. There's nothing we wouldn't do for each other."

THE POWER TO INSPIRE

When you feel defeated by setbacks or difficult times, other people can help you endure your frustrations a little easier with what psychologists call *motivational support*. When others believe deeply in you, your distressing emotions can be eased. Melissa describes her coworkers as "angels who knew I would get through my husband's illness before I did," and Dawn calls her child's daycare provider "a cheerleader who made me believe I was the best mom in the world, even when I wasn't so sure."

Sometimes motivational support can come from people you don't even know. That was the case for me. After my daughter was born, I developed pregnancy-induced arthritis. Usually an active person, my joints now swelled with pain with the smallest amount of exertion. The loss of my former self made me feel sad and self-pitying. My doctor told me I'd just have to learn to live with it, which only compounded my sense of hopelessness.

When I was ready, I decided to start working out at the YMCA. I started slowly by walking on a treadmill. At first, I could walk for only three minutes at a very low speed before my body began to hurt. As luck would have it, I chose to exercise in a room where people had a lot more reasons not to exercise than I did.

There was Harry, a man in his fifties, who was recovering from a stroke. It so incapacitated him that he had been forced to move back home with his mother. Unable to drive, he was so motivated to regain his former strength that he took a taxi to the Y every day just so he could exercise. He never gave up. As I watched him over the course of a year, he went from hobbling into the room on a walker to being able to walk, drive, and eventually work in the twelve-week room as a support to others. There were many others like Harry in that room. One woman was recovering from a mastectomy, but she was there using the weight machines to build up her muscles. And another woman probably weighed more than three hundred pounds when she started riding the exercise bikes, but she kept coming back too.

These people inspired me. As I watched them, I realized I wasn't alone in my experience. It was a slow road, but I'm back to my former self, and I know that the inspiration of people I've never even met helped me get there.

The Importance of Mattering

Getting support from others can be a powerful emotional tool, but so can giving support. Being part of a reciprocal relationship is a key feature of what psychologists call *mattering*. In essence, mattering means you are not only supported and cared for by others, but others depend on and need you as well.

Stephanie Brown and her colleagues at the University of Michigan's Institute for Social Research tracked older married couples for five years to see what impact giving to others had on their longevity. The researchers asked a variety of questions, including "Have you helped a friend, neighbor or relative with shopping, transportation, housework, child care or other tasks in the last year?" and "Are you willing to listen to your spouse if she or he needs to talk?"

The results showed that people who gave support to their spouse and others lived longer than those who did not. The reason is, in

Figure 4. Effects of Social Support on Depression

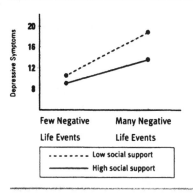

In one study, Sheldon Cohen, professor of psychology at Carnegie Mellon University, and his colleagues found that when people had many negative experiences in their lives, they were less likely to get depressed if they had high levels of social support.

part, because helping others increases your own feelings of emotional well-being. John Taylor, professor of sociology at the University of Miami, and R. Jay Turner, professor of sociology at Florida State University, found this to be true as well. They asked thirteen hundred men and women between eighteen and fifty-five how much they felt they mattered to others. Taylor and Turner asked questions like "How much do other people depend on you, and how much would you be missed if you went away? He found that the more people felt they mattered, the less depressed they were. This was especially true for women.

According to Harvard professor Robert Putnam, if you could quantify happiness (and you can), activities like entertaining people at your home, being part of a bowling team, volunteering, or participating in local politics are the happiness equivalent of more than doubling your income.

Social Support and Good Feelings

When I first designed my LifeSkills course at UCLA, I tried to create a classroom atmosphere that encouraged a sense of connection for the students. It was important to me that the women felt a sense of community among themselves and a sense of caring and understanding from me.

I worked hard to learn the names of all my students by the first week of class. Throughout the ten-week course, many students shared with me their private pains and emotional victories. Others relied on the budding friendships of the women in the class for support. In a large university where it's easy to become a number, I wanted this class to be a home for them. That's because for many women, emotional distress is compounded by the thought that they are the only ones going through a struggle.

To address this perception, I asked the women to answer this question anonymously: what is the greatest stressor in your life right now? I collected their papers and read them to the group. One woman wrote: "There have been many times when I felt alone and depressed, with nowhere to turn. I feel that there is great stress in deciding where I want to take my life. Sometimes I fear that even after coming so far, I will fail. I often find that I compare myself with others. All I see is what they have and what I don't have."

The women in the class pointed out how helpful this seemingly benign exercise was. One student wrote: "One day you asked us to write about the difficulties we are facing in our lives, and you read the responses out loud. I can't tell you how much that affected me. Suddenly I felt like I wasn't alone. Everyone seemed to have the same feelings about life as I did. Somehow I felt connected to everyone in the room. When I left class that day, I felt different. I felt better. Knowing I wasn't alone was like a huge burden lifted off my shoulders."

I saw how caring connections could ease women's emotional distress. Then I began to wonder, are there other ways to get support? Could it come from the Internet, or God, or a pet?

Is the Internet a Form of Support?

Can a plastic and metal box become a social companion? It depends on whom you ask. Some people contend that computers have isolated us from one another and reduced our ability to connect. That may have been true in the early days of the Internet, when its use was largely the domain of men. But today, at least half of the adults who use the Internet are women. And women have brought with them their own style of communication and desire for connection.

According to a survey conducted by Eric Weiser of Curry College, men use the Internet mainly for entertainment and leisure—things that could have the effect of isolating them from others. But women are more likely to use the Internet to send e-mail and find information that will help them and their families—that is, doing things that connect.

For Vicky, e-mail has helped reduce her sense of isolation, a feeling that could easily have led her to sadness or depression. "I have a friend who lives in another state," said Vicky. "We were both stay-at-home moms at the time. We'd both be snowed in with our young kids. So I'd get online and write, 'What did you do today?' And she'd reply, 'I did the laundry, I vacuumed, and I made this cherry pie that is so good. Let me send you the recipe.' We got to hear about each other's life, even if it was mundane. I felt connected to her, even though she wasn't here."

Many women use the Internet as a form of social support because it works. When Georgia was planning her wedding, she was overwhelmed by all the details. Prior to the big day, she was on the computer printing out programs and managing the minutiae of the event. She recalls, "The whole week before my wedding, my friend sent me e-mails reminding me why I was doing this. Like reason 17 ('Because we get to eat cake and dance') or, reason 54 ('Yea! You can finally have sex.') The little e-mails she sent once or twice a day really helped me manage my anxiety. They were cute. It helped lighten a situation that at the time was feeling very serious to me."

E-mail can provide some of the same benefits that face-to-face support can. And there's also the benefit of immediacy. "I like the idea that someone is always there for me," says Georgia. "I can let out my feelings right away, even if it's midnight. In some ways I get the therapeutic benefit of writing in a journal, and I know I'll get a response back."

The connection that e-mail fosters for women can do more than just reduce feelings of sadness or anxiety. Because of the value women place on connection, e-mail can prevent distress from happening in the first place. This is something Carrie realized when she was unable to use her e-mail: "I felt so much more connected when I used e-mail. When our computer broke, I felt like I was going through withdrawal. I was e-mailing my mother-in-law or father-in-law every day just to say, 'Hi, I'm thinking of you, I miss you.' When I couldn't do it, it was almost like I was a junkie coming off heroin. It wasn't because it was just a habit; it was because I missed the connection. It made me happy."

God as a Social Support

Why do people who are religious report less depression, anxiety, and hostility, and have greater life satisfaction than do nonreligious people? Many studies point to the role of social support. The question is, where is the support coming from—their fellow worshippers or God?

When I asked women about the role religion or spirituality played in their lives, many quickly told me about the relationship they have with God. Their descriptions sounded as if they were talking about a friend or family member. Murielle explained, "I talk to God on a daily basis. When I'm faced with things during the day, I have a conversation with God. I have a chat like, 'I wonder what I should do in this situation, God?' When I'm having problems, I look for advice from God. It's like a special friend who's in my soul."

Although most women probably wouldn't phrase it this way, God is part of their social support network, a being that provides comfort, solace, and a feeling of connection. Social psychologist Lee Kirkpatrick and colleagues at the College of William and Mary found that the more women feel they have a personal relationship with God, the less lonely they are, regardless of the other support they have in their lives. Being less lonely means people are also less likely to be depressed or anxious.

Being Part of a Religious Community

For some individuals, the personal connection they have with God is enough to provide them with emotional benefit. For others, being part of a religious community provides the benefit. Studies show that people who attend services and participate in religious activities are happier and healthier than are those who don't. They are so much healthier, in fact, that women who belong to a religious community have a 59 percent less chance of dying over a given period than do those who do not.

According to Harvard professor Robert Putnam, "Connectedness, not merely faith, is responsible for the beneficence of church people." In his research he found that people who attend services on a regular basis seem to know more people, reportedly talking with 40 percent more people in the course of the day. According to Herbert Benson, M.D., the social support provided by a religious community can be a powerful key to reducing distress: "Be it weekly church or synagogue services . . . Bible study or bingo night, confirmation classes, preparation for bar mitzvah or bat mitzvah, potluck suppers or youth groups . . . religious institutions ensure that their members get ample doses, not just of faith but of healthy social interactions."

Are Pets Friends?

One week after newspaper columnist Cindy Adams's husband Joey died, friends gave her an unexpected gift: a tiny Yorkshire terrier puppy. She named the puppy Jazzy because of his frantic jazzed-up energy. In *The Gift of Jazzy*, Cindy wrote, "With Joey gone half a year, I realized that while I was alone, I was not lonely. And part of the not being lonely was having this demanding creature to care for. . . . The lone creature alive who loved me unconditionally— no matter how fat, how tacky, how old my wardrobe."

Social support comes in all forms, including the small hairy kind, and the benefits can be just as substantial as with people. One study showed people over sixty years old reported less anxiety, loneliness, and depression, and had greater life satisfaction one year after adopting a cat than did noncat owners. Some individuals became more social after getting a furry friend. Young single women were less lonely if they owned a dog or a cat. Once again, the caring connection is key. The more emotionally attached you are to your pet, the greater the benefit for you.

This is not news to pet owners. Dot, who has a cocker spaniel, says, "I just love Marvin. He's always happy to see me. If I'm having a bad day, just putting my arms around his big furry neck makes me feel better."

Lior, who lost her husband in a car accident, says her two dogs "are the reason I get out of bed every day."

Annette, who has a dog named Scoop, says, "He knows when I'm upset. Sometimes he comes over to me, puts his head on my lap with a look like, 'If I could take away all your problems, I would do that.' He just loves me without asking for anything back except a pat on the head. Sometimes I talk to him and say, 'You're keeping me sane because I can tell you everything. You know my deepest, darkest secrets.' "

For many, pets become a nonjudgmental confidant in their social support network. And they can have the same powerful effect on your body's ability to withstand stress that a supportive person might. Social psychologist Karen M. Allen and her colleagues at the State University of New York found this out when they asked forty-five women who owned dogs to perform a stressful task: doing math problems out loud.

One group of women tackled the math exercises with only the experimenter in the room. Another group performed the same task while their dogs walked around or sat in the room with the experimenter. The researchers assessed the women's heart rates, blood pressure, and skin moisture, all measures of stress. When mentally calculating the math problems, the women whose dogs were present had significantly lower vital signs than did the women who did not, a sign of calm and well-being. Allen attributes this serenity, in part, to the "social support" of the dogs.

For some people, even fish can reduce emotional distress. One woman says, "Every weekend I take care of the fishpond in my yard. Last week I was out there, and I see this little flash out of the corner of my eye. 'Oh, my gosh! My fish had two babies!' I was so excited. I went from being ho-hum after my long workweek to this feeling of lightness. Then I got worried about them. Will some animal come and try to eat them? I check them every day. It's important to me that they're there. I have a connection with these fish."

So How Much Connection Do You Need?

Being connected with others is a universal desire. Exactly how much connection you need may depend on your temperament type. I asked my client Shannon, "If you were having a terrible day, what would make you feel better—spending time alone or having several of your best friends at your place when you arrive home?" Without hesitation Shannon responded, "I would definitely want all my friends around me."

That's probably because Shannon is an extrovert. People often say that an extrovert is someone who is outgoing, and an introvert is someone who is shy. But this is not true. It actually comes down to how you replenish your energy. Extroverts get energized by spending time with other people. If an extrovert goes to a party, she is probably charged up at the end of the evening and ready to do something else. Introverts, on the other hand, get energized by spending time alone. Being around other people for prolonged periods of time actually drains introverts. According to temperament experts David Keirsey and Marilyn Bates, if an introvert goes to a party, she may want to leave early—not because she is a party pooper, but because she is pooped by the party.

Ask yourself how you replenish your energy. If you are an extrovert, find ways to be with other people. This will help you avoid feeling sad or lonely. If you are upset, you may find that seeking the comfort of others will be your first response to a stressful situation. If you are an introvert, find time to be alone. This will help you minimize feeling overwhelmed or sad. If you are distressed, you may first need some time alone to reflect and recharge before sharing your feelings with others.

An Amazing Story of Support

Eight months after giving birth to twin girls and with a four-year-old son at home, my sister-in-law Cathy was diagnosed with colon cancer. As she and my brother Gary listened to the doctor tell them the news, Cathy recalls, "I thought I was going to crumble." Their hope was that after surgery to remove the tumor, it would be over. But it wasn't over. Cathy needed chemotherapy and radiation. "I realized that I wasn't going back to work from my maternity leave. I understood for the first time that this was going to be a long haul," Cathy said.

As Gary and Cathy told people about their situation, the show of support was immediate. But it didn't come from out of the blue. Both Gary and Cathy are giving people who have helped many others over the years with a listening ear or a helping hand. And their giving was now coming back to them full force. In psychological terms, they mattered, and people wanted them to know they mattered.

As Cathy recalls, "I couldn't believe how many people called to say, 'Tell me what I can do for you.'" Gary's coworkers donated money and gift certificates for food to help them get through the months that Cathy could not work. Gary's boss said, "I will work with you. Bring your wife to her appointments." He did. The first two weeks Gary accompanied Cathy to every single appointment, sometimes as long as five hours—he travelled to the hospital with her, sat with her as she got hooked up for chemotherapy, and stayed there holding her hand.

So many people from Cathy's office volunteered to help her that they had to create a chart just to schedule everyone. Coworkers and friends drove Cathy to the oncologist and the radiologist, baby-sat the children, cooked meals, and did the food shopping. Her coworkers even pooled their vacation time and donated it to Cathy so she would not have to worry about her income during the long ordeal.

As the holidays approached, her friend photographed Cathy's children and sent out her Christmas cards. Gary's parents flew in to help. The hospital adopted Gary and Cathy for Christmas, and Santa Claus arrived at their house with bags of toys and clothes for the children, as well as gifts for Gary and Cathy.

I asked Cathy how this outpouring of social support affected her. She said:

At first it was difficult to accept the help, because I was angry that I had to do this. I was so angry. This was supposed to be my maternity leave, my time with my kids. Why did this happen? Then I had to say to myself, "This is not going to help me. I have to accept this and go on." The support and generosity of everyone helped me do that. It was a turning point for me. If I can have the support of so many people, then I'm going to make it through this.

That's when my attitude changed. All the people in my life gave me the strength to get through it: Gary, my kids, my family, my friends, and the support of Gary's and my coworkers. I thought, "I am going to be here for my children. I'm going to see them get married, and I'm going to see them have their babies, and I'm going to baby-sit their babies. I have to do this. And nothing's going to stop me."

Today Cathy is cancer-free. Her life is forever changed, not only because of the cancer, but because of the power of connection.

How to Create More Connection in Your Life

Maybe you are happy with the connections you have and would like to strengthen them. Or maybe you would like a better social network in your life. Here are some ways to do that.

- **Talk to your partner or others who are close to you.**
  Being able to get and give support requires information.
  What do you need to feel cared for? What does your partner need? Teach your partner how to communicate with you so that you'll be more likely to use him or her as a source of support. Ask your partner to listen in a nonjudgmental way, and refrain from trying to fix your problem unless you ask him or her to do so. If you see your partner is upset, ask what you can do to help—for example, maybe you can talk about a problem, run an errand to help, or just give your partner some time alone.

- **Stay in touch with old friends.** With the busyness of life, it can be easy to fall out of touch with friends, especially if they live far away. So make it a priority to stay connected. Make a phone call, write an e-mail, or send a card. When my mother got a computer, she went online and connected with friends she hadn't talked with in years. Now they e-mail photos of grandchildren and share stories. Although she doesn't see her friends regularly, she feels more connected than she has in years.

  It is helpful to cultivate your friendships while you're feeling good. Sometimes it can be difficult to reach out to others when you're sad, because that requires energy, something that may be in short supply. If your network is already established, it's more likely people will reach out to you when you need it.

- **Find like-minded people.** When I first moved to Los Angeles from New York, I didn't know anyone. One of the ways I met people was by joining a singing class. To be honest, I didn't do it to meet people. I did it because I loved music, but meeting people was exactly what happened. Each week I would get together with this small group of individuals who had lots in common with me. No one knew anyone else before the group started, but as the weeks progressed, we were all having fun and meeting after class to chat.

  If you're looking to expand your social network, try volunteering, join a group or a church, or take a class in something that interests you, be it knitting or money management. The group doesn't need to meet often for you to get the benefits of social support. Once every three or four weeks is enough.

- **Consider a self-help or support group.** In one study, women who had recently lost their husbands participated in a support group with other widows and had one-to-one counseling with women who had successfully come to terms with their own bereavement. After one year, these women were further along in their recovery than was a similar group of women who did not participate. They were less depressed, more focused on the present, and more active in social activities.

This is what happened for Lillian. When her husband died, she was overwhelmed with grief. A friend suggested she join a support group. Not one for joining groups, Lillian was reluctant, but she decided to give it a try. Being around others who had also experienced the loss of their spouse, somehow made Lillian feel less alone. In the group, she was able to say how she felt without worrying about upsetting others. She was able to put her feelings into words.

There are myriad support groups that can help with issues like mothering, working, menopause, overeating, or illness, to name a few. Some are run by professionals, and others are run by the individuals themselves. Go to Appendix B to find a Web site that will link you to a list of more than eight hundred groups.

- **Give to others.** Find manageable ways to matter to others. Pick up your grandson from school, send a card to a friend who is feeling down, or volunteer in your community. The benefits of social support go both ways.

It is clear, as psychologist Daniel Goleman says, that "our toolkit for managing our own emotions involves other people to a very great extent."

In some instances, it is worthwhile to consider expanding your social support to include a therapist. This is the next tool: Emotional Tool 7, psychotherapy.

15

Reaching Out, Reaching In

Tool 7: Psychotherapy

The purpose of psychotherapy is to set people free.

—Rollo May, psychologist

Shoshanna, whom we first met in Chapter 6, is struggling with her love life. She was married briefly right after college. During the next ten years, she seriously dated several men, but says she has not yet found "the one." All the relationships were similar: they often started out with great passion and promise, but then quickly deteriorated into bitterness and unfulfilled expectations.

For almost a year, Shoshanna has been dating Greg. He wants the two of them to be together, yet he is ambivalent about marriage, kids, and even about spending time with each other. Shoshanna is frustrated by the relationship, but is committed to "working things out." She told her friend Laura that she is feeling "stuck and sad." Laura suggested Shoshanna see a therapist.

"Do you think there's something wrong with me?" Shoshanna asked Laura.

"Of course not," Laura said, "but you said yourself that you're stuck, right? So why not find someone who can help you get unstuck? You know I'm always here for you, Shosh, but I really don't know how to help you with this."

Seeing a therapist had never crossed Shoshanna's mind. After all, she was a bright and successful person who knew how to make things happen. But this was different. Maybe it *was* time to get some extra support.

Why Psychotherapy?

Emotional Tool 7 is psychotherapy, and I've chosen it for one reason: it works. In 1952, researcher Hans Eysenck made a startling statement. He said that most people who went to therapy were no happier than people who did not. He believed that with enough time, people generally tend to overcome their problems on their own.

Many psychologists were upset by his remarks, but others took it as a challenge to study scientifically whether his claim was true. Since then, over fifty years of research have unequivocally shown that Eysenck was wrong. For example, Mary L. Smith, professor of education, leadership, and policy studies at Arizona State University, and her colleagues examined 475 studies on psychotherapy and concluded that the average person who receives therapy is better off than 80 percent of similar people who do not. Those who've been in therapy generally report a higher quality of life than do those with similar distress who have not gone into therapy. And the effects of psychotherapy are often enduring. As one woman told me, "Therapy gave me the gift of myself. That was something I didn't get growing up. I learned that I tended to bottle up my emotions to the point where I didn't recognize them anymore. Whether I was angry or sad or lonely, it all felt the same. It just felt bad. It took a while to start to listen to myself and say, 'Okay, what am I feeling? I want to eat ten pints of ice cream. Why? What's going on with me?' Those are skills I use today, even though I'm no longer in therapy. I've learned to step back and say, 'Why am I so

Figure 5. Does Therapy Work?

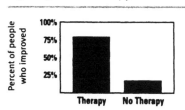

Hundreds of studies on the effectiveness of psychotherapy show that 75 percent of people improve significantly following one year of once-a-week therapy (50 percent improve by five months). Improvement is defined as less anxiety, depression, anger, or stress; better relationships with others; and/or better performance at work. *(Adapted from M. Lambert, 2001)*

upset? It's very useful to be able to recognize those feelings in my body because then I can do something about them. The change in me has been incredibly dramatic. My life is so much better."

The general effectiveness of psychotherapy can be seen in the chart above. Of course psychotherapy is not a cure-all. Your distress may be related to such other problems as a financial catastrophe or a medical condition. How effective therapy is for you will depend on a host of factors, including the type of problem you have, your relationship with your therapist, the skill of your therapist, and your commitment to the process. But according to a 1994 *Consumer Reports* survey, most of the 2,900 people who said they went to therapy reported they had a better life after therapy than before.

Why Not Just Talk to a Friend?

I'm often asked, "Why should I see a therapist when I can just talk to my friend (or my mother or my husband)?" This is a valid question. After all, I am a big advocate of social support. For many people, talking with a caring friend or family member is the emotional tool of choice.

However, there are some situations in which that can be difficult. In certain circumstances, you may be uncomfortable or embarrassed sharing your problems with others, even those close to
you. Or you may be worried about their reactions. One study
found that 85 percent of people who experienced a trauma or up-
heaval in their lives—the death of a loved one, an illness, or other
loss—felt the need to share that experience with others. But many
did not because they didn't want to upset their family and friends.

Sometimes family members or friends may be unable or unwilling to help you. They may mean well, but saying, "Don't worry, it
will be okay," may not cut it. They may feel uncomfortable, because they don't know how to assist you or they are tired of listening to your problems. Shoshanna's friend Laura wanted to help
her, but since Laura was happily married and couldn't relate to
Shoshanna's dilemmas, she didn't know what advice to give to her
friend.

It becomes even more complex when the person you talk with
is invested in your problem. For example, your husband may not
want to see you become more independent for fear you may leave
him. Or your mother may see your suffering as a sign she's been a
bad parent. These types of scenarios may make it difficult for others to put your needs before their own.

The bottom line is this: social support from others is a powerful
emotional tool, but friends cannot do what therapists do. As one
woman told me, "Therapy is not like sitting at lunch and talking to
your girlfriends about something that happened over the weekend.
It's very different. It's a very specific time to work on a problem."

When to Consider Therapy

Although some people go to therapy for personal growth or self-
exploration, here we will focus on psychotherapy as a tool to reduce emotional distress. You might consider therapy if:

- Your distress is persistent; you feel bad no matter what you do.

- You've tried the other Emotional Tools, and they haven't helped much.

- Your feelings are interfering with your life (for example, they make it difficult for you to concentrate at work or take care of your kids; they affect your relationship with your spouse or significant other).

- You have a pattern of negative experiences.

Should Shoshanna Consider Therapy?

I think Shoshanna could benefit from therapy. She's told her friend Laura that she's been feeling sad, and that sadness has been persistent for almost a year. A competent and hard-working woman, Shoshanna is able to function at work and handle life's responsibilities, but she describes her life as "just going through the motions."

She's tried to find ways to feel better. She exercises regularly and has lots of friends to lean on for support. She even keeps fresh flowers on her desk at work, thinking it might cheer her up. But nothing seems to help.

If you look at Shoshanna's life, you will see a clear pattern of negative experience. I said previously that if something happens once, it's an incident; twice, it's a coincidence; and three times, it's a pattern. Shoshanna has a pattern of unhappy relationships. This suggests that her inability to find a sustaining love relationship may be due to more than just bad luck. It may involve deeper issues— the kind of issues that can be readily addressed in therapy. As David Burns, M.D., associate professor of psychiatry and behavioral sciences at Stanford University School of Medicine, writes, "Sometimes a negative feeling becomes a way of life."

How Will Shoshanna Find a Therapist?

Now that Shoshanna has made the decision to go to therapy, how can she find a good therapist? What should she look for? I think one of the better ways is through friends or family. If you know people who have been in therapy, ask them what they liked about the therapist, and if they would recommend that practitioner to others. If you belong to an HMO, you may be offered a choice of several therapists. This was the case for Shoshanna, whose HMO gave her the choice of three therapists. Shoshanna might call all three individuals and ask whether they have experience working with the issue she is concerned about—in her case, a history of relationship difficulties and feelings of sadness.

Good therapists come in all types: psychologists, clinical social workers, mental health counselors, and psychiatrists. What's most important is their competence and the connection you feel with them. To assess their competence, check whether they are licensed to practice. While this doesn't always guarantee that therapists are wonderful, it does indicate that they meet minimum professional standards.

To determine whether you and a particular therapist will be able to connect, pay attention to how she talks with you on the phone. Is she businesslike and abrupt? Does she say you need to schedule a paying session in order to answer basic questions? If so, steer clear. Although you can't expect a therapist to provide a free consultation over the phone, you can expect her to give you basic information and a good feeling about working with her.

Shoshanna called the three therapists referred to her by her HMO. All seemed helpful, but Shoshanna got an especially good feeling from one, psychologist Valerie Keller. She arranged for an appointment to see her.

Is One Type of Therapy Better Than Another?

Therapists practice many different styles of therapy, and each therapeutic school claims to be the best. Cognitive-behavioral therapy is currently one of the more popular therapies. It's preferred in part because it is brief, action-oriented, and goal-focused. In this type of therapy, people examine how their thoughts and beliefs are linked to their feelings and how changing their assumptions about life and themselves can reduce their distress. It is one of the most rigorously researched of all the therapies, with many studies showing that when it comes to conditions like depression, cognitive-behavioral therapy can be as effective as medications like Prozac.

Does this mean you should look only for a therapist who practices cognitive-behavioral therapy? Not necessarily. Therapy of any style can be helpful if it contains certain elements. These include a supportive relationship with the therapist, an opportunity to learn new skills, and an action-oriented approach. Some therapies may give you insight about yourself and your problems, but unless you learn how to move forward, you'll still be unhappy.

What Can Shoshanna Expect in Therapy?

Psychotherapy seems like a mysterious process to many people. Once you understand how it works, however, you'll see that it isn't. The first thing to understand about therapy is that even though you may call your therapist "Doctor," it's not a medical treatment. Your therapist doesn't give you a remedy to make you feel better, as she might if you had the flu. Rather, therapy is a relationship where the two of you work together as a team so you can learn new ways to see yourself and your options in life. The connection you have with your therapist is one of the most crucial components of your therapy. It will be the mechanism through which everything is filtered.

For Shoshanna, the "magic" of therapy will happen by means of three critical factors: (1) the therapeutic alliance, (2) corrective emotional experience, and (3) learning and skill development. In some cases, a therapist may refer you for a physical examination to make sure your distressing feelings are not caused or compounded by a medical condition—for example, a thyroid problem, menopause, PMS, or the use of oral contraceptives. If needed, your therapist might talk with you about medications to help stabilize your mood. However, such medications can only be prescribed by a licensed physician like a *psychiatrist* or *family doctor*.

The Therapeutic Alliance

Shoshanna was nervous about her first appointment. When she arrived, Dr. Keller, dressed in a casual blouse and comfortable pants, greeted Shoshanna warmly. "It's so very nice to meet you," she said. "Please have a seat." Immediately, Shoshanna felt at ease.

"Why don't you tell me what made you decide to come see me?" Dr. Keller asked. As Shoshanna began to talk, she noticed that Dr. Keller was listening intently, as if Shoshanna were the most important person in the world. The doctor nodded frequently as if to say, "I'm with you." She let Shoshanna finish her story without interrupting. Afterward she helped Shoshanna identify some of the feelings she was struggling to describe.

Shoshanna had known Dr. Keller for less than an hour, yet she sensed that she could trust her. This is the *therapeutic alliance*. It's the feeling that the therapist "gets" you. It's the sense that the two of you are a team. There are some who maintain that this alliance alone may be healing.

The therapeutic alliance is not necessarily created during the first session, but you'll know if the potential is there fairly soon. Keep in mind that just because a therapist is nice doesn't necessarily make her compatible with you. You need to find someone whose style and manner fit your needs. Some examples of a good therapeutic alliance follow.

- Megan described her therapist like this: "She was gentle and calm. She was very loving and empathic. I felt a sense of unconditional acceptance from her. Everything I told her, she got, and she understood. She was like a mentor to me."

- Lupe recalls, "I remember telling him secrets that I've never felt comfortable telling anyone else. I felt like I could get them out and leave them safely with him. That was a freeing feeling."

- Myrna says, "I admire people who seem comfortable in their own skin, and she did. She wore bracelets that jingled, and she laughed easily. She participated and challenged and asked questions. She was very human. I liked that. I wanted what she had."

If your therapist interrupts you to take phone calls, seems hurried, or is inattentive, or if you just get a bad feeling about him or her, don't return. One woman told me her therapist talked about her own house-hunting troubles during their meetings. During my graduate training, my supervising psychologist would fall asleep during our group therapy sessions. When I pointed out his napping tendencies, he said, "What is it about you that needs me to be awake?" It was a big red flag!

Several studies have shown that when people work with a therapist who makes them feel understood, cared for, and safe, they feel better more quickly and stay better longer. The reason the therapeutic alliance was so important for Shoshanna is that the trust she developed with Dr. Keller made it easier for her to reveal her true self and allowed the therapy process to work.

The Therapy Process

In ongoing sessions, Shoshanna shared with Dr. Keller her frustrations about not finding a loving relationship. "I try so hard in my relationships, but they never seem to work out. Why doesn't Greg want to commit to me?" Shoshanna asked. But what she really wanted to know was what could she change about herself so that Greg would want her.

"Do you want to be with him?" Dr. Keller asked. "What does he do for you?"

Shoshanna was quiet. She had never asked herself that. She had spent the last year asking herself, "Why doesn't he want to be with me?" but not once did she ask herself, "Is this who I want to be with?" It seemed so obvious, yet the question was almost shocking to her. In their continuing sessions, Dr. Keller helped Shoshanna identify her needs and not apologize for them. Shoshanna learned that she didn't need to change who she was for a man to like her. She learned that it was okay for her to ask for what she wanted.

As Dr. Keller restated Shoshanna's feelings back to her, she acted like a mirror that reflected who Shoshanna really was. Slowly, Shoshanna began to know herself. The power of reflecting back is illustrated in a story by Pulitzer Prize–winning journalist Studs Terkel about his tape recorded interviews with average Americans. He interviewed a young mother at her home, using a tape recorder. After the conversation, her children wanted to hear the sound of their mother's voice on the tape recorder. Terkel complied. As the tape rolled, the woman put her hand to her mouth.

"Oh, God," she gasped.

"What is it?" Terkel asked.

"I never knew I felt that way before," she said.

For Shoshanna, like the woman on the tape recorder, hearing her own words reflected back by Dr. Keller helped her see herself more clearly.

The Corrective Emotional Experience

When Shoshanna was eleven, her father left home to remarry and start a new family. After that, he had little contact with her. Shoshanna told Dr. Keller that she always believed if only she'd been smarter, nicer, and less noisy, her parents would have stayed together. As a result of her childhood experiences, she saw herself as flawed and unlovable.

Her schemas began to play out in her therapy sessions with Dr. Keller. As she felt more connected with her therapist, Shoshanna began to fear that Dr. Keller would disapprove of her. She thought about how she could be the best client possible so that Dr. Keller would look forward to seeing her each week and not feel bothered by her.

This is exactly what Shoshanna did in her relationships with men. She abandoned herself in order to please her partners. She related to men as if she were still eleven and all men were her father. In essence, she denied who she was with the illogical hope that her boyfriend would stay if she was everything he wanted. It was this schema that was not only hurting her romantic relationships, but contributing to her ongoing sadness. It takes a lot of energy to deny who you really are.

This is where Shoshanna's corrective emotional experience began. With her therapist's encouragement, Shoshanna slowly revealed her true self to Dr. Keller. To Shoshanna's amazement, Dr. Keller liked her anyway. She liked her even when she was insecure or scared or crying. Dr. Keller was always there for her. Shoshanna began to understand what it was like to be accepted unconditionally. Because of her relationship with Dr. Keller, Shoshanna began to see herself in a new way. Her belief that she was unlovable was slowly chipped away, and her corrective emotional experience with Dr. Keller helped to heal her past experience with her father.

Learning and Skill Development

Insight can be of limited value if you don't develop a sense of emotional competence and the ability to take action. Since Shoshanna spent so many years denying her feelings, she needed to learn how to recognize them as they arose. To do this, Dr. Keller taught her to observe the thoughts she was having and notice how her body felt. From this, Shoshanna was able to determine if she was angry or sad or anxious. Then Dr. Keller told her to stop, take a deep breath, and feel the feeling without judgment. For Shoshanna, this was groundbreaking.

"She taught me to feel the feeling and to go with it," said Shoshanna, "and I know how to do that now. It's not an abstract thing. I know how to do that, and I've continually come back to that skill whenever I'm upset. I'm not always able to feel a feeling without judging myself, but I'm getting better at it."

Shoshanna learned how to examine her thoughts to determine if they were based on fact or feelings. When she told Dr. Keller that she was unlovable, Dr. Keller challenged her to prove it. "What facts show that you are unworthy of love?" asked Dr. Keller.

Shoshanna offered the list that, on bad days, she often recycles in her head. Dr. Keller worked with Shoshanna to examine the validity of each claim she made.

"How do you know you are unlovable?" asked Dr. Keller.

"Because none of my relationships last. Men leave because I am unlovable," said Shoshanna.

"Is it possible that because you believe you are unlovable that you try to convince men that you're unlovable too? That you're right about your feelings?" she said.

"How would I do that?" asked Shoshanna.

"Since we're playing detective here, how do you think you do that?" asked Dr. Keller.

Shoshanna thought for a moment. "By changing who I am to be what they want?" she asked.

"And what message does that give them?"

Shoshanna paused. "That I'm not good enough."

"And yet," said Dr. Keller, "when you're here with me, you say you are your authentic self, right?"

"Yes, more than I've ever been with anyone," said Shoshanna.

"And do you think I care about you?" asked Dr. Keller.

"Yes, I do."

"Then your belief that you are unlovable must not be true," said Dr. Keller.

Shoshanna began to realize that what she thought was the truth was really just her perception—and an inaccurate one at that. Now whenever she has thoughts that lead her to feeling upset, she tells herself, "Prove it!"

Shoshanna also practiced communication skills so she could express her needs to others, particularly men, in a clear way. Since Shoshanna feared disapproval, she often held back her feelings if she thought they might upset others. Through Dr. Keller, she learned not only that it was all right to have needs, but also how to express those needs in a respectful way. To her surprise, people did not abandon her when she told them how she felt. Each successful attempt to communicate reinforced itself and gave her the confidence to do it again.

Depending on your issue and your therapist's style, you may learn a variety of skills other than—or in addition to—the ones Shoshanna learned. All of these skills will empower you to manage your own emotions. As one woman told me, "I would not have been able to learn what I did, in the depth I did, if I hadn't had individual instruction from my therapist. Because she knew my background and why I interpreted things the way I did, she was uniquely qualified to help me. Now I can figure things out more easily because she taught me how."

How Long Can You Expect Therapy to Last?

In the movie *Annie Hall,* Woody Allen's character Alvy Singer tells Annie that he's been in therapy for fifteen years. Certainly, good therapy will provide you with relief in much less time than that, regardless of what style you choose. However, therapy is not a quick fix. Shoshanna, not knowing much about psychotherapy, was surprised when her life didn't change after the first session. So what can you expect?

How long therapy will last depends on several factors. One is the depth of your issue. The more immobilizing the problem, the longer it may take for you to feel better. There is also a difference between feeling better than you did when you first started therapy and improving the quality of your life. Even so, researchers, spurred on by the cost-containing efforts of managed care, have tried to answer the elusive question, how long does therapy take to work?

Studies have shown that about half of all therapy clients say they feel better by the eighth session. If you see a therapist once a week, that's two months of therapy. Those with more intense symptoms show meaningful improvement after about five to six months. And 75 percent of people show significant change by one year. Everyone is different, so applying rigid expectations to your progress may not be productive.

Therapy may not necessarily have a formal ending. Your therapist should be available to you after therapy ends. It is not uncommon for people to return to their therapist for help in navigating new life transitions or for periodic "booster shots."

How Am I Doing?

Depending upon the issues that bring you to therapy, you may find that your progress has its ups and downs and constant improvements are not always the norm. According to psychologists Jack Engler and Daniel Goleman, "Emotional repair and growth, like any other kind of learning, is often two steps forward and one step back." Changing deeply held belief systems takes work, but coming into therapy with realistic expectations will make the process easier.

So how do you know if your therapy is working? You'll know you're on the right track if you feel safe with and understood by your therapist. You should also begin to feel more capable of making changes in your life, either because your beliefs have changed, or your skills have improved, or both. You can also request a periodic review of your progress. Cognitive therapists often include this as part of the therapy. If your therapist doesn't, talk to him or her about it.

How Does Therapy Affect Your Body?

Is it possible that Shoshanna's sessions with Dr. Keller had a positive effect on her body? It is very likely. When Shoshanna told Dr. Keller about her parents' divorce and the impact it had on her, striking changes may have been taking place in her body.

Shoshanna didn't normally share her story with others, and in fact, it wasn't always appropriate to do so. But talking with Dr. Keller in a safe and private place, she was able to unburden herself not only emotionally, but also physically.

According to psychology professor James Pennebaker of the University of Texas, when people talk about emotional events that they generally don't share with others, several biological changes occur. After revealing their deepest feelings, their blood pressure drops, their muscles become more relaxed, and the moisture on their hands lessens. Holding back or inhibiting your deepest feelings results in subtle body tension. When you let go and stop inhibiting these feelings, it's almost as if a sense of physical relief takes place.

Exciting research is also showing that therapy can produce positive changes in brain function. Arthur Brody, M.D., at UCLA compared a group of depressed individuals. Half the group received interpersonal therapy, an action-oriented therapy, and the other half took Paxil, an antidepressant. At the end of twelve weeks of treatment, both groups showed similar changes in their brain activity. Although no studies were done on Shoshanna's brain, it would not be a leap to suggest that her brain showed comparable changes as a result of her therapy.

After Shoshanna's Therapy

Since Shoshanna now has a clearer sense of her own needs, she knows how to interact with men in a healthier way. She made the decision to end her relationship with Greg. "After Greg, there were a few guys I dated who didn't treat me very well. I just walked away. I learned to ask myself, 'Do I want to be with this person?' not 'Does he want to be with me?' That became my new mantra."

Shoshanna feels much more comfortable with herself, and this change has affected other areas of her life. After years of distance and strain, she made contact with her father. Although it's too soon to tell, Shoshanna is beginning a new relationship with him, but this time she's putting her own needs first, rather than trying to gain his approval.

She has also been dating Joe for several months. She says the best thing about their relationship is that "he makes me feel adored and perfect just the way I am." She can say for sure, "This is someone I want to be with." As for her therapy experience, Shoshanna has this to say: "I don't know where I'd be right now, or how my life would have unfolded if I had not gone to therapy. Being in a happy relationship was a goal for me when I started. Would I have ended up in a committed relationship someday? Maybe. Would it have been the right relationship? Would I have been happy? I can say with certainty, no. I probably would not have met Joe, that's for sure. I probably would have just gone on being miserable and not understood why."

16

The Emotion Tree

A Guiding Formula

> *The significant problems we face cannot be solved at the same*
> *level of thinking we were at when we created them.*

—Albert Einstein, physicist

Now that you've learned about the purpose of your feelings and the seven Emotional Tools, there is one last strategy I've devised to help you. I call it the Emotion Tree.

The Emotion Tree is a type of decision tree that will lead you through the essential steps you need to deconstruct your emotions, determine your core issues, clarify your underlying feelings, and identify which Emotional Tools are right for you. As you will see, the Emotion Tree will help you take all the information you've learned in this book and make it work for you.

Use the Emotion Tree whenever you're feeling distressed. Over time, you may find that you can follow its steps in your head or use only the parts you need. No matter how you use the Emotion Tree, it will guide you toward a better understanding of your distressing feelings and to the Emotional Tools you can use to change them.

Figure 6. The Emotion Tree

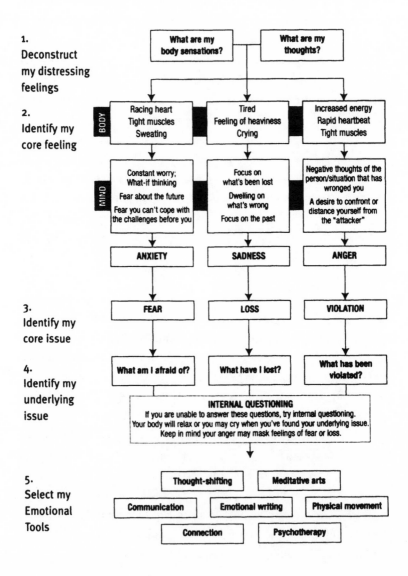

1.
Deconstruct
my distressing
feelings

2.
Identify my
core feeling

3.
Identify my
core issue

4.
Identify my
underlying
issue

5.
Select my
Emotional
Tools

Some people might consider this approach to understanding and shifting feelings too simplistic. After all, they might say, feelings are complex and cannot easily be addressed by strategies, tools, or charts.

While emotions are multilayered and while their origins may reside in a place unavailable to the conscious mind, that doesn't mean you are at their mercy. On the contrary, science has shown that there are numerous strategies you can use to reduce your distress.

Unfortunately, these valuable tools are not taught in any systematic way. That's why the Emotion Tree and the tools of the Emotional Toolkit are designed to guide you through the process of understanding and managing your emotions in a step-by-step, organized way. Take a minute to carefully review the Emotion Tree (on opposite page), and then I'll show you how Nancy used it to reduce her distress.

Nancy and the Emotion Tree

In Chapter 3, we met Nancy, a divorced mother who called to tell me she had been laid off from her job. Nancy used the Emotion Tree to help her reduce her distress by clarifying her feelings and determining what Emotional Tools were best for her.

STEP I: DECONSTRUCT MY DISTRESSING FEELINGS

Nancy started by deconstructing her feelings into body and mind components. "What's happening in my body?" she asked herself.

My stomach is tight. I keep clenching my teeth, and my heart is pounding.

Next she asked, "What kind of thoughts am I having?"

So many thoughts all at once: What if I can't find another job? What if I can't pay my mortgage? What if I can't pay for my son's pre-

*school? I can't sleep because I'm constantly worrying, and I don't
have any answers.*

STEP 2: IDENTIFY MY CORE FEELING

Given Nancy's combination of tense and racing body sensations
along with thoughts characterized by worry and what-if thinking,
it was easy for Nancy to recognize that she was *anxious.*

STEP 3: IDENTIFY MY CORE ISSUE

Once she identified her anxiety, Nancy knew her core issue
was *fear.*

STEP 4: IDENTIFY MY UNDERLYING ISSUE

"What am I afraid of?" Nancy asked herself. It appeared her
fears were monetary ("How will I pay for the mortgage and preschool?"). Still, Nancy decided to use internal questioning to clarify her fears.

Nancy sat in a comfortable chair and relaxed by taking slow,
deep breaths and allowing her body to feel heavy and limp. Given
her level of anxiety, it took a few minutes for this to happen.

When she felt ready, she began by silently saying to herself, "I'm
feeling anxious." She noticed a slight relaxation in her body.
"What else am I feeling?" Words began to pop into her head: *worried, concerned, overwhelmed.* None seemed to produce much of a
bodily reaction, so she went to anxiety's core issue—fear.

"What am I afraid of?" At this point Nancy could easily have
moved into her thinking mind: "Isn't it obvious? I don't know
what my next job will be, and I don't know how I'm going to pay
all my bills." She refrained from doing this and stayed with her
body.

"What am I afraid of?" She waited as her chattering mind ran
all the obvious answers, but none of them produced any type of
body reaction. She was patient. Images of getting notices from the

bank came through her mind. She had images of not being able to pay her son's preschool bills. Then she had an image of her parents. She could feel herself getting tense. She saw her mother saying, "I told you so." Suddenly Nancy's body relaxed deeply, and she began to cry.

For two generations, Nancy's family has owned a furniture business. Her grandparents started the business when they came to the United States. Nancy's father took over the business when his father retired. The legacy of the business and all the sweat that went into building it would be passed on to the family's only child, Nancy.

Nancy, however, had other ideas. After college, she decided she wanted to jump into the world of computers. She had tremendous guilt about letting the family down, yet felt overwhelming sadness when she pictured herself working in the furniture store.

Unable to express these confusing emotions to her family, she expressed only her anger. She yelled about how they were trying to control her. She would show them. She would become rich.

She married her college sweetheart, and the two moved to San Francisco. The couple worked long hours. They were challenged by the excitement of dot.com fever and thrilled with the stock options that piled up in their accounts. Nancy and her husband had a baby boy. Life was sweet.

But life had a way of doing what life does. Things changed. The grueling hours and pressures took their toll on the couple, and they divorced when their son was four. Then just as quickly as it all began, Nancy's career dreams began crumbling. Nancy, a high-level executive, was laid off. The company, along with many others in the area, went bust. Her stock options vanished.

Now Nancy was unemployed (as was her ex-husband) with no job prospects on the horizon. How would she tell her parents? She realized the confident, cocky persona she had adopted was just a disguise to cover the guilt she felt about letting her family down.

She was terrified of calling them. She feared they would say, "I told you so." She feared her career crash would be the second time she let them down. She worried they would walk away from her as she had walked away from them. Although she was nervous about her finances, this was her underlying issue: her fears about finding her way back home to her family and herself. Could she do it?

STEP 5: SELECT MY EMOTIONAL TOOLS

Given her anxiety, Nancy needed to find Emotional Tools that would calm her body and help her manage her worrying mind. She also needed to find a way to cope with her fears about her family's acceptance of her.

Body Tools

Nancy had several friends who were devoted meditators, so she decided to try meditation. After her son was asleep, she began her meditation, breathing in a slow, rhythmic way. For two weeks she practiced, but didn't find herself much calmer. In fact, it was just the opposite. Nancy, a high-energy, active person, found herself becoming more agitated as she fought an overwhelming desire to move her body.

Knowing she needed to find a body tool that worked for her, she decided to try yoga. Since she was too busy to take a class, she bought a yoga video she could follow in the quiet of her evenings. Nancy enjoyed this form of meditative movement because it gave her something concrete to focus on while allowing her to move her body. She was able to find calm by concentrating on the various stretches and poses.

Mind Tools

Nancy needed to find an Emotional Tool for her worrying mind. She began by examining the many deeply held beliefs she had about her life. Using the exercises in Tool 1, thought-shifting, she came to realize that she was being guided by several unsupportive schemas, including "I must succeed at everything" and "I must make my family happy." These schemas generated a constant stream of self-talk that scolded and judged Nancy's every action. These thoughts contributed to Nancy's anxieties and to some unacknowledged sadness about her family.

Nancy decided to challenge her many inaccurate perceptions by writing about them (Tool 4, emotional writing). Through these exercises she came to see her position from another perspective. Among other things, she answered the question, if everything could work out the way I want, what would it look like? Nancy wrote about talking with her family and honestly discussing her guilt and sadness over the past. She wrote about a new beginning for all of them.

In order to face her fears, she needed to develop her communication skills so she could talk with her family in a way that would strengthen, not harm, their relationship. As a result, Nancy spent time learning about communication strategies (Tool 3) and prepared herself to meet with her family.

Shaky about her pending visit, Nancy used Tool 6, connection, and called on an old friend for support. She knew her friend's encouragement and acceptance would give her the confidence she needed to address the feelings she had long denied.

Nancy went to her family's house for dinner. Her heart was pounding as she walked into the living room. She took deep, calming breaths to help relax her tense body. Slowly she began. "I have to start by saying I'm very nervous," she said. "I have so much to tell you, and I want it to come out right." Her parents listened attentively. Nancy went on to explain about her past decisions and how her guilt about letting the family down led her to distance herself from them. She told them how deeply she regretted what had happened and how much she wanted to start again.

Her parents were shocked to hear these words from their feisty daughter. These were the words they longed to hear. In everyone's view, it was time for a new beginning.

Of course this new relationship was not perfect. The members of Nancy's family had to learn to trust one another all over again, and there were small conflicts along the way. But slowly the wounds began to heal. To address her monetary fears, Nancy worked part-time in the furniture store while she looked for a new job. Her anxieties were now manageable.

A WORD ON THE EMOTION TREE

Sometimes with such difficult feelings as sadness or grief, you may need to allow yourself time to experience the emotion before you jump into fixing it. In other cases, such as with a life-threatening illness or troublesome family dynamic, you may need to step away from the problem for a while or even temporarily deny its magnitude.

Ruth's sister was going through a difficult period in her marriage that was causing her much sadness. When she told Ruth about her problems, Ruth said, "Maybe you just need to be sad for a little while before you try to figure out what you're going to do." And that's true. Sometimes you may want to "fix" your feelings because they make other people uncomfortable. Others tell you, "Don't feel that way. . . . Snap out of it. . . . Then do something. . . ." In most cases, these comments are designed to make *them* feel better, not you. The bottom line is to use the Emotion Tree and the Emotional Toolkit in a time and manner that feel right for you.

17

Putting It All Together

Western society promotes outward self-improvement,
not inward development.

—Herbert Benson, physician and researcher

Y ou now have the tools to help you manage life's inevitable ups
and downs. But how will you use them?

I came face-to-face with this question when, halfway into writing this book, my father died. He had been sick for many years, so his death was not a surprise. Still, I wasn't prepared for my reaction. When my mother called to tell me the news, I couldn't breathe. It was as if someone had punched me in the stomach. I was confused and sad and not sure how to get through it. Ironically, it took me a day before I realized that I did know how to get through it: I had my Emotional Toolkit.

Although I felt overwhelmed with grief, I knew my feelings were normal. My intense sadness was just a validation of how much I loved my father. I also knew there were tools I could use to carry me through this difficult time. Even though I really didn't feel like using them, I did anyway.

As an introvert, my initial reaction to things is usually to pull inside. I become solitary and want to be by myself. I wasn't ready to talk to people about my father's death, but I knew that social support would help. So I went to the Internet, where I found stories of other women who lost their fathers (http://atimetogrieve.net). It made me realize I wasn't alone; eventually almost all daughters will grieve the loss of their fathers. After a few days, I was able to talk with friends and family and put my feelings into words. I knew that translating my feelings into words, whether on paper or with others, was important for me to do, so I did.

I started walking as often as I could. Since I'm not an exercise fanatic, many times I had to force myself to go, but I did it. Sometimes I went to the YMCA and walked on the treadmill while my daughter played in the child-care room. Other times, I walked through the neighborhood.

I did brief sitting meditations whenever I found myself getting tense or overwhelmed by my feelings. I knew I needed to meditate when I found myself snapping at people or getting upset by simple things like the terrible food we had on our flight home to the funeral. I breathed deeply, allowed myself to relax, and brought my focus to various parts of my body. Sometimes I had only a few minutes to do this, but it always seemed to help. When I didn't have the quiet or the time I required for a sitting meditation, I would do a meditation-in-action by simply bringing my awareness to what I was doing at that moment, whether I was grocery shopping or cooking dinner.

As for communication, I told my husband exactly what I needed from him during this time so he would know how to support me—like taking care of our daughter so I could go to bed early. Not only did this help me, but it helped him to know what to do at a time when it was hard for him to figure out what I might need.

After a while, my emotions stabilized. My Emotional Toolkit, coupled with time, was helping me cope. I continued to talk with my family and friends. I thought about my faith and my spiritual beliefs.

We flew to New York for my father's memorial service, after which our family would scatter his ashes over the Long Island beaches where my brothers and I grew up. I knew this would be a difficult experience for all of us, and I wasn't so sure how I'd manage.

Each morning while I was staying at my brother's house on Long Island, I went for a brisk walk outside. I practiced my *ujjayi* breathing as I moved. At times, I did an outward meditation as I walked, noticing the colors of the leaves or the smell of the summer air. At other times, I just reflected on whatever thoughts popped into my head, always remembering to focus on the gratitude I felt that I had had my dad in my life long enough to see me graduate college, marry, and have a child of my own.

Throughout the week in New York, my feelings of sadness came and went, and I allowed that to happen. One night we had dinner with the whole family, telling stories and laughing together. Afterward, we stopped at Patsy's, an Italian bakery my family loves. Seeing all the cannolis and other pastries, I thought, "I have to pick up some of these for Dad. They are his favorites." Then I remembered that I no longer had a dad. My eyes filled with tears. But soon we were slurping down Italian ices and laughing again. That's the nature of feelings sometimes. They rise and fall like waves on the ocean. All you can do is ride them.

The day of the service arrived. My husband was by my side throughout the event with his constant reassurance and love. And the presence of my family, supporting each other by just being there, was a great comfort.

Would I have made it through the loss of my father without my Emotional Toolkit? Probably, but I don't think I would have fared as well. Having the tools to guide me when I was too upset to guide myself was a tremendous help.

Using Your Emotional Toolkit

I have used every Emotional Tool in this book. I find that some are better suited to my temperament, and some work better for me at certain times than do others. Through experience, you will learn which Emotional Tools work best for you.

As you go through life, keep in mind that your feelings are messengers that tell you what you need to be happy. They present you with opportunities to learn more about yourself and to make changes in your life as needed. Despite all the subtle messages in our society that suggest you should be happy all the time, your goal with the Emotional Toolkit should not be to eliminate all unpleasant emotions. Rather, the goal is to reduce the amount of time they exist and to decrease the distress that often accompanies them.

As influential psychoanalyst Carl Jung said, "Even a happy life cannot be without a measure of darkness. . . . It is far better to take things as they come . . . with patience and equanimity."

You now have the tools to navigate your emotions as they come, and to do so with a sense of mastery and knowledge. I hope your Emotional Toolkit serves you well.

Class dismissed.

Look with your understanding,
Find out what you already know,
And you'll see the way to fly.

—Richard Bach

Appendix A

Common Questions

I tried internal questioning, but nothing happened. What should I do? As with any skill, internal questioning takes practice, so be patient. One question many people have is, "If I'm not supposed to be 'thinking,' how will the answers about my feelings come to me?" The feeling or issue you're trying to find may come to you as an unforced thought, an image, a sensation, or just a "sense." It's different for each person.

The other tricky part is being able to recognize the sensation of deep relaxation that comes when you accurately identify what you're feeling. Sometimes, it can be a subtle shift. In a way, it's like love. It's hard to define, but when you've found it, you know it.

Don't give up if internal questioning doesn't work at first. Using your body to help you identify feelings is not something most of us are used to doing, and it takes time to learn how to do it. You can also look in the Resource Guide (Appendix B) for more information on a related process, focusing.

What Emotional Tools should I use if I'm feeling sad and anxious at the same time? It's common to feel a mixture of feelings at the same time. When feeling both sad and anxious, you should choose Emotional Tools that address your thinking patterns, specifically examining and shifting your thoughts away from fears of the future (anxiety) and negativity over the past (sadness) to a focus on the present. Mindfulness meditation or meditation-in-action (Tool 2) can help with this. Strengthening your ability to cope with the specific fears you have about the future will reduce their power. Emotional writing (Tool 4) can also help you gain some perspective on the situation triggering your distress. Getting support from others (Tool 6) who have been in a similar situation can also help. Depending on the intensity of your sadness and anxiety, you might also consider psychotherapy (Tool 7).

I find that when I'm stressed out, I lose my patience and snap at people. Does that mean I'm mad or I'm anxious? One of the signs of being stressed out is increased irritability. Oftentimes little things that normally wouldn't bother you when you're calm really push your buttons when you're anxious. Why? During anxiety, your sympathetic nervous system turns on, releasing chemicals that prepare you to protect yourself from danger. In this heightened state, any sense of threat or violation causes you to respond with an intensified reaction, such as snapping at people. Using Emotional Tools to reduce both the body and mind of your anxiety will probably reduce your impatience with others as well.

I've tried to become more aware of my physical sensations, but it's very hard for me. My thoughts seem to dictate my moods. Is this a problem? No, it's not a problem. With practice, many people are able to identify both the body and mind signals of an emotion. Some people find that either their physical sensations or their thoughts are dominant or more easily noticed. The important thing is that you're able to accurately identify the emotion you're feeling. Doing so will allow you to choose the right Emotional Tools for you.

Sometimes I'm overwhelmed by my emotions. I don't know if I just need better coping skills or if I need to go into therapy. Therapy is a coping skill. So is seeking the support of caring friends or family members whom you trust. You don't need to manage everything on your own. As a matter of fact, reaching out to others is an important part of your Emotional Toolkit.

People tell me I should feel bad or upset about certain things, but I just don't. Is that a problem? My rule of thumb is this: if it's not a problem, then it's not a problem. How can you tell if something is a problem for you? Answer these three questions about the issue:

1. Is it causing you to feel distressed?

2. Is it negatively affecting your ability to work or play?

3. Is it negatively affecting your relationships with others?

If you've answered no to all three questions, then this issue is not a problem for you. If you answered yes to one or more of them, you may have a problem that you're not addressing.

There are some feelings I don't like having, like jealousy. I feel guilty or embarrassed for feeling that way and want to stop it immediately, but I can't seem to bring it under control. You are experiencing what I call *meta feelings*. That's when you have a feeling about having a feeling—for example, feeling guilty about being jealous or feeling ashamed about being angry.

The first thing to realize is that a feeling and a behavior are two different things. Feeling jealous about something is different from doing something hurtful to someone because you are feeling jealous. If you recall, we've said that feelings exist for a reason. Your jealousy is giving you some needed information. You have little chance of shifting your distressing feeling if you don't first listen to that information.

Since jealousy can be an indication of anxiety, sadness, or anger, you may want to look at which of these feelings applies to your situation. Are you jealous of someone because you fear he or she will get something you want, like attention or money? Or are you jealous because another person has caused you to lose something you value? Last, are you jealous because you feel another has violated you or your belief system in some way—and gained from it?

Once you determine the source of your jealousy, you'll be able to choose the Emotional Tools that can help you move past the emotion.

Sometimes I fall asleep when I meditate. What can I do to stop that? There are two main reasons why people fall asleep when they meditate. The first one is obvious—they are tired. For many people with busy lives and not enough sleep, sitting down to meditate is the first time they can relax, and their thankful bodies take the opportunity to sleep. According to Michael Baime, M.D., cofounder of the University of Pennsylvania Stress Management Program, most people have this experience at some point in their meditation, including him. Notes Baime, "I live a life just like everyone else. It's too full, and I don't sleep enough and sometimes the first thing that happens when I settle down and actually come into my body and feel it is that I realize how tired I am; how hard I've pushed and I can fall asleep. There's no problem with that. I think if that's what I really need at that moment, that's what I should get."

The other common reason people fall asleep during meditation is related to conditioning. Most people close their eyes only when they go to sleep, so when they close their eyes to meditate, their mind immediately says, "Hey, it's time to sleep." And that's exactly what happens. One way to avoid this is to meditate while sitting upright. Also, if you find yourself getting drowsy or starting to fall asleep, quickly open your eyes without looking at anything in particular, and close them again. This will signal to your brain that it is not time to sleep.

I tend to be pretty sarcastic when I'm upset. I've always been this way. How can I stop? It's a habit, and you can change it. If you are sarcastic with someone, start with an apology: "I'm sorry for what I just said. I'm trying not to talk like that anymore." Over time, you'll become aware of the moment right before a sarcastic comment is about to come out of your mouth. At that point, choose not to say it. You might also want to take a deep breath at that moment. This will take practice, but if you are committed to it, you can stop making sarcastic remarks. Your relationships will be the better for it.

Appendix B

Resource Guide

Recommended Reading

THE SCIENCE OF EMOTIONS

Daniel Goleman (1995). *Emotional Intelligence: Why It Can Matter More Than I.Q.*

An exploration of why becoming aware of your emotions and developing your ability to deal with them are as important as developing your intellectual and academic abilities.

Candace B. Pert, Ph.D., (1997). *Molecules of Emotion: The Science Behind Mind-Body Medicine.*

An examination of the research that proposes the mind and body are one, and its implications for emotional and physical health.

TOOL I: THOUGHT-SHIFTING

Aaron T. Beck (1976). *Cognitive Therapy and the Emotional Disorders.*

How thought-shifting principles are used in psychotherapy. Written by the chief originator of cognitive therapy.

David D. Burns, M.D., (1999). *The Feeling Good Handbook,* revised edition.

A practical book for learning how to manage depression and anxiety.

Dennis Greenberger and Christine Padesky (1995). *Mind Over Mood: Change How You Feel by Changing the Way You Think.*

A helpful workbook that allows you to practice thought-shifting techniques.

TOOL 2: MEDITATIVE ARTS

Herbert Benson, M.D., (1975). *The Relaxation Response.*

The definitive primer on how meditation affects the body. Written by one of the most influential researchers on meditation.

Victor Davich (2004). *8 Minute Meditation: Quiet Your Mind. Change Your Life.*

A practical and simply written guide to starting a mindfulness-meditation practice using eight-minute meditations.

Jon Kabat-Zinn (1994). *Wherever You Go, There You Are: Mindfulness Meditation in Everyday Life.*

An excellent overview of mindfulness meditation. Beautifully written.

TOOL 3: COMMUNICATION

John M. Gottman, Ph.D., and Nan Silver (1999). *The Seven Principles for Making Marriage Work.*

A wonderfully written and well-researched book with the evidence on what really works.

Harriet Lerner, Ph.D., (1997). *The Dance of Anger: A Woman's Guide to Changing the Patterns of Intimate Relationships.*

A practical guide to understanding and managing anger in close relationships using a systems model. Excellent.

Manuel J. Smith, Ph.D., (1975). *When I Say No, I Feel Guilty.*

One of the first books to teach effective communication skills and still a classic.

Deborah Tannen (1990). *You Just Don't Understand: Women and Men in Conversation.*

An intriguing look into how gender influences communication styles and behavior.

TOOL 4: EMOTIONAL WRITING

Louise DeSalvo (1999). *Writing as a Way of Healing: How Telling Our Stories Transforms Our Lives.*

An author and university writing teacher explores how journaling influences emotions.

James W. Pennebaker, Ph.D., (1997). *Opening Up: The Healing Power of Expressing Emotions.*

The definitive book on emotional writing written by the person who invented the field.

TOOL 5: PHYSICAL MOVEMENT

John Douillard (2001). *Body, Mind, and Sport: The Mind-Body Guide to Lifelong Health, Fitness, and Your Personal Best.*

A fascinating look at the mind-body aspects of physical exercise.

Keith W. Johnsgard (1989). *The Exercise Prescription for Depression and Anxiety.*

A wonderful overview of how physical exercise can reduce distress.

Margaret D. and Martin G. Pierce (1996). *Yoga for Your Life: A Practice Manual of Breath and Movement for Every Body.*

An introduction to yoga. Highly recommended by yoga teachers.

TOOL 6: CONNECTION

Dean Ornish, M.D., (1998). *Love and Survival: 8 Pathways to Intimacy and Health.*

An in-depth look at how social connection influences health from a pioneer in mind-body research.

Shelley E. Taylor (2002). *The Tending Instinct: Women, Men, and the Biology of Relationships.*

A treatise by the creator of the "tend and befriend" theory.

TOOL 7: PSYCHOTHERAPY

Jack Engler and Daniel Goleman (1992). *The Consumer's Guide to Psychotherapy.*

An excellent overview of everything you've always wanted to know about psychotherapy.

Resources on Internal Questioning

Internal questioning is an Emotional Tool I adapted from Eugene Gendlin's *focusing* process. For more information on focusing, including how to find a focusing teacher, you can contact the Focusing Institute or read Gendlin's wonderful book, *Focusing.*

Focusing Institute

34 East Lane, Spring Valley, NY 10977

(845) 362-5222

e-mail: info@focusing.org

www.focusing.org

Self-Assessments

David Keirsey and Marilyn Bates (1984). *Please Understand Me: Character and Temperament Types.*

A seventy-item self-test, the Keirsey Temperament Sorter, assesses the reader's temperament and type.

Mindfulness Meditation Instruction

Insight Meditation Society

1230 Pleasant Street, Bare, MA 01005

(978) 355-4378, www.dharma.org

Provides instruction, workshops, and retreats on mindfulness meditation.

Vipassana Support Institute

4070 Albright Ave., Los Angeles, CA 90066

(310) 915-1943, www.shinzen.org

Provides instruction, workshops, and retreats on mindfulness meditation. This is where I learned to meditate from teacher Shinzen Young.

Meditation Audiotapes and CDs

Meditations to Change Your Mood CD with Dr. Darlene Mininni

These are the meditations I teach to my seminar students and private clients.

Available at www.emotionaltoolkit.com

Mindfulness Meditation Practice CDs with Jon Kabat-Zinn

Available at www.mindfulnesstapes.com

Biofeedback Monitors

Jeffers Health Systems

This California-based mail-order company provides an array of biofeedback instruments. The model I used for my LifeSkills class, the Stress Computer, sells for $49.95. Discounts are given for bulk orders.

Exercise Videos and CDs

Basic Yoga Workout for Dummies with Sara Ivanhoe

This is an excellent place to start if you're new to yoga or want to review some of the fundamental poses.

Tai Chi: Exercise for Lifelong Health and Well-Being with Tricia Yu

A good introduction to tai chi.

Yoga Mind and Body by Ali MacGraw, featuring yoga master Erich Schiffmann

This beautifully photographed tape is for an intermediate level. However, beginners can use it as well. Simply adapt the poses to meet the needs of your body.

Web Sites

Walking Lessons for the Absolute Beginner

Tips on everything from how to pick the right walking shoes to how to move your arms when you walk.

http://walking.about.com/library/weekly/aa122699a.htm?once=true&

Audiotapes, CDs, and Music for Walking

A guide to Web sites that offer music audiotapes for walkers. The tapes vary by walking level and type of music. Some provide coaching and tips during the music.

www.walking.about.com/cs/music/a/audio.htm

How to Start a Stress Support Group

Eight suggestions for starting your own group.

http://stress.about.com/library/blsupgr.htm?terms=starting+a +stress+support+group

The Self-Help Sourcebook Online

A database with over eight hundred self-help support groups, information on starting groups, and opportunities to register and link with others.

http://mentalhelp.net/selfhelp/

How to Find a Therapist

To find a therapist in your area, you can contact any of the following organizations:

Academy of Cognitive Therapy

To find a cognitive therapist, call (610) 664-1273 or go to the academy's Web site (www.academyofct.org) and click on Referrals for a list of qualified clinicians in your area.

American Association for Marriage and Family Therapy

To find a marriage and family therapist in your area, call (202) 452-0109 or go to www.aamft.org and click on Therapist locator.net.

American Psychological Association

Call (800) 964-2000 to be directed to a local office for a referral. Tell the person whether you want to find a psychologist who works in a specific town or one who has a specialty working with the issues that concern you.

The Focusing Institute

To find a therapist who uses the focusing technique in therapy, call the Focusing Institute at (845) 362-5222 or go to www.focusing.org.

References

Adams, C. (2003). *The Gift of Jazzy*. New York: St. Martin's.

Alexander, C., et al. (1993). Effects of the transcendental meditation program on stress reduction, health, and employee development: A prospective study in two occupational settings. *Anxiety, Stress and Coping, 6,* 245–262.

Allen, K., et al. (1991). Presence of human friends and pet dogs as moderators of autonomic responses to stress in women. *Journal of Personality and Social Psychology, 61*(4), 582–589.

Anderson, E., & Lambert, M. (2001). A survival analysis of clinically significant change in outpatient psychotherapy. *Journal of Clinical Psychology, 57,* 875–888.

Antonuccio, D., et al. (1995). Psychotherapy versus medication for depression: Challenging the conventional wisdom with data. *Professional Psychology: Research and Practice, 26*(6), 574–585.

Austin, J. (2001). *Zen and the Brain*. Cambridge, MA: MIT Press.

Babyak, M., et al. (2000). Exercise treatment for major depression: Maintenance of therapeutic benefit at 10 months. *Psychosomatic Medicine, 62,* 633–638.

Bach, R. (1970). *Jonathan Livingston Seagull*. New York: Avon.

Baime, M. (2001, June 20). From transcript of *Fresh Air* with Terry Gross. Minnesota Public Radio.

Baumeister, R., & Leary, M. (1995). The need to belong: Desire for interpersonal attachments as a fundamental human motivation. *Psychological Bulletin, 117*(3), 497–529.

Beauchamp-Turner, D., & Levinson, D. (1992). Effects of meditation on stress, health and affect. *Medical Psychotherapy, 5,* 123–132.

Beck, A. (1963). Thinking and depression: Idiosyncratic content and cognitive distortions. *Archives of General Psychiatry, 9,* 324–333.

Beck, A. (1976). *Cognitive Therapy and the Emotional Disorders*. New York: Meridian.

Beck, A., & Rush, J. (1989). Cognitive therapy. In H. Kaplan & B. Sadock (Eds.), *Comprehensive Textbook of Psychiatry* (vol. 2, 5th ed., 1541–1550). Baltimore, MD: Williams & Williams.

Belle, D. (1987). Gender differences in the social moderators of stress. In B. Barnett, et al. (Eds.), *Gender and Stress* (257–277). New York: Free Press.

Benson, H. (1975). *The Relaxation Response*. New York: Avon.

Benson, H. (1996). *Timeless Healing: The Power and Biology of Belief*. New York: Fireside.

Berger, B., & Motl, R. (2000). Exercise and mood: A selective review and synthesis of research employing the profile of mood states. *Journal of Applied Sport Psychology, 12,* 69–92.

Berger, B., & Owen, D. (1992). Mood alteration with yoga and swimming: Aerobic exercise may not be necessary. *Perceptual and Motor Skills, 75,* 1331–1343.

Berkman, L. (1985). The relationship of social networks and social support to morbidity and mortality. In S. Cohen and S. L. Syme (Eds.), *Social Support and Health* (pp. 241–262). Orlando, FL: Academic Press.

Berkman, L. (1995). The role of social relations in health promotion. *Psychosomatic Medicine, 57,* 245–254.

Berkman, L. and Syme, S. (1979). Social networks, host resistance and mortality: A nine-year follow-up study of Alameda County residents. *Journal of Epidemiology, 109,* 186–204.

Blumenthal, J., et al. (1999). Effects of exercise training on older patients with major depression. *Archives of Internal Medicine, 159,* 2349–2356.

Bogart, G. (1991). The use of meditation in psychotherapy: A review of the literature. *American Journal of Psychotherapy, 45,* 383–412.

Borkovec, T., et al. (2002). Disclosure and worry: Opposite sides of the emotional processing coin. In J. Pennebaker (Ed.), *Emotion, Disclosure and Health* (pp. 47–70). Washington, D.C.: American Psychological Association.

Borysenko, J. (1987). *Minding the Body, Mending the Mind.* Reading, MA: Addison-Wesley.

Boswell, P. & Murray, E. (1979). Effects of meditation on psychological and physiological measures of anxiety. *Journal of Consulting and Clinical Psychology, 47(3),* 606–607.

Bourne, E. (1990). *The Anxiety and Phobia Workbook.* Oakland, CA: New Harbinger.

Brody, A. (2001). Regional brain metabolic changes in patients with major depression treated with either Paroxetine or Interpersonal Therapy. *Archives of General Psychiatry, 58,* 631–640.

Brown, S., et al. (2003). Providing social support may be more beneficial than receiving it: Results from a prospective study of mortality. *Psychological Science, 14(4),* 320–327.

Burns, D. (1999). *The Feeling Good Handbook.* New York: Plume.

Cameron, J. (1992). *The Artist's Way: A Spiritual Path to Higher Creativity.* New York: Tarcher/Putnam.

Cameron, L., & Nicholls, G. (1998). Expression of stressful experiences through writing: Effects of a self-regulation manipulation for pessimists and optimists. *Health Psychology, 17(1),* 84–92.

Chang, E., & D'Zurilla, T. (1996). Irrational beliefs as predictors of anxiety and depression in a college population. *Personality and Individual Difference, 20(2),* 215–219.

Chess, S., and Thomas, A. (1996). *Temperament: Theory and Practice.* New York: Brunner/Mazel.

Chess, S., and Thomas, A. (1999). *Goodness of Fit: Clinical Applications from Infancy Through Adult Life.* New York: Brunner-Routledge.

Chopra, D. (1989). *Quantum Healing.* New York: Bantam Books.

Cobb, S. (1976). Social support as a moderator of life stress. *Psychosomatic Medicine, 38,* 300–313.

Cohen, S., & Hoberman, H. (1983). Positive events and social supports as buffers of life change stress. *Journal of Applied Social Psychology, 13*(2), 99–125.

Cohen, S., Sherrod, D., & Clark, M. (1986). Social skills and the stress-protective role of social support. *Journal of Personality and Social Psychology, 50*(5), 963–973.

Cohen, S., & Wills, T. A. (1985). Stress, social support, and the buffering hypothesis. *Psychological Bulletin, 98*(2), 310–357.

Collins, N., et al. (1993). Social support in pregnancy: Psychosocial correlates of birth outcomes and postpartum depression. *Journal of Personality and Social Psychology, 65*(6), 1243–1258.

Csikszentmihalyi, M. (1990). *Flow: The Psychology of Optimal Experience.* New York: Harper Perennial.

Dalai Lama, & Cutler, H. (1998). *The Art of Happiness: A Handbook for Living.* New York: Riverhead.

Damasio, A. (1995). *Descartes' Error: Emotion, Reason and the Human Brain.* New York: Avon.

Damasio, A. (2000). *The Feeling of What Happens: Body and Emotion in the Making of Consciousness.* New York: Harvest.

Davidson, R., et al. (2003). Alterations in brain and immune function produced by mindfulness meditation. *Psychosomatic Medicine, 65,* 564–570.

DeBerry, S., Davis, S., & Reinhard, K. (1989). A comparison of meditation-relaxation and cognitive/behavioral techniques for reducing anxiety and depression in a geriatric population. *Journal of Geriatric Psychiatry, 22,* 231–247.

Deffenbacher, J., et al. (1996). Evaluation of two cognitive-behavioral approaches to general anger reduction. *Cognitive Therapy and Research, 20*(6), 551–573.

Delmonte, M. (1985). Meditation and anxiety reduction: A literature review. *Clinical Psychology Review, 5,* 91–102.

DeSalvo, L. (1999). *Writing as a Way of Healing: How Telling Our Stories Transforms Our Lives.* Boston: Beacon.

DeVries, H. (1981). Tranquilizer effect of exercise: A critical review. *Physician and Sport Medicine, 9*(11), 47–55.

Domar, A., et al. (2000). Impact of group psychological interventions on pregnancy rates in infertile women. *Fertility and Sterility, 73*(4), 805–811.

Douillard, J. (2001). *Body, Mind, and Sport: The Mind-Body Guide to Lifelong Health, Fitness, and Your Personal Best.* New York: Three Rivers.

Elliott, R., Greenberg, L., & Lietaer, G. (2004). Research on experiential psychotherapies. In *Bergin and Garfield's Handbook of Psychotherapy and Behavior Change* (5th ed.). New York: Wiley.

Engler, J. & Goleman, D. (1992). *The Consumer's Guide to Psychotherapy.* New York: Fireside.

Epstein, M. (1995). *Thoughts Without a Thinker*. New York: Basic.

Eysenck, H. J. (1952). The effects of psychotherapy: An evaluation. *Journal of Consulting Psychology, 16,* 319–324.

Francis, M., & Pennebaker, J. (1992). Putting stress into words: The impact of writing on physiological, absentee, and self-reported emotional well-being measures. *American Journal of Health Promotion, 6*(4), 280–287.

Freud, S. (1966). *The Complete Introductory Lectures on Psychoanalysis.* (J. Strachey, Trans.). New York: Norton (Original works published 1917, 1933).

Friedman, R. (2002, August 27). Like drugs, talk therapy can change brain chemistry. *New York Times.* Retrieved from www.nytimes.com/2002/08/27/health/-psychology/27BEHA.html.

Fuller, G. (1977). *Biofeedback: Methods and Procedures in Clinical Practice.* San Francisco: Biofeedback Institute of San Francisco.

Furness, J. B., & Costa, M. (1987). *The Enteric Nervous System.* New York: Churchill Livingstone.

Gendlin, E. (1981). *Focusing.* New York: Bantam.

Gershon, M. (1998). *The Second Brain.* New York: Harper Perennial.

Gilligan, C. (1982). *In a Different Voice: Psychological Theory and Women's Development.* Cambridge: Harvard University Press.

Goldman, B., Domitor, P., & Murray, E. (1979). Effects of zen meditation on anxiety reduction and perceptual function. *Journal of Consulting and Clinical Psychology, 47*(3), 551–556.

Goleman, D. (1995). *Emotional Intelligence: Why It Can Matter More Than I.Q.* London: Bloomsbury.

Goleman, D. (2003, February 4). Finding happiness: Cajole your brain to lean to the left. *New York Times.*

Goode, E., & Wagner, B. (1993, May 24). Does therapy work? *U.S. News & World Report,* pp. 57–65.

Goodman, G., & Esterly, G. (1988). *The Talk Book: The Intimate Science of Communicating in Close Relationships.* New York: Ballantine.

Gottlieb, B. (1985). Social support and community mental health. In S. Cohen & S. L. Syme (Eds.), *Social Support and Health* (pp. 303–326). Orlando, FL: Academic.

Gottman, J., & Silver, N. (1999). *The Seven Principles for Making Marriage Work.* New York: Three Rivers.

Grossman, L. (2003, January 20). Can Freud get his job back? *Time.*

Hall, S. (2003, Sept. 14). Is Buddhism good for your health? *New York Times,* pp. 46–49.

Hays, K. (1999). *Working It Out: Using Exercise in Psychotherapy.* Washington, DC: American Psychological Association.

Hays, L., & Seeger, P. (1949). "If I Had a Hammer." New York: Ludlow Music.

Helminski, K. (2001). *The Pocket Rumi Reader.* Boston: Shambala.

Holahan, C., & Moos, R. (1981). Social support and psychological distress: A longitudinal analysis. *Journal of Abnormal Psychology, 90*(4), 365–370.

Hollon, S. (1996). The efficacy and effectiveness of psychotherapy relative to medications. *American Psychologist, 51*(10), 1025–1030.

Hollon, S., & Beck, A. (2004). Cognitive and cognitive behavioral therapies. In *Bergin and Garfield's Handbook of Psychotherapy and Behavior Change* (5th ed.). New York: Wiley.

Iyengar, B. D., & Menuhin, Y. (1995). *Light on Pranayama: The Yogic Art of Breathing.* New York: The Crossroad Publishing Company.

Jin, P. (1989). Changes in heart rate, noradrenaline, cortisol and mood during tai chi. *Journal of Psychosomatic Research, 33*(2), 197–206.

Johnsgard, K. (1989). *The Exercise Prescription for Depression and Anxiety.* New York: Plenum.

Jordan, J., et al. (1991). *Women's Growth in Connection: Writings from the Stone Center.* New York: Guilford.

Jung, C. (1927). *The Structure and Dynamics of the Psyche: Collected Works* (Vol. 8). Berlin: Europaische Revue.

Kabat-Zinn, J. (1994). *Wherever You Go, There You Are: Mindfulness Meditation in Everyday Life.* New York: Hyperion.

Kabat-Zinn, J., et al. (1992). Effectiveness of a meditation–based stress reduction program in the treatment of anxiety disorders. *American Journal of Psychiatry, 149,* 936–943.

Kabat-Zinn, J., et al. (1998). Influence of a mindfulness meditation–based stress reduction intervention on rates of skin clearing in patients with moderate to severe psoriasis undergoing phototherapy (UVB) and photochemotherapy (PUVA). *Psychosomatic Medicine, 60,* 625–632.

Kagan, J. (1994). *Galen's Prophecy: Temperament in Human Nature.* New York: Basic.

Katz, A., & Bender, E. (1976). *The Strength in Us: Self-Help Groups in the Modern World.* New York: New Viewpoints.

Keirsey, D., & Bates, M. (1984). *Please Understand Me: Character and Temperament Types.* Del Mar, CA: Prometheus Nemesis Book Company.

Kiecolt-Glaser, J., et al. (1985). Psychosocial modifiers of immunocompetence in medical students. *Psychosomatic Medicine, 46,* 7–14.

King, L. (2001). The health benefits of writing about life goals. *Personality and Social Psychology Bulletin, 27*(7), 798–807.

Kirkpatrick, L., et al. (1999). Loneliness, social support, and perceived relationships with God. *Journal of Social and Personal Relationships, 16*(4), 513–522.

Kleck, R., & Strenta, A. (1980). Perceptions of the impact of negatively valued physical characteristics on social interaction. *Journal of Personality and Social Psychology, 39*(5), 861–873.

Klinger, E. (1993). Clinical approaches to mood control. In D. Wegner and J. Pennebaker (Eds.), *Handbook of Mental Control.* New Jersey: Prentice-Hall.

Kornfield, J. (1995). *The Roots of Buddhist Psychology.* Boulder, CO: Sounds True Audio.

Kovach, R. (2002, May). Studs Terkel on the art of interviewing. *Writer, 115*(5).

Lambert, M. (2001). The effectiveness of psychotherapy: What has a century of research taught us about the effects of treatment? *Oklahoma Psychologist, 1,* 12–13.

Lambert, M., Garfield, S., & Bergin, A. (2004). Overview, trends, and future issues. In *Bergin and Garfield's Handbook of Psychotherapy and Behavior Change* (5th ed.). New York: Wiley.

Lambert, M., & Ogles, B. (2004). The efficacy and effectiveness of psychotherapy. In *Bergin and Garfield's Handbook of Psychotherapy and Behavior Change* (5th ed.). New York: Wiley.

Lange, A., et al. (1997). Cognitive treatment through positive self-verbalization: A multiple case study. *Behavioural and Cognitive Psychotherapy, 25,* 161–171.

Langer, E. (1989). *Mindfulness.* New York: Addison-Wesley.

Lasn, K., & Grierson, B. (2000, Sept.–Oct.) America the blue. *Utne Reader,* pp. 74–81.

Lazar, S. W., et al. (2000). Functional brain mapping of the relaxation response and meditation. *NeuroReport, 11*(7), 1581–1585.

Leary, M., et al. (2003). Finding pleasure in solitary activities: Desire for aloneness or disinterest in social contact? *Personality and Individual Differences, 35*(1), 59–68.

Leavy, R. (1983). Social support and psychological disorder: A review. *Journal of Community Psychology, 11,* 3–21.

Lehman, P., Ellard, J., & Wortman, C. (1986). Social support for the bereaved: Recipients' and providers' perspectives on what is helpful. *Journal of Personality and Social Psychology, 54,* 438–446.

Lepore, S. (1997). Expressive writing moderates the relation between intrusive thoughts and depressive symptoms. *Journal of Personality and Social Psychology, 73*(5), 1030–1037.

Lepore, S., et al. (1993). Social support lowers cardiovascular reactivity to an acute stressor. *Psychosomatic Medicine, 55,* 518–524.

Lepore, S., & Greenberg, M. (2002). Mending broken hearts: Effects of expressive writing on mood, cognitive processing, social adjustment and health following a relationship breakup. *Psychology and Health, 17*(5), 547–560.

Lerner, H. (1997). *The Dance of Anger: A Woman's Guide to Changing the Patterns of Intimate Relationships.* New York: HarperCollins.

Lewis, J. (2004). *Women's voices: Quotations by women,* from http://womenshistory.about.com/library/qu/blqulist.htm.

Levinson, D. (1986). A conception of adult development. *American Psychologist, 41,* 3–13.

Lutgendorf, S., & Ullrich, P. (2002). Cognitive processing, disclosure, and health: Psychological and physiological mechanisms. In S. Lepore & J. Smyth (Eds.), *The Writing Cure: How Expressive Writing Promotes Health and Emotional Well-Being* (pp. 177–196). Washington, DC: American Psychological Association.

Martin, S., et al. (2001). Brain blood flow changes in depressed patients treated with interpersonal psychotherapy or venlafaxine hydrochloride. *Archives of General Psychiatry, 58,* 641–648.

May, R. (1981). *Freedom and Destiny*. New York. Norton.

McCraty, R., et al. (1995). The effects of emotions on short-term power spectrum analysis of heart rate variability. *American Journal of Cardiology, 76*(14), 1089–1093.

McCullough, M., Emmons, R., and Tsang, J. (2002). The grateful disposition: A conceptual and empirical topography. *Journal of Personality and Social Psychology, 82*(1), 112–127.

McCullough, M., et al. (2000). Religious involvement and mortality: A meta-analytic review. *Health Psychology, 19*(3), 211–222.

Meichenbaum, D., & Deffenbacher, J. (1988, Jan.). Stress inoculation training. *Counseling Psychologist, 16*(1), 69–90.

Meichenbaum, D. (1985). *Stress Inoculation Training*. New York. Pergamon.

Meichenbaum, D., & Novaco, R. (1985). Stress inoculation: A preventative approach. *Issues in Mental Health Nursing, 7*(1–4), 419–435.

Meichenbaum, D., & Cameron, R. (1974, Summer). The clinical potential of modifying what clients say to themselves. *Psychotherapy, Research and Practice, 11*(2), 103–117.

Microsoft (2001). Women's use of Internet affects purchasing decisions: MSN study explores what women want online, from www.microsoft.com/presspass/-press/2001/Apr01/04-09PurchasePR.asp.

Miller, J. B. (1976). *Toward a New Psychology of Women*. Boston: Beacon.

Najavits, L., & Strupp, H. (1994). Differences in the effectiveness of psychodynamic therapists: A process-outcome study. *Psychotherapy, 31*, 114–123.

Nakano, K. (1991). The role of coping strategies on psychological and physical well-being. *Japanese Psychological Research, 33*(4), 160–167.

Newberg, A., D'Aquili, E., & Rause, V. (2001). *Why God Won't Go Away: Brain Science and the Biology of Belief*. New York: Ballantine.

Nolen-Hoeksema, S. (1993). Sex differences in control of depression. In D. Wegner & J. Pennebaker (Eds.), *Handbook of Mental Control*. New Jersey: Prentice-Hall.

Northrup, C. (1998). *Women's Bodies, Women's Wisdom*. New York: Bantam.

Ornish, D. (1998). *Love and Survival: 8 Pathways to Intimacy and Health*. New York: Harper Perennial.

Pargament, K. (1990). God help me: Religious coping efforts as predictors of the outcomes to significant negative life events. *American Journal of Community Psychology, 18*(6), 793–824.

Payne, L., & Usatine, R. (2002). *Yoga Rx: A Step-by-Step Program to Promote Health, Wellness, and Healing for Common Ailments*. New York: Broadway.

Pearl, J., & Carlozzi, A. (1994). Effect of meditation on empathy and anxiety. *Perceptual and Motor Skills, 78*, 297–298.

Peck, M. S. (1978). *The Road Less Traveled: A New Psychology of Love, Traditional Values and Spiritual Growth*. New York: Touchstone.

Pennebaker, J., Colder, M., & Sharp, L. (1990). Accelerating the coping process. *Journal of Personality and Social Psychology, 58*(3), 528–537.

Pennebaker, J., & Seagal, J. (1999). Forming a story: The health benefits of narrative. *Journal of Clinical Psychology, 55*(10), 1243–1254.

Pennebaker, J. (1993). Social mechanisms of constraint. In D. Wegner & J. Pennebaker (Eds.), *Handbook of Mental Control.* New Jersey: Prentice-Hall.

Pennebaker, J. (1997). *Opening Up: The Healing Power of Expressing Emotions.* New York: Guilford.

Pennebaker, J. (2002). Emotion, disclosure, and health: An overview. In J. Pennebaker (Ed.), *Emotion, Disclosure and Health* (pp. 3–10). Washington, DC: American Psychological Association.

Persons, J., et al. (1996). Psychodynamic therapists' reservations about cognitive-behavioral therapy. *Journal of Psychotherapy: Practice and Research, 5*(3), 203–212.

Persons, J., & Burns, D. (1985). Mechanisms of action of cognitive therapy: The relative contributions of technical and interpersonal interventions. *Cognitive Therapy, 9*(5), 539–551.

Pert, C. (1997). *Molecules of Emotion: The Science Behind Mind-Body Medicine.* New York: Touchstone.

Petrie, K., Booth, R., & Pennebaker, J. (1998). The immunological effects of thought suppression. *Personality Processes and Individual Differences, 75*(5), 1264–1272.

Philpot, V., & Bamburg, J. (1996). Rehearsal of positive self-statements and re-structured negative self-statements to increase self-esteem and decrease depression. *Psychological Reports, 79,* 83–91.

Putnam, R. (2000). *Bowling Alone: The Collapse and Revival of American Community.* New York: Simon & Schuster.

Quenk, N. (2000). *Essentials of Myers-Briggs Type Indicator Assessment.* New York: Wiley.

Rimé, B. (2002). Mental rumination, social sharing, and the recovery from emotional exposure. In J. Pennebaker (Ed.), *Emotion, Disclosure and Health* (pp. 271–291). Washington, DC: American Psychological Association.

Roemer, L., & Borkovec, T. (1993) Worry: Unwanted cognitive activity that controls unwanted somatic experience. In D. Wegner & J. Pennebaker (Eds.), *Handbook of Mental Control.* New Jersey: Prentice-Hall.

Roth, A., & Fonagy, P. (1996). *What Works for Whom? A Critical Review of Psychotherapy Research.* New York: Guilford.

Schulz, R., & Rau, M. (1985). Social support through the life course. In S. Cohen & S. L. Syme (Eds.), *Social Support and Health* (pp. 129–149). Orlando, FL: Academic.

Schwartz, C., & David, E. (2002). To everything there is a season: A written expression intervention for closure at the end of life. In S. Lepore & J. Smyth (Eds.), *The Writing Cure: How Expressive Writing Promotes Health and Emotional Well-Being* (pp. 257–278). Washington, DC: American Psychological Association.

Schwartz, R. M. (1986). The internal dialogue: On the asymmetry between positive and negative coping thoughts. *Cognitive Therapy and Research, 10,* 591–605.

Seligman, M. (1993). *What You Can Change and What You Can't: The Complete Guide to Successful Self-Improvement.* New York: Fawcett.

Seligman, M. (1995). The effectiveness of psychotherapy: The *Consumer Reports* study. *American Psychologist, 50*(12), 965–974.

Seligman, M. (1998). *Learned Optimism.* New York: Pocket Books.

Shapiro, S., Schwartz, G., & Bonner, G. (1998). Effects of mindfulness-based stress reduction on medical and premedical students. *Journal of Behavioral Medicine, 21*(6), 581–599.

Shea, M., et al. (1992). Course of depressive symptoms over follow-up: Findings from the National Institute of Mental Health treatment of depression collaborative research program. *Archives of General Psychiatry, 49,* 782–787.

Sheehan, G. (1989). *Self-discovery.* Retrieved 2003 from www.georgesheehan.com/essays/essay30.html.

Sheehy, G. (1977). *Passages: Predictable Crises of Adult Life.* New York: Bantam.

Siegel, S., & Alloy, L. (1990). Interpersonal perceptions and consequences of depressive-significant other relationships: A naturalistic study of college roommates. *Journal of Abnormal Psychology, 99,* 361–373.

Singelis, T., Choo, P., & Hatfield, E. (1995). Love schemas and romantic love. *Journal of Social Behavior and Personality, 10*(1), 15–36.

Singh Khalsa, D., & Stauth, C. (2001). *Meditation as Medicine.* New York: Fireside.

Slattery, J. M., et al. (2002). *Gender-specific use of natural coping strategies and their perceived effectiveness.* Poster presented at the annual meeting of the Eastern Psychological Association, Boston, MA.

Smith, M. (1975). *When I Say No, I Feel Guilty.* New York: Dial.

Smith, M. L., Glass, G. V., & Miller, T. I. (1980). *Benefits of Psychotherapy.* Baltimore: Johns Hopkins University Press.

Smith, W. P., Compton, W., & West, B. (1995). Meditation as an adjunct to a happiness enhancement program. *Journal of Clinical Psychology, 51*(2), 269–273.

Smyth, J. (1998). Written emotional expression: Effect sizes, outcome types, and moderating variables. *Journal of Consulting and Clinical Psychology, 66*(1), 174–184.

Spera, S., Buhrfeind, E., & Pennebaker, J. (1994). Expressive writing and coping with job loss. *Academy of Management Journal, 37*(3), 722–733.

Sperry, L., et al. (1996). *Treatment Outcomes in Psychotherapy and Psychiatric Interventions.* New York: Brunner/Mazel.

Spiegel, D., et al. (1989, Oct.–Dec.). Effect of psychosocial treatment on survival of patients with metastatic breast cancer. *Lancet,* v. 2, 888–91.

Steptoe, A., et al. (1989). The effects of exercise training on mood and perceived coping ability in anxious adults from the general population. *Journal of Psychosomatic Research, 33*(5), 537–547.

Strunk, D., & DeRubeis, R. (2001). Cognitive therapy for depression: A review of its efficacy. *Journal of Cognitive Psychotherapy: An International Quarterly, 15*(4), 289–297.

Strupp, H. (1996). The tripartite model and the *Consumer Reports* study. *American Psychologist, 51*(10), 1017–1024.

Szalay, L., & Brent, J. (1967). The analysis of cultural meanings through free verbal associations. *Journal of Social Psychology, 72,* 161–187.

Tamres, L., et al. (2002). Sex differences in coping behavior: A meta-analytic review and an examination of relative coping. *Personality and Social Psychology Review, 6*(1), 2–30.

Tannen, D. (1990). *You Just Don't Understand: Women and Men in Conversation.* New York: Ballantine.

Task Force on DSM-IV (1994). *Diagnostic and Statistical Manual of Mental Disorders* (4th ed.). Washington, DC: American Psychiatric Association.

Tavris, C. (1989). *Anger: The Misunderstood Emotion.* New York: Touchstone.

Taylor, H. (2002). The Harris Poll 78. Internet penetration at 66% of Adults Nationwide, from www.harrisinteractive.com/harris_poll/printerfriend/index.asp?PID=295.

Taylor, J., & Turner, J. (2001). A longitudinal study of the role and significance of mattering to others for depressive symptoms. *Journal of Health and Social Behavior, 42,* 310–325.

Taylor, S. (2002). *The Tending Instinct: How Nurturing Is Essential to Who We Are and How We Live.* New York: Holt.

Taylor, S., et al. (2000). Biobehavioral responses to stress in females: Tend-and-befriend, not fight-or-flight. *Psychological Review, 107*(3), 411–429.

Tennen, H., & Affleck, G. (1999). *Finding benefits in adversity.* In C. R. Synder (Ed.), *Coping: The Psychology of What Works.* New York: Oxford University Press.

Terkel, S. (1967). *Division Street America.* New York: Random House.

Thase, M. (2001). Neuroimaging profiles and the differential therapies of depression. *Archives of General Psychiatry, 58,* 651–653.

Tice, D., & Baumeisterk, R. (1993). *Controlling anger: Self-induced emotion change.* In D. Wegner & J. Pennebaker (Eds.), *Handbook of Mental Control.* New Jersey: Prentice-Hall.

Tsutsumi, T. (1998). Comparison of high and moderate intensity of strength training on mood and anxiety in older adults. *Perceptual and Motor Skills, 87,* 1003–1011.

Turlington, C. (2002). *Living Yoga: Creating a Life Practice.* New York: Hyperion.

Turner, D., & Bateson, P. (1988). *The Domestic Cat: The Biology of Its Behavior.* Cambridge, UK: Cambridge University Press.

Twenge, J. (2000). The age of anxiety? Birth cohort change in anxiety and neuroticism, 1952–1993. *Journal of Personality and Social Psychology, 79*(6), 1007–1021.

Uhde, T., & Nemiah, J. (1989). Anxiety disorders. In H. Kaplan & B. Sadock (Eds.), *Comprehensive Textbook of Psychiatry* (vol. 2, 5th ed., pp. 952–972). Baltimore, MD: Williams & Williams.

Vachon, M., et al. (1980). A controlled study of a self-help intervention for widows. *American Journal of Psychiatry, 137,* 1380–1384.

Wang, Y., et al. (1992). Acute psychological response following exercise and exercise plus relaxation. *American College of Sports Medicine.*

Watson, D. (2000). *Mood and Temperament.* New York: Guilford.

Watson, D., & Tharp, R. (1985). *Self-Directed Behavior: Self-Modification for Personal Adjustment.* Monterey, CA: Brooks/Cole Publishing.

Weiser, E. (2000). Gender differences in Internet use patterns and Internet application preferences: A two-sample comparison. *CyberPsychology & Behavior, 3*(2), 167–178.

Williams, R., & Wallace, A. (1989). *Biological Effects of Physical Activity.* Champaign, IL: Human Kinetics.

Wills, T. A. (1985). Supportive functions of interpersonal relationships. In S. Cohen & S. L. Syme (Eds.), *Social Support and Health* (pp. 257–277). Orlando, FL: Academic.

Wright, D., & Cox, E. (1967). A study of the relationship between moral judgment and religious belief in a sample of English adolescents. *Journal of Social Psychology, 72,* 135–144.

Wylie, M. S. (2002, Nov.–Dec.). The untold story: Carol Gilligan on recapturing the lost voice of pleasure. *Psychotherapy Networker.*

Yeung, R. (1996). The acute effects of exercise on mood state. *Journal of Psychosomatic Research, 40*(2), 123–141.

Young, S. (1994). Purpose and method of Vipassana meditation. *Humanistic Psychologist, 22,* 53–61.

Zasloff, R. L., & Kidd, A. (1994). Loneliness and pet ownership among single women. *Psychological Reports, 75,* 747–752.

Zimbardo, P. (2001). *Hans Strupp on psychodynamic therapy* from the Discovering Psychology series, from www.learner.org/discoveringpsychology/index.html.

Sign up for Dr. Mininni's Free E-newsletter

To receive Dr. Mininni's tips for emotional wellness, news about upcoming events, and opportunities to boost your happiness, sign up for her free monthly e-newsletter at www.emotionaltoolkit.com.

Contact Dr. Mininni at:

dmininni@emotionaltoolkit.com

65128929R00200